THE UNIVERSITY

THE TRICKSTER OF SEVILLE AND THE STONE GUEST

EL BURLADOR DE SEVILLA Y EL CONVIDADO DE PIEDRA

Don Juan taunting the statue from a production of **El burlador de Sevilla** *directed by Miguel Narros at the Teatro Español, Madrid 1966–7 by courtesy of the Centro Nacional de Documentación Teatral, Madrid.*

Aris & Phillips Hispanic Classics

Tirso de Molina

The Trickster of Seville
and the Stone Guest

Translated with an introduction and notes by
Gwynne Edwards

Aris & Phillips Hispanic Classics
are published by
Oxbow Books, Park End Place, Oxford OX1 1HN

ISBN 0-85668-3019-0

A CIP record for this book is available from the British Library.

Printed and bound by Antony Rowe Ltd, Eastbourne

CONTENTS

To
Paul Chamberlain

INTRODUCTION

The Spanish drama of the sixteenth and seventeenth centuries has many points of contact with its Elizabethan counterpart and is for that reason immediately accessible to the English-speaking reader. During the period in question Spain achieved, of course, immense economic and political power and became during the reigns of Charles V (1517-1556) and Philip II (1556-1598) the most influential country in Europe, enjoying territorial domination of the Low Countries and Italy, not to mention its increasing role in the exploration and exploitation of the Americas. Undoubtedly, the emergence of Spain as a great political and economic power lies at the heart of the great flowering of artistic activity that took place in the seventeenth century – the age of Cervantes, Velázquez, Lope de Vega, Tirso de Molina and Calderón –, though by that time the nation's political power was fast declining. Within that outburst of creative genius, the drama occupied a prime position and achieved between about 1580 and the death of Calderón in 1681 a vigour, inventiveness and quality unequalled before or since. In this respect, as in others, Spanish drama of the Golden Age rivals Elizabethan drama, though in terms of output Shakespeare's 36 plays cut a poor figure alongside Lope de Vega's 800, Tirso de Molina's 300, and Calderón's 120. During the one hundred years in question the theatre in Spain presents a spectacle of constant and continuous development. By the end of the sixteenth century, the principal towns and cities had fixed theatres, the *corrales*, as opposed to the groups of itinerant actors who in the earlier part of the century had performed in town and village squares. By the 1630s the more elaborate Court theatres had come into being, notably in the Buen Retiro just outside Madrid, where technical innovation and ingenious stage-designers made possible the presentation of complex plays and highly elaborate stage-effects. If, in conjunction with the development of the *corrales*, or public theatres, and the more sophisticated Court theatres, account is also taken of the vigorous tradition of religious plays or *autos sacramentales* that were performed throughout this period to celebrate the festival of Corpus Christi, some idea may be formed of the richness of what on its own merits has come to be called Golden-Age drama[1].

vii

I. THE SPANISH *COMEDIA*

The Spanish *comedia* of the seventeenth century – *comedia* is simply used to mean 'play' – was fashioned in large part by Lope de Vega (1562-1635), building on and perfecting the experiments of a number of lesser dramatists of the late sixteenth century. During the first half of the sixteenth century, when there were no established public theatres or acting companies in Spain, drama was for the most part associated with the Court or the Church and reveals little of the truly popular character that was to distinguish its later development. Thus Juan del Encina (1468?-1530?), initially a courtier and later an archdeacon and canon, wrote both highly artificial pastoral *églogas*, or eclogues, and religious pieces. Similarly, Gil Vicente (1465?-1537?), a dramatist at the Portuguese Court from 1502 to 1536, wrote for a sophisticated bilingual court audience, producing romantic comedies, morality plays, allegorical fantasies and pastoral works, eleven of them in Spanish. The work of a third dramatist, Bartolomé de Torres Naharro (1485?-1520?), reveals both a marked Italian influence and a knowledge of classical theory which makes his contribution to the later drama quite significant. But none of these dramatists, though important in their way, suggest the emergence of the *comedia* of Lope de Vega as clearly as do the group of writers who appeared in the latter part of the sixteenth century.

Although Lope de Rueda (1509?-1565) is an influential rather than outstanding dramatist, his short comic plays or *pasos* are the clear predecessors, both in their lively, down-to-earth prose dialogue and their sharply-drawn characters and situations, of the strong comic element in the drama of the seventeenth century. This popular comic strain is to be found too in the short pieces or *entremeses* of Cervantes (1547-1616), a great admirer of Rueda. It is, though, in the serious drama of the last twenty-five years of the sixteenth century that the most significant changes are to be seen. Juan de la Cueva (1550?-1610), Cervantes, Lupercio Leonardo de Argensola (1559-1613) and others wrote plays in which the influence of classical tragedy is strong, though in some of them the subject is Spanish, thus anticipating the highly nationalistic character of the theatre of Lope and his followers. Secondly, we see a movement away from the five-act classical format to a play of four and, in some cases, three acts, the structure to be adopted by Lope himself. Again, there are numerous examples of the breaking of the classical unities of place and time and evidence too of the variety of metre and stanza-forms which Lope would advocate so strongly. And finally, all these changes were taking place at a time when theatres were themselves beginning to evolve. The stage was set for the emergence of the true seventeenth-century *comedia*.

The dramatic formula worked out by Lope in his plays and advocated in a poetic essay of 1609, the *Arte nuevo de hacer comedias en este tiempo*, may be described briefly as follows: the play has a three-act structure, corresponding to the exposition of the situation, its complication and dénouement; the strict separation of serious and comic elements is abandoned, even though the predominant mood of a given play may range from tragic, to tragic-comic, to comic; the unities of action, time and place are greatly relaxed, for the main plot is often interwoven with one or more sub-plots, the time-span of the events portrayed in a play usually extends beyond twenty four hours and in some instances covers many years, and the action, far from being limited to a single setting, ranges widely, moving not only from inside to outside, and town to town, but also from country to country; the language of the play is accommodated to the subject-matter and the status of the speaker, which, given the mixture of serious and comic elements mentioned above, means in turn a mixture of styles and language, embracing kings, noblemen, servants, soldiers and peasants; a variety of metre and stanza forms is used, corresponding to the dramatic requirements of given situations, but the backbone of the *comedia* is, in fact, the eight-syllable line with assonance in alternate lines, the traditional line of Spanish ballad poetry distinguished above all by its capacity to inject pace and vitality into the spoken word; subject-matter avoids, on the whole, classical material (Calderón is the exception here) and draws instead on Spanish history, legend and literature, as well as on Italian sources; and finally, the aim of the *comedia* is, in the tradition of classical literature, to entertain and delight and at the same time to teach – an idea encapsulated in the phrase *deleitar aprovechando* which is, curiously enough, the title of a book by Tirso de Molina.

The dramatic formula outlined above, so different from French classical theatre yet so reminiscent of Elizabethan drama, was practised by Lope in all his writing for the stage, was received enthusiastically by a theatre-going public eager for novelty and excitement, and provided the model which Lope's contemporaries and successors followed and adapted in their different ways. Lope's own drama is one of immense variety. On the one hand there are plays like *Fuente Ovejuna* or *Peribáñez* in which history and the clash of nobles and peasants provide the material for the portrayal of essentially human and individual conflicts, combining emotional impact and didactic intention. On the other, the Bible provided Lope with much material, as in the case of *La hermosa Ester*, his dramatisation of the Book of Esther. Thirdly, there are delightful comedies of intrigue, often revolving around the theme of love, such as *La discreta enamorada, Amar sin saber a quien* and *Las bizarrías de Belisa*. And finally there are much darker, more tragic plays, many of them focusing on the code of personal honour and the consequences of its loss: such is *El castigo sin venganza*, a particularly grim piece which ends in bloodshed and anguish, and is one of the finest tragedies written in the Golden Age. It has to be said, nevertheless, that the volume and variety of Lope's theatre makes any categorization impossible, as indeed is the case with many of the dramatists who followed in his footsteps: Tirso de Molina (1581?-1648), Pérez de Montalbán (1602-38), Vélez de Guevara (1579-1644), Ruiz de Alarcón (1581?-1639) Mira de Amescua (1574?-1644) and Calderón de la Barca (1600-81). The list is incomplete, but it is sufficient to give some idea of the dynamism of the theatre of seventeenth-century Spain which Lope helped so much to generate[2].

II. THE GOLDEN AGE *CORRAL*

Although mention has been made of the Court theatres, the development of the *comedia* took place in the public theatres or *corrales* and was influenced greatly by the physical characteristics of such spaces. As the word suggests, a *corral* was in fact a courtyard, rectangular in shape and overlooked by the backs of houses. It was also therefore largely exposed to the sky. The stage, situated at one end of the rectangle, projected into it. The central area of the auditorium, the *patio*, was nothing more than a large space where the commoners stood to watch the play. A few rows of seats ran along the sides of the theatre arranged in tiers, and above these were the windows of the surrounding houses which served as boxes, *aposentos*, and which were often hired by the wealthy on an annual basis. At the back of the theatre, at ground-floor level, were the entrances, one for men and one for women, as well as the theatre bar or *fruteria*, while at first-floor level were to be found the enclosures specifically set aside for women of the lower classes and unflatteringly known as *cazuelas*, or stewpots. Finally, at second-floor level, directly above the *cazuelas*, was another enclosure, the *tertulia*, which was reserved for the clergy.

The stage itself consisted of a projecting apron, a mid-stage and back-stage area. There was no proscenium arch or curtain. Part of the back-stage was usually curtained off and its curtains could be drawn back to reveal an inner space or to disclose some dramatic 'discovery'. Above the stage was a gallery which ran round the theatre at first-floor level and which could be brought into use when the stage-action required, as, for example, the top of a mountain or the battlements of a castle. At a level higher still the balcony of a house might be used to represent Heaven, and the various levels could be linked to the stage by ladders and ramps which could be used by the actors to move from one level to another. In the floor of the stage a trapdoor might be employed to suggest a pit or even Hell itself, belching forth smoke and even flames. The more sophisticated public theatres possessed various kinds of stage-machinery such as rocks which could open, and the wealthier acting companies seem to have had an excellent stock of costumes, though it has to be said that characters of whatever period wore contemporary costume. In general, scenery was simple and, since the theatres were exposed to the skies and performances took place in daylight, audiences were obliged and were, of course, accustomed to using their imaginations. Undoubtedly, the performance of plays presented those audiences with a vigorous, swift-moving and exciting spectacle.

A typical afternoon performance in a *corral* would commence with musicians playing and singing. Then would come the *loa*, a kind of prologue recited or sung in praise of an individual, the audience, or the play, and followed by the performance of the play itself. Between the acts short farces would be presented - *entremeses* and *sainetes* -, so that there was no interval in the modern sense to interrupt the continuous flow of the action and allow a restless Spanish audience to become bored. Not without cause did Lope himself comment in his *Arte nuevo* on this aspect of Spanish theatre-goers as well as on their craving for entertainment. It was this, indeed, which meant that a run of any given play was usually of no more than two or three days.

As for the actors themselves, they were organized into companies in the cities, each company coming together during Lent and beginning the theatrical year at Easter. The theatre-going season would then last until Lent came round once more. Each acting company was headed by an *autor de comedias*, a manager, not to be confused with the dramatist who would be known as the *poeta* or *ingenio* and from whom the manager of a company would obtain his plays. An acting company would contain about four young actors, including the lead-actor or *primer galán*, two men specializing in elderly parts (*barbas*), two comedians (*graciosos*), and six actresses, including the female lead or *primera dama*. While these companies performed for most of the time in the *corrales*, they might also be called upon for performances in the Court theatres as they developed over the years, an order which they could hardly refuse to comply with but which created difficulties for the management of the *corrales* and greatly inconvenienced the theatre-going public of Madrid whose two public theatres, the Corral de la Cruz and the Corral del Príncipe, founded in 1579 and 1582 respectively, were deprived of plays for many weeks at a time.

The theatres of the Golden Age came into being as providers of income for charitable institutions, in particular hospitals, and they were indeed both the owners and the beneficiaries of Madrid's two public theatres. Initially the running of these theatres was placed in the hands of lessees, but by the seventeenth century they had become the equivalent of theatre managers whose responsibilities involved both the hiring of acting companies and the general administration of the entire organization, a part of the daily box-office takings and the cost of the lease of the theatre going to the hospitals. Later on the ownership and administration of the theatres would be taken over by the Town Council itself, and the hospitals then received an annual subsidy. The link between the theatres and the hospitals also had an important consequence in relation to the frequency with which plays were performed and the length of time for which they ran. At first plays were performed only on Sundays and holidays, but the financial needs of the hospitals meant that eventually performances were given on most days of the week. This being the case, and Madrid having a relatively small population with an enormous appetite for the theatre, a given play was unlikely to run for more than a week, a factor which in turn accounts for the vast productivity of the dramatists of the Golden Age.

Finally, it is important to draw attention to the kind of public which went to the theatre. In Madrid this evidently embraced all sections of the population. The standing area, by far the largest part of the auditorium, would have been occupied by the ordinary people, including the noisier elements – servants and soldiers – who both abused or applauded the actors and argued amongst themselves. The rows of seats along the sides of the theatre would clearly be taken by wealthier and more educated members of the public, and the balconies and rooms overlooking the stage, some of which were reserved for town offcials, would be rented by the nobility. Even the King had a 'box' at the Corral de la Cruz. The audience, in short, consisted of a great cross-section of the public, in consequence of which the dramatists were obliged to appeal to a variety of tastes ranging from the 'groundlings' to the monarch. In those circumstances it is hardly surprising that the theatre of the Golden Age should be distinguished by its variety as well as its vitality[3].

III. TIRSO DE MOLINA
Life

    Tirso de Molina is the pseudonym of Fray Gabriel Téllez who was born in Madrid, probably in 1580. Nothing certain has been discovered about his parentage, although the theory has been advanced by Doña Blanca de los Ríos that he was the illegitimate son of the Duke of Osuna. An entry in one of the parish registers of Madrid for March 9, 1584, refers to Gabriel, son of Gracia Juliana and an unknown father, while some words added in the margin and subsequently crossed out were deciphered by Doña Blanca as '*Tz. Girón, hijo del Dq. Osuna*', i.e., Téllez Girón, son of the Duke of Osuna[4]. Most scholars have dismissed the evidence for the theory as far too flimsy, but if it is in fact correct and the Gabriel Téllez mentioned there was the child who later became Tirso de Molina, the dramatist was the son of one of the most famous noblemen and public figures of the Golden Age. The strongest contradictory evidence to the above is to be found in documents, one of which points to Tirso's birth in 1583, while the other – a personal statement – indicates that he was born in 1580.

    In 1600 Tirso became a novice in the Mercedarian Order in Guadalajara and, on completion of his novitiate, became a friar of the order. Undoubtedly, he would have undergone a very thorough training in theology, though his works are certainly not cramped or inhibited in any way by the oppressive weight of dogma. 1606, 1607 and the years 1612-15 find him in the house of the Mercedarian Order in Toledo, and it seems likely that there he met Lope de Vega, then a resident of that city. At all events, documentary evidence shows that in 1612 Tirso sold three plays to an actor-manager in Toledo. Clearly, his interest in the theatre was increasing, and the years immediately following witnessed the composition of some of his very best work.

New portrait of Tirso de Molina by Anthony Stones, 1985.

In 1616 Tirso was sent with six monks of the order to the West Indian island of Santo Domingo where he remained and taught theology for two years. It was probably the expedition to the Caribbean which allowed Tirso to become acquainted with the ports of Lisbon and Seville respectively, both of which were to figure prominently in *The Trickster of Seville*. After his return from Santo Domingo, he lived in Toledo, and in 1620 moved to his birthplace, Madrid, commencing there a period of intense literary activity and participation in literary competitions which seems to have ended abruptly in 1625. On March 6 of that year, the *Junta de reformación*, a body appointed to safeguard public morality, accused Maestro Téllez, otherwise known as Tirso, of writing profane works and recommended the King, Philip IV, to banish the dramatist to a remote house of his order where, under threat of excommunication, he be forbidden to write *comedias*. Although in 1626 Tirso was made prior of a Mercedarian friary at Trujillo in Extremadura, a long way off from Madrid, it seems unlikely that this was in response to the accusation of the *Junta*. He remained at Trujillo until 1629, after which he may have moved to Toledo. At all events he was promoted in 1632 to the position of historian of the Order of Mercy. In 1634 he returned to Madrid and over the next two years, assisted by a nephew, published four volumes of his plays. In 1640 a member of his own order, Fray Marcos Salmerón, an official visitor to the friary of the Order of Mercy in Madrid, instructed that no inhabitant of the friary should have in his possession any book of profane plays or poetry or write prose or poetry which attacked or criticised the government of the day. Tirso, choosing to ignore the instruction, was banished for a time to Soria but later returned to Madrid. In 1645 he became prior of the friary of the Order of Mercy in Soria. Two years later he moved to Almanzán, also in Soria, where he died in 1648.[5]

Drama

Tirso's dramatic work can on the whole be categorized rather more easily than that of the prolific Lope, though in the last resort any attempt at classification has its dangers. Broadly speaking, Tirso can be said to have written (a) comedies, (b) historical plays, and (c) religious dramas.

The comedies are, for the most part, about love, particularly jealousy, and involve a group of lovers, a tangle of relationships, and thus a complex plot. Amongst them are some skilfully written and amusing pieces, such as *Don Gil de las calzas verdes*, but as a comic dramatist Tirso is considered by many critics to have lacked both the inventiveness and the dramatic technique of Lope de Vega and to have lapsed too often in the comedies into cliché and the mechanical working-out of a well-tried dramatic formula. On the other hand, the comedies are often distinguished by an insight into character which is a feature of Tirso's drama as a whole. Thus, *El vergonzoso en palacio* contains some interesting examples of female psychology – a sister far bolder than her bashful suitor, and another sister, averse to men, who falls in love with a portrait of herself in male costume. Other plays reveal women who are ambitious and forceful and who to that extent suggest a reversal of traditional roles. In general, though, in accordance with the formula of comedy, character is subordinated to plot, and it was left to Tirso's more serious work to develop this aspect of his art.

As far as the historical plays are concerned, there is a good deal of unevenness, but also some very fine pieces. Tirso's best-known historical play, *La prudencia en la mujer*, has as its protagonist Queen María, widow of Sancho IV of Castile and León, and deals with her struggle to retain the throne for her son, Ferdinand, in a time of political upheaval. The strength of the play lies, clearly, in the presentation of the courageous and heroic central figure surrounded by treacherous and scheming enemies, as well as in its powerful and stirring language, while the relevance of its message to the contemporary political situation – the manipulation of the young Philip IV by the powerful Count-Duke of Olivares – adds a further ring of authenticity. Another chronicle-play of considerable interest and power is *Antoña García* in which the country-girl, Antoña, takes up the cause of the Catholic Kings, Ferdinand and Isabella, in defiance of the local feudal overlord. Once more Tirso turns historical material into powerful and exciting theatre and creates in the main character an enormously vital and appealing heroine.

Tirso's religious plays consist of powerful dramas based on biblical stories and works whose themes are religious in a more general sense. Amongst the former are *La venganza de Tamar*, a dramatisation of the story of King David's warring children; *La mujer que manda en casa*, based on the story of Jezebel and Naboth; and *La mejor espigadera*, which takes its material from the Book of Ruth. Tirso, of course, brought his theological training and knowledge to bear on the dramatic treatment of the material in question, but above all these are plays which portray human conflict at crucial moments in the history of a people. Nothing illustrates the point better than *La venganza de Tamar*, generally acknowledged to be one of Tirso's very finest works. On a human level the fatal attraction of Amnon, David's son, for his half-sister, Tamar; his violation of her; his murder by her brother, the envious and ambitious Absalom: all the complexity of individual and collective motivation is convincingly and movingly set before us. On a broader level, the sense of individuals as part of a greater, unfolding pattern in which sin, guilt and punishment are closely interwoven, contributes to a feeling of universality.

Amongst the plays that deal with religious material in a more general sense, *El condenado por desconfiado* is particularly outstanding and, along with *The Trickster of Seville*, is probably Tirso's best-known play. The intellectual background to the play has to do with the theological controversy waged at the end of the sixteenth century between the Molinists and the Banezians over the extent to which Divine Grace enables a man to achieve salvation. In the controversy the Molinists held free-will to be of enormous importance, almost to the exclusion of the role of God's grace, while the Banezians clung to the totally different view that man was virtually predestined. Tirso's play embodies the different viewpoints in its two central characters: Paulo, the hermit who believes that Divine Grace is not available to the true sinner, convinces himself that confession of his sins is useless, and is doomed; and Enrico, the criminal who, for all his terrible crimes, believes in God's mercy, repents, and is saved. But if *El condenado por desconfiado* is a play of ideas, it is, more than that, a play about human conflict and dilemma, and in this respect Paulo and Enrico are two of the most memorable characters in the whole of Golden-Age drama: the former an apparently pious man beset by doubt, arrogantly rebelling against the fate which he thinks God has in store for him; the latter a passionate, instinctive monster of a man redeemed by love of his father, which leads him finally to trust in God's mercy. Undoubtedly, it can be argued that the play's religious preoccupations limit its broader appeal, particularly to an age in which religious values have declined. On the other hand, it cannot be denied that in terms of characterization, construction and emotional impact, *El condenado por desconfiado* is a very great play[6].

Tirso and the Lopean *comedia*

As we have seen, Lope's views on the drama had been expressed in 1609 in the *Arte nuevo de hacer comedias*. His enthusiasm for a new form of drama which broke the stranglehold of Classicism led in the years that followed to an often fierce controversy in which individuals took up entrenched positions and in which Tirso himself came down very firmly on Lope's side. In 1621 he wrote, for example, a miscellany of stories, plays and poems entitled the *Cigarrales de Toledo* in which a group of well-to-do people leave Toledo for their estates and proceed to entertain themselves. The performance of Tirso's own *El vergonzoso en palacio* leads to a discussion on theatre and to a discourse by one of the characters which amounts to Tirso's defence of Lope's dramatic practice. Above all, Tirso argues, the aim of the drama should be the imitation of life. In this context any attempts to preserve the unity of time and to suggest something as complex as a love-affair in an action covering twenty-four hours is the very opposite of life-like, as indeed is the strict separation on the stage of the serious and the comic. The argument that the ancients deserve respect for their achievements is not to say that their work cannot be improved upon. Indeed, times change and taste changes accordingly, demanding a new art of which Lope is justifiably the champion:

> Lope, having established the *comedia* and endowed it with its present subtlety and perfection, is great enough to lead a school of his own; and those amongst us who regard ourselves as his followers should consider ourselves fortunate to have such a master, and should always defend his teachings against those who violently impugn them.[7]

There are, of course, essential differences between Tirso and Lope as dramatists. Firstly, Tirso clearly lacked that gift for spontaneity and sheer inventiveness which led to Lope's being known as the *monstruo de naturaleza*, a dramatist as creative as Nature itself. On the other hand, as earlier remarks have perhaps suggested, Tirso's intellect was greater than Lope's so that many of his works have a greater profundity and seriousness, and in that sense look forward to the more intellectual drama of Calderón. Again, Tirso's insight into character and the working of the human mind, sharpened no doubt by his experience as a priest, is sharper and deeper than Lope's and to that extent has been regarded by some

xviii

critics as more Shakespearean.[8] In terms of dramatic technique, Tirso tends to be the more careful of the two writers in the construction of his plots and, although *The Trickster* is not a good example, reveals in many of his plays a striking ability to interweave in different proportions main and sub-plots, or two plots of equal importance, as is the case in the brilliantly constructed *El condenado por desconfiado*.

IV. THE TRICKSTER OF SEVILLE
The two versions

Two early printed versions of the play exist: *El burlador de Sevilla y convidado de piedra* was published in a collection of plays dated 1630 and is stated there to be a '*comedia famosa del Maestro Tirso de Molina*'; another version, entitled *Tan largo me lo fiáis*, was published by itself, with no date, and carrying the words '*comedia famosa de Don Pedro Calderón*'.[9] The problems surrounding the accurate dating and priority of seventeenth-century printed texts is indeed complex, and is not the concern of this Introduction, but the general conclusions to be drawn from the available evidence are as follows: the differences between the two versions, which involve the names of some of the characters (Don Juan's father is one), certain speeches (*Tan largo* has in Act I a speech not on Lisbon but on Seville), individual scenes and the use of particular verse-forms, point on balance to *Tan largo's* being, despite all its imperfections, closer to Tirso's original. It derives in the printed form we have, which may well be as late as 1660, from earlier printings. The text of *El burlador*, on the other hand, is probably a version constructed from the memory of a number of people: possibly Tirso himself; a company of actors; or a memory-man used by a company to pirate the play of another company. In conclusion, it has to be recognized that both versions are imperfect and somewhat removed from the original play. In terms of theatre *El burlador* is often better than *Tan largo*, no doubt because it owes something to people working in the theatre, and it is the version which is generally available in modern editions.

Authorship

As the earlier discussion has shown, the name of Tirso de Molina appears on the title-page of *El burlador de Sevilla* in the collection of plays dated 1630, while *Tan largo* is attributed to Calderón. The latter possibility is not, in fact, one that has ever been taken seriously, but it is an indication of the problems that often surround both the authorship and dating of

Golden-Age plays. Indeed, an argument has been put forward for Andrés de Claramonte as the *refundidor* or reviser of the 1630 version of *El burlador*.[10] Four of the play's lines appear in one of his own plays, *Deste agua no beberé*; he was a known plagiarist; and he also had his own company of actors. A reasonable hypothesis is that Claramonte revised an earlier version of *El burlador* for a performance by his own company and was thus responsbile for some of its corruptions. Be this as it may, there is nothing to suggest that Tirso was not the original author of the play. The style is generally consistent with his work; the versification corresponds on the whole to Tirso's practice; and the suggested date of composition is clearly well within the period of his writing for the theatre. Even if the play does not form part of the *Partes* or collections of Tirso's work (each *Parte* containing twelve plays), its omission, given the circumstances surrounding the publication of such volumes, does not mean that Tirso did not write *El burlador*.

Date

The actual date of composition of the original play from which *El burlador* and *Tan largo* derive is pure supposition. Tirso was, as we have seen, in Seville in 1616 on his way to the Indies, but he was also there on his return in 1618. In 1619 Philip III visited Lisbon, which may account for the speech about Lisbon in *El burlador*. The title-page of the latter in the collection dated 1630 states that it was performed by Roque de Figueroa who, records indicate, did not have his own company until 1624, while in 1625 there is evidence of the performance in Naples of a play called *Il convitato di pietra*, probably in Spanish, by the company of Pedro Osorio. In short, it seems that the original certainly existed by 1625 and may well date back to 1616. It does not seem likely that the play was written before 1616.[11]

Sources

Attempts have been made by various scholars to discover a source for Tirso's Don Juan amongst his contemporaries. One such theory, held for quite a long time, was that he was modelled on Miguel de Mañara Vincentelo de Lesca, reputed to be an infamous libertine who subsequently changed his ways. The discovery that Mañara was born in Seville in 1626 and was therefore only a child when Tirso wrote his play is sufficient indication of the perils of flying such kites. Other historical models have also been suggested, including Mateo Vázquez de Leca, a Sevillian, nephew of Philip II's secretary, who is said

xx

to have lived a scandalous youth and who was born in 1571. The most convincing, if any are convincing, is, however, Don Pedro Téllez Girón, Marquis of Peñafiel and later to become the notorious Duke of Osuna. In his own lifetime (1579–1624) Don Pedro's adventures were indeed scandalous. During his teenage years, his father found it impossible to control him, he married early but continued to indulge in numerous affairs, he frequently broke his word, lied, obtained money under false pretences, and even killed a man in a brawl. An idea of his notoriety can be gleaned from the fact that his exploits became, not long after his death, the subject of a play, *Las mocedades del duque de Osuna*, by Cristóbal Monroy y Silva. Morevoer, Don Pedro's official residence was at Osuna, a town near Seville, and he therefore made Seville the focal point of his various activities, making his mark in a city known for its crime and general sleaziness. In addition, it seems that he had a particular liking for the sexual trick, the *burla*, so favoured by Tirso's Don Juan. And finally, as far as a personal link with Tirso is concerned, there is the intriguing possibility that, as Doña Blanca de los Ríos has suggested, Don Pedro Téllez Girón may have been his half-brother, in which case the portrayal of Don Juan and his scandalous behaviour can be seen as Tirso's reaction to and rebuke of someone who would not recognise him as a Girón.[12]

A second line of argument suggests that particular features of *The Trickster* are to be found in Italian religious drama supposedly of the fifteenth and sixteenth centuries, in particular in a play called the *Ateista fulminato*. The play deals with the seduction of Leonora by Count Aurelio and his punishment by the statues of the girl's parents who drag him down to Hell. A promising theory turns out in the end to be supported by extremely flimsy evidence, for it has now been proved that this play belongs to the end of the seventeenth century and, far from influencing *The Trickster*, is influenced by it. Another suggested dramatic source is *Leonzio, ovvero la terrible vendetta di un morto*, first performed at the Jesuit school of Inglostadt in 1615. Count Leonzio, a follower of Machiavelli, kicks a skull which he finds near a cemetery and invites it to dinner. The invitation is taken up by an enormous figure who proves to be Leonzio's grandfather, sent by God to punish the young man, who splits his skull and takes him to Hell. While this plot lacks some of the essential ingredients of the Don Juan play, in particular the return-invitation motif, it clearly reflects important elements of a legend widely known throughout Europe and in which the most probable source for *The Trickster* is to be found.

This legend, part of ancient European folklore and frequently found in ballad form, describes a young man who is in many versions on his way to church and comes across a skull or a skeleton which he kicks or insults and mockingly invites to dinner. The dead man, in the form of a ghost, skull, skeleton or even statue, appears and invites the young man to eat with him, on which occasion he is either punished by death or escapes because he is protected by a holy relic.

As far as the Hispanic versions of the tale are concerned, all but one contain the return-invitation motif and most suggest that the young man is on his way to church not to hear Mass but to look at the girls. Clearly, these elements are both prominent in *The Trickster*, the second in the character of Don Juan himself, the former leading to the play's climactic scene in the church. Of particular interest here is the work done many years ago by Marcelino Menéndez Pelayo and Ramón Menéndez Pidal in relation to popular ballads in the provinces of Burgos, León and Segovia. A ballad discovered in León in the village of Cureña contains the following elements: a young man goes to church to look at the girls; he sees a skull at the roadside, kicks it and invites it to supper; the skull arrives in time for the meal and invites the young man to eat with him in the churchyard; the young man accepts the invitation and, protected by a religious relic he is wearing, escapes with a warning. A second ballad which Menéndez Pidal says was recited to him in 1905 in Riaza in the province of Segovia, is even more interesting in relation to *The Trickster* and for this reason is given here in my own translation:[13]

> There was a young man, the story says,
> Who went to church to say his prayers.
> Once there he knelt, his prayer began,
> Close to the figure of a stone man.
> The youngster pulled the statue's beard,
> And said to him, as though he heard:
> 'You're a respectable old sod!
> Who would have thought that this young bod
> Would one day have the nerve to dare
> To tug the thin and scrawny hair
> Of your chin? Why don't you tonight
> Turn up at my place for a bite
> To eat? I know you won't agree.
> Your belly's not exactly pretty.
> On the contrary, it's long and thin.
> I doubt that you'll eat anything.'
> At that the young man took his leave;

How could he, after all, conceive
What the consequences might be
Of that outrageous affrontery?
And so it was around nightfall
The dead man came to pay his call.
The servants said: 'Who's at the door?'
Came the reply: 'Only a poor
Lost soul who's looking for a meal.
Go quick, ask your master if he'll
Accommodate the man he's asked
To come to share his evening repast.'
The servants hurried with this news.
It left the master all confused.
Within his bones he felt a chill;
With sudden fear his heart stood still.
But, even so, the master said:
'Invite him in, although he's dead.'
The servants went and lit two flares
So the stone man could climb the stairs.
They placed a chair in front of him
That, if he wished, he could sit in.
'Eat all you want', the young man said.
'The food's ready. Get yourself fed!'
'Thank you', the corpse replied. 'I'm fine.
I've only come to see you dine.
But I'd like to know if you'll agree
To share another meal with me
In the churchyard, tomorrow night'.
The young man rose when it was light,
Got quickly dressed, left his abode,
To San Francisco's church he rode
And there called for a man of God,
Confessing his sins as best he could.
The priest, granting him confession,
Gave him a cross for his protection.
So the youngster, when darkness came,
Made his way to the church again.
There he beheld a pick and spade,
And an open grave freshly made.
Nine o'clock and everything silent,
The dead man kept his grim appointment.
'Now, my fine fellow, come and eat.
For you I've prepared a real treat:
Scorpions and vipers for our dinner,
Accompanied by gall and vintage vinegar.'

xxiii

The young man viewed this grisly sight,
And suddenly lost his appetite.
'You can be glad', the dead man said,
'You've just partaken of holy bread.
Otherwise I'd force you to join in,
Make you account for a life of sin.
Always remember what I've said.
Don't make fun of those that are dead.
Instead, pray that their souls find rest,
Or you'll become my permanent guest.
Take heed out there, all you sinners,
Unless you wish to come to dinner.'

While there are great similarities between both the León and the Riaza ballads, the latter not only has a stone figure but emphasizes the hostile relationship between him and the young man. The date of the ballads cannot be ascertained with any certainty, but it seems quite likely that they preceded Tirso's play and that he knew them. As a source for *The Trickster*, they appear to be a very likely possibility, though they cannot, given their brevity, flesh-out the characters. It was left to Tirso to create the character of Don Juan, and in doing that he had many models in contemporary Spanish drama. The measure of his success may be gauged by the extent to which Tirso's protagonist, the first-ever Don Juan, inspired so many later writers and musicians to produce their variations on the original.

V. ANALYSIS OF THE PLAY
Themes

Like its Elizabethan counterpart, the drama of the Golden Age is both entertaining and instructive: a case, as has been pointed out, of *deleitar aprovechando*. Its moral emphasis and thus the importance of theme has been greatly emphasized and probably over-stated by A.A. Parker in numerous studies over the last forty years, but it would, of course, have been inconceivable that the theatre of a country as fervently Catholic as seventeenth-century Spain should not have placed due emphasis on moral issues.[14] In this respect the action of *The Trickster* revolves around a cluster of themes.

The principal theme of *The Trickster* is undoubtedly the theme of justice, embodied in the words of the statue as it destroys Don Juan:

                         His fate provides the lesson
           You should heed, for each man reaps the harvest
           Of his deeds.   (Act III, 973-75)
Whether or not Don Juan is damned is not specifically stated,
but his punishment, extremely painful and without confession,
is certainly a case of divine retribution for an offence which,
over and above all others, is an offence against God. This
consists essentially of an assumption by Don Juan that the
mercy of God will be available to him, as it were, on demand,
and that there is therefore no need to ask for it until the very
last moment: the source of his oft-repeated 'Plenty of time for
me to pay that debt!' The dangers of last-minute repentance
and of taking too much for granted were, indeed, frequently
emphasized by theologians and moralists in sixteenth and
seventeenth-century Spain and would certainly not have been
lost on a contemporary audience.
       While the offence against God is Don Juan's most serious
crime, divine retribution may be seen as a kind of
blanket-punishment covering a range of other misdemeanours,
most of them social.[15] The seductions perpetrated on Isabela,
Tisbea, Aminta and other women in the past involve deception
on Don Juan's part, and, as often as not, a violation of the
accepted laws of hospitality and friendship, as well as honour.
Thus, Tisbea and the fishermen care for and entertain Don
Juan and are cruelly taken advantage of, as are Aminta and
Batricio later in the play. Similarly, Don Juan uses his
friendship with Mota to further his designs on Ana and violates
the trust she places in him to seek entry to her house. And
having done so, and murdered her father to facilitate his own
escape, he has no scruples about allowing Mota to take the
blame for his misdeeds. The deliberate flaunting of accepted
standards of behaviour is not, though, something practised by
Don Juan alone. Isabela and Ana indulge in secret and illicit
affairs, scorning conventional moral attitudes and, in Ana's
case, deceiving a trusting father. Don Pedro Tenorio is guilty,
in protecting his wayward nephew, of disloyalty to the King of
Naples, while the King himself prefers to shut his eyes to much
that is going on around him. And at the other end of the social
scale, Aminta's father, Gaseno, is quite prepared to forget his
obligations to his proposed son-in-law, Batricio, if there is the
chance of her marrying a nobleman.
       Amongst the play's social themes, honour is especially
important.[16] As a nobleman or *caballero*, Don Juan possesses the
honour conferred on him by noble birth, as indeed do many of
the other characters in the play. Yet his and their behaviour

are often the opposite of what we would regard as honourable in the moral sense and point to the distinction between honour as reputation, social standing and public image, and honour as virtue, a theme much explored by Golden-Age dramatists. The two men in the play who are honourable in both senses of the word are Don Diego Tenorio, Don Juan's father, and Don Gonzalo de Ulloa. Other characters like Duke Octavio and Doña Ana fall below that standard, for their respective involvement in secret love affairs is immoral and a danger to their own and their families' good name. As for Don Juan, his 'honourable' status as a nobleman is denied by practically everything he does, from his failure to keep his promises to his defiance of the King's commands. Even the apparently honourable gesture of keeping his promise to the statue has to be weighed against Don Juan's self-interested desire of not wishing to be regarded as a coward. In short, Tirso's presentation of the theme of honour as it is embodied in Don Juan and most of the play's other characters serves to pinpoint the degree to which honour, in its true moral sense, has been devalued by a society bent on largely material pleasures, be it the pursuit of sex, status or money.

The latter is, of course, at the heart of two of the play's themes: the pursuit of pleasure and the passage of time. The traditional theme of 'enjoy life while you can', so typical of Renaissance attitudes, is embodied above all in Don Juan's breathless sexual journey through the play, but that philosophy, as the quotation indicates, is circumscribed by the inescapable fact of time running out, eloquently voiced by Catalinón in the phrase: 'Live now and pay later!' (Act II, 314). The theme of life's brevity and of the sands of time running through one's fingers is, indeed, all-pervasive in Spanish literature of the seventeenth century, the Baroque's disillusioned response to a Renaissance exuberance long disappeared as much as the austere reminder of a fervently Catholic Spain to those who would put too much faith in the fleeting pleasures of the physical and temporal world. To that extent *The Trickster*, far from being a jaunty catalogue of sexual adventures, voices the much more sombre thoughts of an age that was fully conscious of the proximity of life and death.

Characterization

Much has been written by many critics over many years about Don Juan, and a good deal about Tirso's Don Juan.[17] What we, the audience, know about him, however, is no more or less than the dramatist chooses to place before us in terms of action and word in the space of the two hours or more that the performance of the play requires. What, then, can we say about Don Juan Tenorio as the result of that observation? What, indeed, can we say about the other characters in the play?

Don Juan

The first thing to be said is that, whatever subsequent ages have made of him, Don Juan is not a great lover. Rather, the key to his character lies in the play's title, *The Trickster of Seville*, and it is the trick, the *burla*, the deception as much as the physical enjoyment of women which fascinates him. Thus it is not only the irresistible beauty of a woman that attracts him to her or the sensual pleasure of the encounter that lingers with him afterwards – on the contrary, it is the challenge to ingenuity and the winning of the victory that provide the stimulation and the sense of triumph. To that extent Don Juan, like his friend the Marquis of Mota, is a typical, dissolute, irresponsible Sevillian nobleman who delights in fooling and deceiving women. But he enjoys too mocking and getting the better of people in general. The attempted deception of Doña Ana is, for example, tied up with the deception of Mota to whom Don Juan delivers a false version of her message. After the seduction of Isabela in Act I, he leaves his uncle, Don Pedro, with the impression that he will lie low in Milan or Sicily but confides in the audience that he will head for Spain. Banished from Seville by the King, Don Juan defiantly returns. And seeing the statue of Don Gonzalo de Ulloa in the church, he mocks it by tugging at its beard and inviting it to dinner. In short, nothing is sacred or inspires reverence in Don Juan. He is the personification of that youthful arrogance and flippancy often to be found in the aristocracy.

If, on the other hand, Don Juan were nothing more than this, he would scarcely impress himself so firmly upon our imagination or have become a source of inspiration to other writers and musicians. The truth is, clearly, that there are in *The Trickster* clues to Don Juan's character and meaning that go deeper than that superficial, stock gallant mentioned above. The first occurs, surely, when in the opening scene, in reply to Isabela's inquiry about his identity, he describes himself as 'a man who's nameless' (Act I, 15). Though flippant, the remark invests this stanger in a woman's room at night with a sense of mystery and power that is increasingly in evidence as the action unfolds. In Act III, entering Aminta's bedroom at night, Don Juan observes: 'The hours of darkness are my special hours' (208). Earlier in the play Don Pedro Tenorio describes Don Juan's escape from the palace of the King of Naples in terms which invest him with daemonic significance: 'But I am quite convinced the very devil/Had in that person taken human form' (300-01). Cradled in Tisbea's lap, he makes an almost miraculous recovery for a man who has just been dragged from the sea, and the persistent allusions to fire, though part and parcel of the conventional language of love, have the effect - both here and elsewhere - of transforming him into an elemental force, an impression heightened constantly by the dynamism of his movement through the play, the darkness which frequently surrounds him, the devastation that he so often leaves in his wake, the galloping horses that bear him away, and the sheer energy and magnetism that seem to distinguish him from ordinary mortals. It is, though, Don Juan's final confrontation with the statue, the challenge flung out to those forces and powers beyond human understanding, that transform Don Juan from a merely flippant rebel against social norms into a much more heroic embodiment of the human spirit ranged against insurmountable odds. If it can be argued that Don Juan's refusal to be cowed by the statue stems from arrogance and self-esteem, and is therefore to be viewed negatively, it cannot be denied that the spectacle of such defiance in the face of dangers whose magnitude are not lost on him - Tirso very effectively suggests Don Juan's contained terror - is inspiring. Although crimes are punished and the moral lesson is set before us, Tirso seems in the closing scenes of his play to have created a figure with whose heroic stand he is, despite himself, in sympathy. In this original Don Juan Tenorio the seeds of later, more romantic and heroic versions have already been sown.

Isabela and Ana

Of the two noblewomen we only in fact see Isabela, for Ana never appears on stage. What both women have in common is their indulgence in secret love-affairs and their evident willingness on that account to run the risk of dishonour in relation both to themselves and their families.[18] As far as Isabela is concerned, there is little evidence in the play of any real love for Duke Octavio. After her seduction by Don Juan, she is much more concerned that Octavio will marry her and thus save her reputation. Later, the arranged marriage to Don Juan is less important to her than continuing gossip about her conduct, and when she finally marries Octavio there is nothing to indicate any enthusiasm. As for Ana, her letter to Mota stems from the King's decision to marry her to Octavio and points to a genuine desperation on her part, even though Mota is presented to us as a less than desirable catch. She is, perhaps, somewhat less calculating than Isabela, but on the other hand is not averse to deceiving her father. Neither woman is shown to be particularly virtuous, for all their beauty and social standing.

Tisbea and Aminta

Tisbea is by far the most interesting and intriguing female character in the play. In one sense she is a traditional literary type modelled on the disdainful shepherdesses of sixteenth-century pastoral novels: beautiful but aloof from her many male admirers. On the other hand, it is the sense of Tisbea's individuality, of the contradictions in her character, and of the powerful passions which boil beneath the cool and beautiful exterior which are the source of her real fascination for us. Her delight in the sufferings of her suitors stems not from her indifference to passion but from her belief in her own control of the situation.[19] It is this which is tested by Don Juan's arrival and which, after a teasing but dangerous game with him, begins to crumble. Having held the upper hand over the local fishermen, Tisbea discovers that, inasmuch as she finds Don Juan difficult to resist, he has the upper hand over her. Abandoned by him, her outrage, which is far more desperate than that of her disappointed suitors, seems directed as much at herself, conscious as she is of her own part in her downfall, as against Don Juan's treachery. Greater self-knowledge has been obtained only at great expense, leaving Tisbea with the proof that men are not to be trusted but also with the more disturbing question, previously not really asked of her, of the extent to which, in given circumstances, she can trust herself.

In comparison, Aminta is far less complex, a naïve country girl who is flattered and overwhelmed by the attentions of a courtier. In general she is also intrinsically more honest and virtuous than the other women in the play. She is annoyed by the fact that the arrival of Don Juan upsets Batricio; she protests when he enters her bedroom at night; although flattered by his attentions, her good sense tells her not to trust him; and she accepts his offer of marriage only when he leads her to believe that Batricio has abandoned her. She clearly does not merit the fate which Isabela, Ana and Tisbea bring upon themselves largely as the consequence of their misdemeanours. That she suffers is a comment less upon herself than upon the malice and self-interest of other people.

Octavio and Mota

Of the two noblemen Octavio is by far the better morally, though he is certainly not without fault. His secret affair with Isabela is less than admirable, though he is genuinely distraught by the news of her misdemeanours in the palace. On the other hand, he does not seem to mind the proposed marriage to Ana and, when that does not materialize, accepts Isabela without any obvious enthusiam. In general Octavio seems to be presented as a conventional *caballero*, conscious of his honour and social standing and set-up by Tirso to be mocked and poked fun at on that account.

Mota is another Don Juan but on an altogether different level. He is given to the same *burlas* or deceptions but without the same success. Don Juan's cheeky disregard for social convention and given individuals becomes in Mota a disagreeable callousness, the deception of sophisticated noblewomen and the cheating of ignorant whores. No doubt Mota regards himself as a sharp man-about-town but is easily duped by Don Juan himself and even obliged to suffer the consequences, albeit temporarily, of the latter's murder of Don Gonzalo. There is almost nothing to be said in favour of this idle, immoral, boastful and callous rake. The only possible explanation of Ana's interest in him is that she is unaware of his true character, and it does seem most unlikely that marriage to her will change him in any fundamental way.

Batricio and Gaseno

Although a shepherd, Batricio's concept of his own honour is that of a nobleman, a fact which allows Tirso to present this rustic in a comic manner. His willingness to yield Aminta to Don Juan to safeguard his *own* honour thus removes the sympathy we might otherwise feel for this unfortunate lover and renders his manipulation by Don Juan, comic. He completely lacks the resolution of peasants in other Golden-Age plays for whom their honour is, as much as reputation and name, their own integrity.

Gaseno, Aminta's father, is a social climber, less interested in his daughter's happiness than in the enticing possibility that her marriage to Don Juan will make her a lady and enhance his own standing. His pretentiousness is equalled only by his foolishness, and his protests at the outcome of events, though morally justified in themselves, are on his lips incongruous and comic.

xxx

Don Pedro and Don Diego Tenorio

Don Pedro, who is Don Diego's brother and Don Juan's uncle, is in a sense Don Juan thirty or more years on. As a young man he must have been very like his nephew in matters of seduction, and in questions of expediency shows now the same duplicity which in earlier years must have characterized his amorous exploits. The amorous *burla* of earlier years simply becomes Don Pedro's *burla* of the King of Naples and then of Octavio, both of them conducted with the kind of *panache* revealed by Don Juan himself in his various seductions. The parallel between uncle and nephew is further reinforced in the sense that both deceive others only to be deceived themselves: Don Pedro is himself fooled by Don Juan, despite the latter's promises, and Don Juan, as we have seen, is finally and fatally deceived by the stone guest. If Don Juan is the irresponsible, devil-may-care young courtier of his day, Don Pedro is the typical courtier-politician for whom duplicity passes for diplomacy.

Don Diego could not be more different. Like his brother, he occupies an important and influential position at Court, in this case the Spanish Court, but unlike Don Pedro he is never guilty of deceiving the King. Whenever Don Diego seeks to protect Don Juan, he does so out of concern for family honour, frequently upbraids his son for his scandalous behaviour, and, having failed to convince him of the error of his ways, commends his punishment to God. His failure to control Don Juan points, perhaps, to an earlier over-indulgence of the young man for which Don Diego, to judge by the severity of his warnings, now feels responsibility.

Don Gonzalo de Ulloa

Before his death at Don Juan's hands, Don Gonzalo strikes us as an extremely conventional figure. He is certainly rather stiff – even if the long Lisbon speech found its way into the play for reasons other than characterization –, highly deferential to the King, conventionally obsessive in relation to his honour, yet apparently ignorant of his daughter's secret meetings with Mota. His death is, of course, unjustified, though it is in part due to his lack of self-control, and prompts a certain sympathy, but on the whole Tirso portrays him, as he does so many of the characters, ironically.

The King of Naples

He appears only in Act I in relation to the indiscretions of Isabela and is presented by Tirso as a ruler who, above all, is anxious to protect his good name. In order to achieve that he prefers to have others – in this instance Don Pedro Tenorio – hush up possible scandals, but in placing his trust in such people he shows himself to be less than circumspect. In the King of Naples Tirso is clearly criticising the power invested in royal favourites by seventeenth-century Spanish monarchs.

Alfonso XI of Castile

Throughout the play King Alfonso is shown to be attempting to patch up the havoc created by Don Juan and to be in that respect a patcher and a botcher – in short, far removed from the idealized monarchs of many Golden-Age plays. No sooner has he arranged the marriage of Ana to Don Juan than news of the Isabela affair forces him to change his plan, while he appeases Octavio with the offer of Ana's hand in marriage. Subsequently, Mota is wrongly arrested on his orders and, when released, is allowed to marry Ana at her request. The King's bewilderment is exemplified by the play's final scene when he is bombarded by complainants. He is rescued, moreover, not by any decisive action on his part but by news of Don Juan's death at the hands of the statue. If in the course of the play Tirso presents a nobility which is self-seeking and corrupt, he also portrays a monarch who is less than ideal.

Catalinón

Catalinón is a particularly good example of the *gracioso*, the comic character of Golden-Age drama. In *The Trickster* the fact that he is the servant of a man as reckless and as scornful of all social and even divine constraints as Don Juan serves to highlight the traditional self-interest of the *gracioso* – particularly his concern for saving his own skin. The calamitous situations in which Catalinón finds himself in this play are more extreme than those confronting most *graciosos* and thus allow for highly amusing scenes, notably in the confrontations with the stone guest. In addition, though far from being a moral man himself, the *gracioso* was often used by Golden Age dramatists to express moral sentiments, usually in relation to his master's imprudent behaviour. In some respects, indeed, Catalinón's moral outrage at Don Juan's behaviour, particularly in regard to less fortunate girls like Aminta, seems to be perfectly genuine. This, combined with moments of weakness in which self-interest silences him, makes Catalinón an interesting and credible character, and he is certainly one of the most colourful of Golden Age *graciosos*.

Language

In the *Arte nuevo de hacer comedias* Lope de Vega had recommended that the dramatist's aim should be to imitate Nature, but at the same time made his characters speak in verse. On the other hand, he argued that the language of the play should never be so obscure as to make comprehension impossible and in practice aimed to create a dramatic style which, despite its imagery and sometimes ornate poetic elaboration, was clear, direct and capable of carrying the action swiftly forward. As one of Lope's principal supporters, Tirso largely followed his example in matters of language, and *The Trickster* is indeed distinguished by its racy, cut-and-thrust dialogue. In general too, in accordance with Lope de Vega's recommendations, language matches the social status of the characters, the earthiness of Catalinón contrasting, for example, with the more refined utterances of the noblemen. The principal exception to this rule is Tisbea, a fishergirl who indulges in poetic conceits more appropriate to a lady of the Court, yet the apparent incongurity is easily explained by Tisbea's belief in her own superiority.

In any Golden-Age play imagery is, much more than a purely decorative element, a pointer to the play's themes and is, more often than not, used systematically.[20] This is particularly true of *The Trickster*, for while there is nothing very original or subtle about its imagery, it does in fact underpin the play's dominant themes. In this respect the allusions to fire are important. On the one hand the image of fire evokes passion, be it Tisbea's or Don Juan's, but it may refer just as much to ardour as to destructive force. In addition, fire, as in the chapel scene, points to hell and damnation, or, by means of allusions to Troy in flames, links present to past treachery, thereby universalizing the particular situations of the play. Similarly, daemonic imagery occurs on a number of occasions and in a variety of ways, but always in association with Don Juan. His uncle describes him as 'the very devil' (I, 300) and Batricio believes that 'the devil sent him straight to us' (II, 677). The association is deepened by Don Juan's frequent allusions to darkness, while Catalinón's descriptions of him as 'the scourge of women' (I, 895) and 'a locust to all women!' (I, 436) add to our impression of Don Juan as a destructive and evil force.

The allusive nature of the play's imagery, repeatedly transforming the particular into the universal, may be illustrated too in relation to Tisbea, notably her allusion to the peacock's tail. Using this image to describe the beauty of the ship's sails (I, 487-93) destroyed by the assault of the waves, she fails to grasp, as we do not, the relevance to herself of this traditional embodiment of beauty and pride. The effect of the image, especially for an age accustomed to emblems, would have been – and still is for the most part – to underline Tisbea's shortsighted arrogance and simultaneously to place it in the context of the folly of pride in general, as though she were the example or text around which the ensuing sermon, the play itself, is constructed.

The same effect is achieved by means of the metaphor of payment which in one form or another threads its way through the play's dialogue. Thus Don Juan is warned repeatedly of the debt that he will finally have to pay. He repays Tisbea's kindness by deceiving her. Ana pays dearly for the deception of her father, while Mota acknowledges that he will be obliged to pay for a trick gone wrong. Don Diego's warning to his erring son refers to the payment that God will ultimately demand, and the idea of the reward linked to the actions of the individual is summed up in the statue's concluding words:

> His fate provides the lesson
> You should heed, for each man reaps the harvest
> Of his deeds.   (III, 973-4)

Clearly, much of the imagery has a strong didactic purpose and must be related to the moral purpose of the play as a whole. In this context the allusive, universalizing nature of many of the images makes sense too, for their effect is to transform individual episodes and characters into general examples that have a relevance to all of us.

Staging

Many of the points made earlier in relation to the Golden Age stage can be illustrated by reference to *The Trickster*.[21] A reading of the play reveals very clearly the continuous flow of the action and its movement through both time and space: from day to night, Italy to Spain, court to seashore to countryside. The dialogue itself is used by the dramatist, given the lack of scenery and the fact that the performance would have taken place in daylight, to inform the audience of the location and time of a given episode: the opening scene in the palace at night; Tisbea on the sea-shore by day; Don Juan and Mota in the streets of Seville at night; Aminta and Batricio in the countryside by day. The uninterrupted flow of the action and the frequent entrances and exits of different characters also allow us to see the importance of the two doors situated at either side of the back-stage. Thus at the beginning of Act I

Don Juan makes his exit from the palace. Not long afterwards, when Don Pedro Tenorio arrives to arrest Octavio, he enters by one of the doors. And in Act III both doors are used in a particularly striking way when Don Juan and Catalinón leave the stage, their exit suggesting their entrance into the church, only to emerge through the other door, the stage itself now becoming the interior of the church. It is a moment which suggests very vividly the great flexibility of the Golden-Age stage and its demands upon the imagination of the audience.

The so-called 'discovery space', a curtained area of the back-stage, is used on several occasions. Thus, when in Act III Don Juan enters Aminta's bedroom, it seems likely that this inner stage would be used. Again it would clearly be the place for Don Gonzalo's tomb in the church. In the same act the trap-door in the stage would have allowed the statue to drag Don Juan down to the lower regions, to the accompaniment of much noise and, probably, thunderflashes. In contrast, there seems to be no occasion in the play when the upper levels – the gallery and the balconies – would have been used, for there is no reference to mountains or to Heaven, and when in Act I Don Juan makes his escape by means of 'this high balcony' (106), he merely exits through one of the doors, for the action is taking place on the stage itself.

As far as costumes are concerned, they would have been seventeenth-century, despite the fact that the action is set in medieval times. Of particular interest in this respect, of course, is the way in which the statue would have been presented. It is more than likely played by an actor, dressed either to suggest the polychrome statues of the period or simply in grey cloak and gloves with his face masked. Another possibility is that the actor would have worn armour. And yet another, though less likely, is that the statue would have been represented by some kind of automaton, which the better-off companies of Tirso's time would have been able to afford and which was also within the capability of current technology.[22] At all events, we can well imagine how a seventeenth-century audience would have been transfixed by the appearance of a figure from the afterlife.

Don Juan after Tirso
Don Juan is, with Hamlet, Faust and Don Quixote, one of the great figures of world literature, yet few people on hearing his name would think of Tirso's Don Juan. In part this is due to a lack of familiarity with the literature and culture of Spain in comparison to, say, a much closer acquaintance with

Mozart's opera *Don Giovanni*, but it is explained too by the fact that in the popular imagination Don Juan has come to signify much more than the character created by one man or, indeed, a group of writers taken together and extending from Tirso to Bernard Shaw. Clearly, Don Juan is the expression of something deeply embedded in human nature, be it sexual desire or the pursuit of ideal beauty, and Tirso, in creating the first Don Juan, caught something of that. The writers and composers who followed Tirso also did so in varying degrees, adapting the Don Juan figure in the light of their own or their age's particular preoccupations.[23]

Molière's *Dom Juan ou le Festin de Pierre* was written only some thirty-five years after Tirso's play, was not based directly on it, and is very different from it, above all in its presentation of Don Juan as a thinking, sophisticated, self-justifying seducer rather than as a man of action. Molière has embodied in his protagonist the libertine and religious sceptic of his age, the self-absorbed sensualist intent on justifying and continuing his way of life at all costs. He thus transformed the Don Juan character into a figure who is much more intellectual and psychologically interesting, but who at the same time lacks the drive and passion of Tirso's hero and who, since he does not believe in the supernatural forces which confront him in the form of the statue, does not suggest the same kind of reckless and heroic challenge.

Mozart's *Don Giovanni*, first performed in 1787, brings together different elements from earlier versions of the story, for Da Ponte's libretto is an extremely effective synthesis of *The Trickster* and *Dom Juan* in particular. For this reason Don Giovanni retains the passion and vitality of Tirso's character as well as the wit and sophistication of Molière's Dom Juan. Nevertheless, Mozart's protagonist is still very much the cynical realist concerned solely with his own pleasure and in that sense is closer to Molière. The eighteenth century in general was less concerned with the religious aspects of Don Juan's pursuit of pleasure than with the pursuit of pleasure itself.

In the nineteenth century, in accordance with the preoccupations of Romanticism, the Don Juan story took a different turn. Hoffman's short story, *Don Juan*, presents the character as someone in search of the ideal woman and who, in his disappointment, wreaks his vengeance on man and God. He is also shown to be irresistible as far as women are concerned. This new conception of Don Juan, personifying romantic attitudes, influenced Hoffman's successors greatly, amongst them Alfred de Mussett, Hans Bethge, Nikolaus Lenau and

Alexander Pushkin. In Spain itself José Zorrilla's *Don Juan Tenorio*, first performed in 1844, portrays its hero as a ruthless seducer in pursuit of personal pleasure and therefore returns in a sense to Tirso's Don Juan. On the other hand, the Romantic element is to be seen in the fact that Don Juan Tenorio is a religious sceptic and is saved finally by the love of a pure woman. In short, Zorilla achieved an effective synthesis of the old and the new.

A reaction against the nineteenth-century Don Juan described above is to be found in the nineteenth century itself in the criticisms of such writers as Stendhal and Georges Sand who objected, for example, to Don Juan's devaluation of love and to his victimization of women. Despite such attacks, he continued to fascinate and draw different responses from different writers, and in the twentieth century has engaged the attention of creative writers as diverse as George Bernard Shaw, Albert Camus, Jean Anouilh and Henri de Montherlant. Shaw, whose *Man and Superman* belongs to the very beginning of the century, predictably uses the figure of Don Juan as a mouthpiece to voice his own ideas. The play deals with the idea of the Life Force and the roles of Man and Woman in relation to it, but in the course of the play Shaw reveals that Man is in fact used by Woman as an instrument to achieve her function of procreation, and Don Juan, far from being the pursuer, is the pursued. It is an interpretation which virtually closes the door on any further variation of the Don Juan myth. For Camus, whose collection of essays, *Le Mythe de Sisyphe*, published in 1942, contains a study of Don Juan, he is no mystic in search of pure love but a man who is constantly aware of the absurdity of human existence in the face of death and who therefore resolves to enjoy the life he has in the way he considers best: the enjoyment of women. In this respect the protagonist of Anouilh's *Ornifle ou le Courant d'air*, performed in 1955, is very similar, though the character is certainly small-scale. De Montherlant's *Don Juan*, written three years later, has a protagonist who is sixty-six years old, a man who is therefore facing death, who is conscious of the desperate need to squeeze every drop of pleasure out of life and who is, in more ways than one, a return to Tirso's obsessive seducer. Clearly, in the twentieth century, in accordance with its complex character, the Don Juan theme has undergone and is still likely to undergo varied and diverse treatments.

VI   THE TRANSLATION

In terms of metre and rhyme Golden-Age drama reveals certain marked differences from its Elizabethan counterpart. The *comedia* was not in fact tied to a single metre, and lines in a given play may be found to consist of seven, eight or eleven syllables. It is, however, the eight-syllable line which was by far the favourite of Golden-Age dramatists, and for a very good reason: it allows the dialogue to move swiftly and enabled the dramatists to create that sense of pace and movement in the play which, as we have seen, Lope de Vega felt essential if the interest of a Spanish audience was to be maintained.

As far as rhyme is concerned, Golden-Age drama is distinguished by its variety of rhyming stanza forms: eight-line *octavas*, ten-line *décimas*, five-line *quintillas*, four-line *redondillas*, three-line *tercetos*, all using the octosyllabic line. The most common and important form of all was, however, the *romance*, characterized not by full rhyme but by assonance: see, as a typical example, ll. 375-516 of Act I of *The Trickster* in which alternate lines have the characteristic *romance* pattern of repeated stressed and unstressed vowels – ros<u>a</u>, ol<u>a</u>s, sol<u>a</u>, etc. The line is again octosyllabic. In short, Golden-Age drama has a shorter line and a much greater degree of rhyme than Elizabethan drama with its normally unrhymed iambic pentameter.

In undertaking translations into English of Golden-Age plays, different translators have chosen different approaches. As far as *The Trickster* is concerned, Roy Campbell's translation of 1959 is for the most part in iambic pentameter and employs a considerable amount of rhyme.[24] The experience of those directors I have consulted is that Campbell's translation is unreadable and unactable. The explanation for this seems to me to have nothing to do with the fact that Campbell's chosen metre was iambic pentameter but much to do with his decision to use rhyme. Firstly, rhymes in English are often very difficult to find. Secondly and more importantly, the need to use them, once the decision has been taken, imposes severe restrictions on the translator, in particular the inescapable demand to twist the syntax into a shape which allows the rhyming word to fall into the right place. Rhyme becomes thus a self-imposed straight jacket and the lines themselves acquire the kind of inversions and cumbersome 'poetic' effects which literally sinks the translation in terms of its actability. Campbell's choice of individual words and phrases which he must have considered literary and poetic but which in reality give his translation a cumbersome and old-fashioned feel is a further drawback. The following example from Act I illustrates very well the points made above:

Don Pedro	The king sent me.
Octavio	Well if the king's kind thought
	Bend to me thus, I reck my life as naught
	To serve my liege, and would not count the cost
	If in the cause of honour it were lost.
	Tell me, my lord, what planet of good cheer,
	What stroke of goodly fortune, brought you here
	To say I am remembered by the King? (pp.241-2)

A prose translation does, of course, avoid the problems inherent in metre and rhyme, as may be seen in Robert O'Brien's version, published three years after Campbell's.[25] Above all, prose immediately eliminates the awkward inversions often imposed by rhyme and therefore allows for a word-order which is straightforward, natural and speakable. On the other hand, a prose version lacks the pulse and the discipline of metre, two of the essential ingredients of Golden-Age and Elizabethan theatre, the framework within which, as in a piece of classical music, emotion is contained and a constant tension between content and form established. Prose dissipates all this. And it dissipates too the pleasure to be derived from listening to verse.

Although he has not translated or adapted any of Tirso's plays, Adrian Mitchell has in recent years produced versions of Calderón's *El alcalde de Zalamea, La vida es sueño* and *El gran teatro del mundo*. Working from a literal English prose version of the Spanish text, he has set himself the extremely difficult task of retaining for the most part both Spanish metres and rhyme schemes, and it would be churlish to deny the vigour and the effectiveness on stage of his versions. The following example, from Act I of *El alcalde de Zalamea*, is in octosyllables and the four-line *redondilla* - a bb a:[26]

SERGEANT	You're a minority of one
CAPTAIN	I'm wrong?
SERGEANT	No sir, let's say that I'm
	Sure there's no way of killing time
	Better than - doing it for fun,
	With no love guff. A patch of grass,
	A bottle and a loaf or two
	And a ripe peasant princess who
	Can't tell her elbow from her arse. (pp. 6-7)

A very different passage, in which Mitchell has in fact

abandoned the assonance of the Spanish *romance* for blank-verse, but in octosyllabic lines, reveals Isabel's strong emotions at the beginning of Act III:

> I was torn with anxieties.
> My mind full of a thousand fears,
> Each fear chained to another fear.
> I could not breathe, or see, or hear.
> I wandered. I fell down. I ran
> Without a guiding star or light,
> All through the forest till I fell
> And lie, exhausted at your feet.   (p.76)

The difference in quality between Mitchell's and Campbell's lines is self-evident. It is, of course, to do with language – Mitchell's is simpler, more natural – but it is also very much to do with the fact that, when as in the first of the two examples he employs rhyme, the syntax is really that of prose.

In my own attempt to produce a version of *The Trickster*, I have been very conscious of the need to maintain the syntax of prose as far as possible, for it is this which makes the lines speakable, as in Tisbea's quite poetic description in Act I of a sinking ship:

> Stranded there, it's like some lovely peacock,
> The sails in imitation of the tail,
> Their beauty and dazzling brightness commanding
> The sailors' eyes, ravishing their sight.
> The movement of the waves plucks at its feathers;
> Its loveliness and pride begin to fade,
> And all its splendour's slowly stripped away.
>   (ll. 487-93)

The decision to opt for iambic pentameter was taken as the result of discussions with several theatre directors, all of whom felt that this is the metre in which British actors feel most at ease. There are, of course, disadvantages, the most important of which is the need to lengthen the original line by two or more syllables and thus introduce more words. To that extent the result is not a translation but a free adaptation, and the reader should always bear this in mind. Nevertheless, the experience of participating in a workshop at Theatre Clwyd, Mold, in the autumn of 1984 proved to me the effectiveness of this version on the stage and opened the eyes of those present to the qualities of Tirso's play, previously unknown to them. For that opportunity I wish to express my gratitude to the then associate director, Paul Chamberlain, and his actors.

NOTES TO THE INTRODUCTION

1. On the general background see N.D. Shergold, *A History of the Spanish Stage from Medieval Times until the End of the Seventeenth Century* (Oxford, 1967); H.A. Rennert, *The Spanish Stage in the Time of Lope de Vega* (New York, 1909; 2nd ed., 1963); Margaret Wilson, *Spanish Drama of the Golden Age* (Oxford and London, 1969); and E.M. Wilson and D. Moir, *The Golden Age: Drama 1492-1700. A Literary History of Spain*, Vol. 3. Ed. R.O. Jones (London, 1971).

2. For the development of the *comedia* the reader is recommended to the studies mentioned above, as well as to J.P. Wickersham Crawford, *Spanish Drama before Lope de Vega* (Philadelphia, 1922; 2nd revised ed., 1937; 3rd revised ed., 1967); H.J. Chaytor (ed.), *Dramatic Theory in Spain* (Cambridge, 1925); Duncan Moir, 'The Classical Tradition in Spanish Dramatic Theory and Practice in the Seventeenth Century', in *Classical Drama and its Influence*, ed. M.J. Anderson (London, 1965), 191-228; and R. Schevill, *The Dramatic Art of Lope de Vega together with 'La dama boba'* (Berkeley, 1918).

3. The most detailed study of the Golden-Age *corrales* is that by N.D. Shergold, *A History of the Spanish Stage*. See in particular chapters 7 and 14.

4. See Blanca de los Ríos, *Tirso de Molina. Obras dramáticas completas*, vol.I (Madrid 1946), lxxv.

5. For an account of Tirso's life and career see the relevant chapter in Margaret Wilson, *Spanish Drama of the Golden Age*, and, for a more detailed history, Blanca de los Ríos, *El enigma biográfico de Tirso de Molina* (Madrid, 1928).

6. Two of Tirso's best religious plays are to appear in this present series (Aris and Phillips *Hispanic Classics*): *Tamar's Revenge* (*La venganza de Tamar*) in a translation by John Lyon (1987) and *Damned for Despair* (*El condenado por desconfiado*) in a translation by Nicholas Round (1986). In his introduction to *Tamar's Revenge* John Lyon explains the theatrical background, and the main themes and characteristics of Tirso's drama, while Nicholas Round in *Damned for Despair* describes the religious and intellectual background to the period and provides a substantial bibliography to up-date the standard reference works by Williamson, Placer and Dorst.

7. See Margaret Wilson, *Spanish Drama of the Golden Age*.

8. On Tirso's contribution to Golden-Age drama in terms of

characterization and intellectual depth, see in particular
I.L. McClelland, *Tirso de Molina. Studies in Dramatic
Realism* (Liverpool, 1948).
Detailed comparisons of the two versions have been
undertaken by Gerald E. Wade and Robert J. Mayberry,
'*Tan largo me lo fiáis* and *El burlador de Sevilla y el
convidado de piedra*', *Bulletin of the Comediantes*, XIV, I
(1962), 1-16; María Rosa Lida de Malkiel, 'Sobre la
prioridad de ¿*Tan largo me lo fiáis*? Notas al *Isidro* y a *El
burlador de Sevilla*', *Bulletin of Hispanic Studies*, XLII
(1965), 18-33; and Albert E. Sloman, 'The Two Versions of
El burlador de Sevilla', *Bulletin of Hispanic Studies*, XLII
(1965), 18-33. For the text of *Tan largo*, see *Tan largo
me lo fiáis*, ed. Xavier A. Fernández (Madrid, 1967).
There is a detailed discussion of Claramonte's rôle by
Gerald E. Wade, *El burlador de Sevilla y convidado de
piedra* (New York, 1969), 6-11.
See, for example, the arguments put forward by H.A.
Rennert, *The Spanish Stage in the Time of Lope de Vega*,
and Joseph C. Fucilla, '*El convidado de piedra* in Naples
in 1625', *Bulletin of the Comediantes*, X, I (1958), 5-6.
Many critics have discussed possible contemporary models.
The different views and arguments are neatly and
conveniently brought together by Gerald E. Wade, *El
burlador de Sevilla y convidado de piedra*. See in
particular pp. 29-35.
For the background to the literary and folkloric origins of
The Trickster, the reader is recommended to Dorothy
McKay, *The Double Invitation in the Legend of Don Juan*
(Stanford and London, 1943), Leo Weinstein, *The
Metamorphoses of Don Juan* (Stanford, 1959), and R.
Menédez Pidal, 'Sobre los orígenes de *El convidado de
piedra*', in *Estudios literarios*, 6th ed., (Buenos Aires,
Colección Austral, 1946), pp. 89-113). For the ballads
discussed and translated here, see the latter, pp. 95-109.
One of the most influential of A.A. Parker's studies has
been *The Approach to the Spanish Drama of the Golden
Age*, Diamante, VI (London 1957).
See, in particular, J.E. Varey, 'Social Criticism in *El
burlador de Sevilla*', *Theatre Research International*,
2(1977), 197-221.
On the question of honour see C.A. Jones, 'Honor in
Spanish Golden-Age Drama: Its Relation to Real Life and to
Morals', *Bulletin of Hispanic Studies*, XXXV (1958),
199-210, and P.N. Dunn, 'Honour and the Christian
Background in Calderón', *Bulletin of Hispanic Studies*,

XXXVII (1960), 75–105, reprinted in *Critical Essays on the Theatre of Calderón*, ed. B.W. Wardropper (New York, 1965), 24–60.

17. The most detailed study of the play as a whole, and in particular its characters, is that by Daniel Rogers, *Tirso de Molina. El burlador de Sevilla. Critical Guides to Spanish Texts* (London, 1977). See too Gerald E. Wade, 'The Character of Don Juan of *El burlador de Sevilla*', in *Hispanic Studies in Honor of Nicholson B. Adams*, ed. J.E. Keller and K.-L. Selig. University of North Carolina Studies in the Romance Languages and Literatures, LIX (Chapel Hill, North Carolina, 1966), 167–78.

18. See in this respect A.A. Parker, 'Los amores y noviazgos clandestinos en el mundo dramático-social de Calderón', *Hacia Calderón: Segundo coloquio anglogermano* (Berlin, New York, 1970), 79–87.

19. On this point see Melveena McKendrick, *Woman and Society in the Spanish Drama of the Golden Age:a study of the 'mujer varonil'* (Cambridge, 1974), 158–9.

20. On the play's imagery, see C.B. Morris, 'Metaphor in *El burlador de Sevilla*', *Romanic Review*, LV (1964), 248–55, and D. Rogers, *Tirso de Molina, El burlador de Sevilla...*, 55–60.

21. See D. Rogers, *Tirso de Molina. El burlador de Sevilla...*, 21–25, and J.E. Varey, 'The Staging of Night Scenes in the "Comedia"', *The American Hispanist*, II, 15 (1977), 14–16.

22. See J.E. Varey, *Historia de los títeres en España (desde sus orígenes hasta mediados del siglo XVIII)* (Madrid, 1957), 24–90.

23. The most detailed study is that by Leo Weinstein, *The Metamorphoses of Don Juan* (Stanford, 1959).

24. Roy Campbell's version is to be found in *The Classic Theatre. VOLUME III: Six Spanish Plays* ed. Eric Bentley (New York, 1959).

25. Robert O'Brien's prose version, *The Rogue of Seville*, is published in *Spanish Drama*, ed. Angel Flores (New York, 1962).

26. *The Mayor of Zalamea or The Best Garrotting Ever Done*, adapted by Adrian Mitchell (Edinburgh, 1981).

THE TRICKSTER OF SEVILLE AND THE STONE GUEST
EL BURLADOR DE SEVILLA Y EL CONVIDADO DE PIEDRA

HABLAN EN ELLA LAS PERSONAS SIGUIENTES

DON DIEGO TENORIO, *viejo*
DON JUAN TENORIO, *su hijo*
CATALINÓN, *lacayo*
EL REY DE NÁPOLES
EL DUQUE OCTAVIO
DON PEDRO TENORIO
EL MARQUÉS DE LA MOTA
DON GONZALO DE ULLOA
EL REY DE CASTILLA
DOÑA ANA DE ULLOA

FABIO, *criado*
ISABELA, *duquesa*
TISBEA, *pescadora*
BELISA, *villana*
ANFRISO, *pescador*
CORIDÓN, *pescador*
GASENO, *labrador*
BATRICIO, *labrador*
RIPIO, *criado*
AMINTA, *villana*

The Spanish text reproduced here is based on the edition of Américo Castro, originally published in 1910 in the *Clásicos Castellanos* series. See 6th edition (Madrid, 1958). Where Castro has made amendments or suggested variations on the text, these have been included.

DRAMATIS PERSONAE

DON DIEGO TENORIO, *an old man*
DON JUAN TENORIO, *his son*
CATALINÓN, *a servant*
THE KING OF NAPLES
DUKE OCTAVIO
DON PEDRO TENORIO
THE MARQUIS DE LA MOTA
DON GONZALO DE ULLOA
THE KING OF CASTILE
DOÑA ANA DE ULLOA

FABIO, *a servant*
ISABELA, *a duchess*
TISBEA, *a fishergirl*
BELISA, *a peasant-girl*
ANFRISO, *a fisherman*
CORIDÓN, *a fisherman*
GASENO, *a peasant*
BATRICIO, *a peasant*
RIPIO, *a servant*
AMINTA, *a peasant-girl*

JORNADA PRIMERA

Salen Don Juan Tenorio y Isabela, duquesa

Isabela	Duque Octavio, por aquí podrás salir más seguro.	
D. Juan	Duquesa, de nuevo os juro de cumplir el dulce sí.	
Isabela	¿Mis glorias serán verdades, promesas y ofrecimientos, regalos y cumplimientos, voluntades y amistades?	5
D. Juan	Sí, mi bien.	
Isabela	Quiero sacar una luz.	10
D. Juan	Pues ¿para qué?	
Isabela	Para que el alma dé fe del bien que llego a gozar.	
D. Juan	Mataréte la luz yo.	
Isabela	¡Ah, cielo! ¿Quién eres, hombre?	
D. Juan	¿Quién soy? Un hombre sin nombre.	15

---

1   Octavio: Isabela believes the man who has just made love to her to be Octavio, her lover. Neither she nor we suspect that he may not be Octavio until he objects to her bringing a light.

2   unseen by anyone: Isabela's wish that 'Octavio' should depart without being seen arises from the fact that she fears for her reputation. Her affair with Octavio is clearly conducted in secret, a situation generally disapproved of in seventeenth-century Spain on both moral and social grounds. Should Isabela's relationship with Octavio become common knowledge, her reputation in the eyes of others will inevitably be diminished, and should Octavio subsequently abandon her, her chances of finding a husband will be slight indeed. Clandestine affairs abound in the literature of Golden-Age Spain, partly because they provided writers with highly dramatic material, but they evidently had their counterpart in real life. Clandestine marriages had been recognized by the Roman Catholic Church until 1563 when the Council of Trent prohibited them. The secret affair between individuals who meet on the understanding of marriage continued to be a favourite subject with Spanish writers, including Cervantes, Tirso de Molina and Calderón de la Barca, long after the Council of Trent. Isabela's affair with Octavio has the added complication and danger of being conducted in the Royal Palace, thereby violating palace decorum. For a discussion of clandestine relationships see A.A. Parker, 'Los amores y noviazgos clandestinos en el mundo dramático-social de Calderón', *Hacia Calderón: segundo coloquio anglogermano* (Berlin, New York, 1970), 79-87.

4   My vow of marriage: Isabela's insistence on marriage points to the fact that her relationship with Octavio is not merely frivolous. On the other hand, she and Octavio are social equals and there seems to be no obstacle to their marriage, a circumstance which underlines the folly and imprudence of their secret meetings. See the reaction of Octavio's

ACT I

Enter Don Juan Tenorio and Isabela, a duchess

Isabela	Quickly, Octavio, follow me through here
	And you'll escape unseen by anyone.
D. Juan	Duchess, my faithful promise I renew.
	My vow of marriage I insist is true.
Isabela	If dreams could only be reality, 5
	And promises and love's sweet flattery,
	The gifts and offerings inspired by love,
	Were really signs of a heart that's firm and true!
D. Juan	Of course they are, my love.
Isabela	Then let me bring
	A light.
D. Juan	But why on earth do you need a light? 10
Isabela	So that my soul can in the sight of you
	Find confirmation of my happiness.
D. Juan	You bring a light, I swear I'll put it out!
Isabela	Heaven help me! Tell me truthfully! Who are you?
D. Juan	I'll tell you who I am: a man who's nameless. 15

---

servant, Ripio, Act I, 227-230.

10   A light: in the public theatres, the *corrales*, of seventeenth-century Spain, where *The Trickster* would have been performed, there was no artificial lighting and plays were therefore performed in the afternoon (see the section on staging in the Introduction). Invariably, the dramatist used the dialogue to locate the time and the place of the action. As a further aid to the suspension of disbelief, the costumes and the movements of the characters would also have been important. Here Isabela probably leads 'Octavio' by the hand to the door through which he is to make his escape, their movement across the stage suggesting the uncertainty and insecurity of people in a darkened room. On this particular aspect of Golden Age plays there is an interesting article by J.E. Varey, 'The Staging of Night Scenes in the "Comedia"', *The American Hispanist*, II, 15 (1977), 14-16.

14   Who are you?: while Isabela's failure to distinguish between her lover, Octavio, and a total stranger might seem puzzling, there are a variety of explanations: the thrill and the danger of a clandestine meeting sweep aside all reason; possibly, from the moment of Don Juan's entry and initial embrace, there is no further conversation between them; it is conceivable that Isabela knows the man to be a stranger but, like the other women in the play, finds him irresistible. Ambiguity of motive and intention is certainly a feature of Tirso's presentation of his characters and adds greatly to the fascination of the play.

15   a man who's nameless: much has been made of Don Juan's reply to Isabela in terms of its symbolic suggestion, i.e., Don Juan as the male sex-force. While this is true, it is also important to realize that he is here taunting Isabela, delighting in the trick he has played on her, joking at her expense, his flippancy contrasting delightfully with her confusion.

5

Isabela	¿Que no eres el duque?
D. Juan	No.
Isabela	¡Ah, de palacio!
D. Juan	Detente:
	dame, duquesa, la mano.
Isabela	No me detengas, villano.
	¡Ah, del rey! ¡Soldados, gente! 20

Sale el Rey de Nápoles con una vela en un candelero

Rey	¿Qué es esto?
Isabela	*[Ap.]* ¡El rey! ¡Ay, triste!
Rey	¿Quién eres?
D. Juan	¿Quién ha de ser?
	Un hombre y una mujer.
Rey	*[Ap.]* Esto en prudencia consiste.
	¡Ah, de mi guarda! Prendé 25
	a este hombre.
Isabela	¡Ay, perdido honor!

Vase Isabela. Salen Don Pedro Tenorio, embajador de España, y Guarda

D. Ped.	¡En tu cuarto, gran señor,
	voces! ¿Quién la causa fué?
Rey	Don Pedro Tenorio, a vos
	esta prisión os encargo. 30
	Siendo corto, andad vos largo;
	mirad quién son estos dos.
	Y con secreto ha de ser,

20+ The King of Naples: the action of the play occurs before 1350, a time at which only Sicily belonged to Spain. The King of Naples at this time was Roberto, who ruled from 1309 to 1343 (see Pedro Salazar de Mendoza, *Monarquía de España*, I (Madrid, 1770), 337). Spanish dramatists of the Golden Age were, however, notoriously indifferent to historical accuracy, as will be seen later. In general terms the spirit of Tirso's play is much more seventeenth than fourteenth century, especially in relation to the picture of social manners which Tirso gives us and the criticism which he makes of the characters' behaviour.

23 Do you need more proof?: an addition to the original.

24 prudence might be called for here: as has been pointed out, the lovers' rendezvous constitutes a violation of palace decorum and, were the matter to become public knowledge, a slur upon the personal honour of the King. His immediate concern is therefore for his reputation, which will best be protected by the prudent action of having the matter dealt with quickly and, above all, secretly.

Isabela	You mean you aren't the Duke?
D. Juan	Of course I'm not!
Isabela	Assist me, guards, at once! I beg of you!
D. Juan	Oh, don't play hard to get! Give me your hand!
Isabela	I order you to set me free at once!

Isabela   I order you to set me free at once!
          Guards! Soldiers! Courtiers! I need your help!   20
    The King of Naples appears, holding a candle

King   What's all this noise?

Isabela   *[Aside]*   The King himself! I'm lost!

King   Who's in there? Speak!

D. Juan   Who do you think it is?
          A man and woman! Do you need more proof?

King   *[Aside]* I think that prudence might be called for here.
          Attend here quickly! Guards! Arrest this man   25
          Immediately.

Isabela   My reputation's ruined!
    Isabela leaves. Enter Pedro Tenorio, the Spanish
    ambassador, with guards

D. Ped.   My lord, it's very rare there's such commotion
          In your quarters. What's the cause of it?

King   Don Pedro, I command you see to it
          That this arrest is made with utmost speed.   30
          Force might be needed; use it if you must.
          Attempt to identify the guilty pair.
          At every step proceed with utmost caution,
          For there's cause, I think, for some suspicion,
          And if it proves to be the thing I fear,   35

26+   **Pedro Tenorio, the Spanish ambassador**: although a foreigner, Don Pedro is portrayed very much as the King of Naples' right-hand man, entrusted here with the execution of a very delicate matter. The question of the monarch's reliance on those near to him, especially on royal favourites or *privados*, was one which preoccupied greatly Spanish dramatists of the seventeenth century and may be related to contemporary political events. During the reigns of Philip III (1598-1621) and Philip IV (1621-1665) the influence of royal favourites such as the Duke of Lerma and the Count - Duke of Olivares became very great indeed, and the moral issues posed by such developments were reflected in many plays of the time. Notable examples are: Lope de Vega's *Las mudanzas de fortuna*; Tirso de Molina's *Privar contra el gusto*; Pérez de Montalbán's *Cumplir con su obligación*; Vélez de Guevara's *El conde don Pero Vélez*; and Mira de Amescua's *La próspera fortuna de don Álvaro de Luna* and *La adversa fortuna de don Álvaro de Luna*. In *The Trickster* the responsibilities of the monarch and his reliance on others are suggested in the relationship of the King of Naples with Don Pedro and later in that of King Alfonso of Castile with Don Diego. The fact that Pedro and Don Diego are brothers helps, amongst other things, to spotlight this theme.

que algún mal suceso creo,
porque si yo aquí lo veo   35
no me queda más que ver.

Vase el Rey

D. Ped.   Prendelde.
D. Juan   ¿Quién ha de osar?
Bien puedo perder la vida;
mas ha de ir tan bien vendida,
que a alguno le ha de pesar.   40
D. Ped.   ¡Matalde!
D. Juan   ¿Quién os engaña?
Resuelto en morir estoy,
porque caballero soy
del embajador de España
Llegue; que solo ha de ser   45
quien me rinda.
D. Ped.   Apartad;
a ese cuarto os retirad
todos con esa mujer.

Vanse Guarda

Ya estamos solos los dos;
muestra aquí tu esfuerzo y brío.   50
D. Juan   Aunque tengo esfuerzo, tío,
no le tengo para vos.
D. Ped.   ¡Di quién eres!
D. Juan   Ya lo digo:
tu sobrino.
D. Ped.   *[Ap.]*   ¡Ay, corazón,
que temo alguna traición!   55
¿Qué es lo que has hecho, enemigo?
¿Cómo estás de aquesa suerte?
Dime presto lo que ha sido.
¡Desobediente, atrevido!. . .
Estoy por darte la muerte.   60
Acaba.
D. Juan   Tío y señor;
mozo soy y mozo fuiste;
y pues que de amor supiste,
tenga disculpa mi amor.

---

36   turn my royal eyes elsewhere: in making no attempt to discover the
truth for himself, the King of Naples reveals a lack of resolution and
purpose which was certainly characteristic of both Philip III and Philip
IV. It seems likely that Tirso wrote *The Trickster* between 1616 and
1625. For obvious political reasons he could not portray the King of
Castile in an overtly unfavourable light. In the play, therefore, it is
the King of Naples who is shown to be the more blameworthy, but this

	I'd rather turn my royal eyes elsewhere.	
	The King leaves	
D. Ped.	Get hold of him!	
D. Juan	Who'll be the first to dare?	
	If it's the case my own life's to be lost,	
	I'll guarantee the cost will be so high,	
	That none of you will want to pay the price.	40
D. Ped.	Finish him off!	
D. Juan	Let no one be deceived!	
	I promise you I'm not afraid to die,	
	For I'm a man of some nobility,	
	Not unrelated to the Spanish embassy.	
	Come on then, now! The fight is man to man.	45
	Whoever wins, wins single-handed.	
D. Ped.	Leave us!	
	Wait in the other chamber, all of you!	
	Ensure the woman's guarded properly.	
	The guards go out	
	Well, here we are, you rascal, man to man.	
	We'll have a demonstration of your spirit.	50
D. Juan	I've lots of spirit, uncle, have no doubt,	
	But your presence stops me showing it.	
D. Ped.	Who are you, man?	
D. Juan	I've said already, uncle.	
	Your nephew.	
D. Ped.	*[Aside]* Heavens above, what is he saying?	
	Might this not be an act of treachery?	55
	[Aloud] What have you been about, you wretched boy?	
	What can it be you're doing in the palace?	
	I want to know, so out with it at once!	
	You are a bold and disobedient fellow.	
	I'd like to put an end to all your tricks!	60
	Explain yourself immediately!	
D. Juan	My good lord,	
	I'm a young man, as you were also young.	
	You knew everything there was to know of passion,	
	So my obsession you will understand.	

---

would not have prevented a contemporary Spanish audience from drawing similar conclusions about their own ruler.

44 Not unrelated to the Spanish embassy: Don Juan ensures thus that his uncle, in order to avoid any scandalous gossip concerning himself, will dismiss the palace guards. It is one of the many examples in the play of his manipulation of both people and situations. At this moment his identity is concealed by the fact that he has drawn his cloak over his face, so that as yet Don Pedro does not know whom he is dealing with.

	Y, pues a decir me obligas	65
	la verdad, oye y diréla:
	yo engañé y gocé a Isabela
	la duquesa. . .
D. Ped.	No prosigas,
	tente. ¿Cómo la engañaste?
	Habla quedo o cierra el labio.	70
D. Juan	Fingí ser el duque Octavio. . .
D. Ped.	No digas más, calla, basta.
	[Ap.] Perdido soy si el rey sabe
	este caso. ¿Qué he de hacer?
	Industria me ha de valer	75
	en un negocio tan grave.
	Di, vil: ¿no bastó emprender
	con ira y con fuerza extraña
	tan gran traición en España
	con otra noble mujer,	80
	sino en Nápoles también
	y en el palacio real,
	con mujer tan principal?
	¡Castíguete el cielo, amén!
	Tu padre desde Castilla	85
	a Nápoles te envió,
	y en sus márgenes te dió
	tierra la espumosa orilla
	del mar de Italia, atendiendo
	que el haberte recebido	90
	pagaras agradecido,
	iy estás su honor ofendiendo,
	y en tal principal mujer!
	Pero en aquesta ocasión
	nos daña la dilación;	95
	mira qué quieres hacer.
D. Juan	No quiero daros disculpa,
	que la habré de dar siniestra.

---

75 *Some kind of cunning*: the King has ordered Don Pedro to arrest the intruder, but the revelation of the latter's identity and its implications for Don Pedro's reputation lead him to put self-interest before loyalty to the King. As the action unfolds, all the characters are seen to be less than admirable. These scenes take place, as we have seen, at night. In the play as a whole, as in so many Golden Age plays, darkness is not merely a cover for the subterfuges of the characters but also a metaphor for their moral defects. On this aspect of the play see J.E. Varey, 'Social Criticism in *El burlador de Sevilla*', *Theatre Research International*, 2(1977), 197–221.

	But since you force me to confide in you	65
	This little episode, I will, so listen:	
	I've tricked and just seduced sweet Isabela,	
	The duchess. . .	
D. Ped.	What? Good Lord above! I'll hear	
	No more. Deceived her? How did you deceive	
	Her? Just speak quietly or hold your tongue	70
D. Juan	I just pretended I was Duke Octavio. . .	
D. Ped.	Stop. Not another word. You've said enough.	
	[Aside] I'm lost if news of this affair gets out	
	And reaches the King's ears. What can I do?	
	Some kind of cunning's the sensible thing	75
	In any matter as perilous as this.	
	[Aloud] Speak up, you rascal! Wasn't it enough	
	For you to carry out with such bravado	
	That act of unforgivable deception	
	Against a Spanish lady of distinction?	80
	Was there any need to repeat it here	
	In Naples, in the royal palace too,	
	And with a woman of such noble birth?	
	I pray that Heaven'll grant your just reward!	
	I know your father's been obliged already	85
	To pack you off to Italy from Spain,	
	But then, as soon as Italy's friendly shore	
	Extends its welcome, letting you set foot	
	Here on its foamy sand, rightly convinced	
	The guest's obligation's to his host,	90
	And that kindness will with kindness be repaid,	
	You straight away reject that solemn trust,	
	And with a woman of such high distinction!	
	But now the sticking-point's been reached, it's clear	
	Delay is but a further aggravation.	95
	Consider well, my lad, what's best for you.	
D. Juan	For me to say I'm not to blame	
	Would be a lie, so there's no point in that.	

---

84   just reward!: the first allusion in the play to divine justice. Subsequently Don Juan is warned of God's punishment by many of the characters. The play is wholly concerned with divine justice rather than divine mercy and must be seen within the religious context of seventeenth-century Spain.

90   The guest's obligation's to his host: Don Juan flouts his obligation to those who offer him shelter and hospitality on a number of occasions. It provides but one example of his disrespect for all social and moral values.

	Mi sangre es, señor, la vuestra;	
	sacalda, y pague la culpa.	100
	A esos pies estoy rendido,	
	y ésta es mi espada, señor.	
D. Ped.	Alzate y muestra valor,	
	que esa humildad me ha vencido.	
	¿Atreveráste a bajar	105
	por ese balcón?	
D. Juan	Sí atrevo,	
	que alas en tu favor llevo.	
D. Ped.	Pues yo te quiero ayudar.	
	Vete a Sicilia o Milán,	
	donde vivas encubierto.	110
D. Juan	Luego me iré.	
D. Ped.	¿Cierto?	
D. Juan	Cierto.	
D. Ped.	Mis cartas te avisarán	
	en qué para este suceso	
	triste, que causado has.	
D. Juan	*[Ap.]* Para mí alegre, dirás.	115
	Que tuve culpa, confieso.	
D. Ped.	Esa mocedad te engaña.	
	Baja, pues, ese balcón.	
D. Juan	*[Ap.]* Con tan justa pretensión	
	gozoso me parto a España.	120

Vase Don Juan y entra el Rey

D. Ped.	Ejecutando, señor,	
	lo que mandó vuestra alteza,	
	el hombre. . .	
Rey	¿Murió?	
D. Ped.	Escapóse	
	de las cuchillas soberbias.	
Rey	¿De qué forma?	

---

101   Offence: the offence to which Don Juan refers is both his seduction of
Isabela and his compromising of his uncle's honour and reputation. In
theory Don Pedro's killing of his nephew would cleanse any stain upon
his reputation, but in practice would lead only to gossip and
speculation, given the nature of life at Court. Don Juan's histrionic
submission to his uncle's will is made in full knowledge of that fact and
is entirely consistent with his ironic and mocking attitude to everything
around him.

106   high balcony: in the *corrales* a gallery supported by pillars ran across
the back of the stage and could be used for balcony-scenes. Here, on
the other hand, Don Pedro instructs Don Juan to leap down from the
level, i.e., the stage-level, on which they are standing. His exit would
therefore be made, as was Octavio's, through one of the two doors at
the back of the stage, in which case the balcony is not actually visible.

	But my blood, uncle, is the same as yours,	
	So spill it now and punish me for this	100
	Offence; I kneel here humbly at your feet.	
	Take this sword! Kill me if that's your wish!	
D. Ped.	Get up and show me you've more nerve than that!	
	Humility has overcome my anger.	
	See if your nerve will get you to the ground	105
	By means of this high balcony.	
D. Juan	I'll fly,	
	Uncle! Your faith in me has given me wings!	
D. Ped.	Well, the truth is my main concern's to help,	
	So fly to Sicily as best you can,	
	Or maybe Milan, and seek refuge there.	110
D. Juan	I'm on my way!	
D.Ped.	You promise me?	
D. Juan	I promise.	
D. Ped.	My letters will inform you of the end	
	Of this affair, this sorry tale for which	
	You, nephew, bear responsibility.	
D. Juan	*[Aside]* But, even so, it's turned out well for me!	115
	[Aloud] I confess, uncle, all the fault was mine.	
D.Ped.	Your youth, my boy, is leading you astray.	
	But down the balcony and on your way!	
D. Juan	*[Aside]* I think my uncle's gone and said it all.	
	I fancy making Spain my port of call.	120

Don Juan leaves. The King appears

D. Ped.	Your majesty, we tried our very best
	To carry out your orders. I'm afraid
	The fellow. . .
King	Is he dead?
D. Ped.	Got right away,
	Escaping the fierce thrusts of all our swords.
King	How did he manage that?

109-10 Sicily...Milan: see 20+, note. Milan did not come under Spanish rule until 1535.

119-20 I think...call: it is important to draw attention to the dramatist's use of the 'aside' in relation to Don Juan. The fact that the stage of the seventeenth-century *corral* jutted out into the auditorium made communication between actor and audience a feature of Golden-Age plays, as was the case indeed in Elizabethan theatre, and in this context the 'aside' came to be a particularly useful convention. In *The Trickster* Don Juan's relationship with the audience is very important, his 'asides' allowing him to take the audience into his confidence, making them his accomplices in his tricks and deceptions, and thereby – for much of the play – winning their sympathies. The audience, privileged witnesses to the deception of others, can take as much delight in their undoing as does Don Juan himself.

13

D. Ped.	Desta forma:	125

Aun no lo mandaste apenas,
cuando, sin dar más disculpa,
la espada en la mano aprieta,
revuelve la capa al brazo,
y con gallarda presteza,   130
ofendiendo a los soldados
y buscando su defensa,
viendo vecina la muerte,
por el balcón de la huerta
se arroja desesperado.   135
Siguióle con diligencia
tu gente; cuando salieron
por esa vecina puerta,
le hallaron agonizando
como enroscada culebra.   140
Levantóse, y al decir
los soldados: "¡muera, muera!",
bañado de sangre el rostro,
con tan heroica presteza
se fué, que quedé confuso.   145
La mujer, que es Isabela,
que para admirarte nombro,
retirada en esa pieza,
dice que es el duque Octavio
que, con engaño y cautela.   150
la gozó.

Rey   ¿Qué dices?

D. Ped.   Digo
lo que ella propia confiesa.

Rey   *[Ap.]* ¡Ah, pobre honor! Si eres alma
del hombre ¿por qué te dejan
en la mujer inconstante,   155
si es la misma ligereza?
¡Hola!

---

125   Let me explain: Don Pedro invents the story of the intruder's escape,
filling his account with lurid and melodramatic details in order to add
conviction. In performance, gesture and delivery play an important part
in this essentially histrionic performance.

149   Octavio: Don Pedro, far from being told this by Isabela, distorts the
information given to him by Don Juan.

153   fragile honour: the theme of honour in its various forms was a favourite
with most dramatists of the Golden Age and figures prominently in many
plays. Whether or not the honour situations presented on the stage
correspond closely to real life or were used by dramatists for theatrical
effect is a subject which has been much debated. See, for example,
C.A. Jones, '*Honor* in Spanish Golden-Age Drama: Its Relation to Real

D. Ped.   Let me explain: 125
                No sooner had you told us to arrest him
                Than he, without a word and quick as light,
                Went for his sword, brandished the naked steel
                Before our eyes, using his cloak to bind
                His arm, and made a swift assault upon   130
                Your soldiers, making thus defence attack,
                Confronting us with quite unusual boldness.
                But conscious then, no doubt, that death was close
                At hand, he made a dash for it, and threw
                Himself into the garden from a window.   135
                The guards went after him as best they could,
                Rushed quickly down the stairs, made their way out
                Into the garden by some other door,
                And found him lying there, rolling about
                And twisting like a serpent facing death.   140
                Then suddenly, he's up and on his feet;
                Your men are closing in to make the kill;
                His face is just a mask of blood, occasioned
                By the fall, when, all at once, inspired by
                Some superhuman agency, he's gone!   145
                The woman is the Duchess Isabela
                I name her to amaze you even more.
                The guards have her a prisoner in this chamber.
                She claims the man involved is Duke Octavio,
                Who, by some cunning stratagem, has just   150
                Seduced her.
King   Are you sure?
D. Ped.   All I can say
                Is what the girl's already said to me.
King   [Aside] Oh, fragile honour, source and very essence
                Of man's existence, yet your pure wholeness
                Relies entirely on fickle woman,   155
                Herself the very image of inconstancy!
                [Aloud] You there!

Life and to Morals', *Bulletin of Hispanic Studies*, XXXV (1958), 199–210. As far as the drama is concerned, Lope de Vega had drawn attention to the popularity of honour as a dramatic subject in his *Arte nuevo de hacer comedias (The New Art of Writing Plays)*, a poetic essay on the writing of plays published in 1609:

        Cases of honour are by far the best.
        They move the passions of each spectator.

In the plays of the Golden Age a man's honour – honour in the sense of reputation and good name – is often threatened or lost as a result of the vulnerability of the female members of his family, especially wives, sisters and daughters, to the attentions of marauding males of the Don Juan variety.

Sale un Criado

Criado   ¡Gran señor!

Rey   Traed
delante de mi presencia
esa mujer.

D. Ped.   Ya la guardia
viene, gran señor, con ella.   160

Trae la Guarda a Isabela

Isabela   [Ap.] ¿Con qué ojos veré al rey?

Rey   Idos, y guardad la puerta
de esa cuadra. Di, mujer:
¿qué rigor, qué airada estrella
te incitó, que en mi palacio,   165
con hermosura y soberbia,
profanases sus umbrales?

Isabela   Señor . . .

Rey   Calla, que la lengua
no podrá dorar el yerro
que has cometido en mi ofensa.   170
¿Aquél era el duque Octavio?

Isabela   Señor. . .

Rey   ¡Que no importan fuerzas,
guarda, criados, murallas,
fortalecidas almenas
para amor, que la de un niño   175
hasta los muros penetra!
Don Pedro Tenorio: al punto
a esa mujer llevad presa
a una torre, y con secreto
haced que al duque le prendan,   180
que quiero hacer que le cumpla
la palabra o la promesa.

Isabela   Gran señor, volvedme el rostro.

Rey   Ofensa a mi espalda hecha
es justicia y es razón   185
castigalla a espaldas vueltas.

Vase el Rey

D. Ped.   Vamos, duquesa.

Isabela   Mi culpa
no hay disculpa que la venza;

---

170   Offence: see 24, note.

175   a mere boy: Cupid.

186   My back is turned: the King of Naples both turns his back on and
closes his eyes to the truth of the matter. He is concerned only with

A *servant enters*

Servant	Your majesty!
King	I want the woman

In front of me at once, so fetch her from
The other chamber.

D. Ped.   The guards already
Have her here, my lord. Here is the lady   160

A guard enters with Isabela

Isabela   *[Aside]* Such is my shame, I daren't look at the King!

King   Leave us in private and ensure the door's
Securely guarded. Now, madam. The truth!

What cruel destiny or hostile fate
Obliges you, and in the royal palace,   165
To use your beauty and your high position
To stain my own unblemished reputation?

Isabela   Your majesty. . .

King   Silence! No words of yours
Can hope to gild the seriousness of this
Offence against my noble royal presence.   170
Can it be true Octavio was the man?

Isabela   Your highness. . .

King   Are not bolts and bars enough,
As well as servants, guards, high battlements,
Thick walls and watchtowers, all well-protected,
To keep out love, to stop a mere boy   175
From breaking through such strong and stout defences?
Don Pedro, I command two things of you:
Take the woman with you and tell the guards
To place her in the tower; then proceed
In secret and arrest the man, Octavio.   180
I'll force him to make good his word to her;
A promise is to be a promise kept.

Isabela   Your majesty, why turn your back on me?

King   Since the offence took place behind my back,
The punishment's appropriate and just: 185
My back is turned towards the one who's guilty.

The King leaves

D. Ped.   Come with me, duchess!

Isabela   My offence is such,
There's not an explanation will erase it!

---

hushing up any potential palace scandal.

191   It's early: a good example of the way in which Golden-Age dramatists
used the dialogue to locate the time and place of the action. See 10,
note.

17

	mas no será el yerro tanto	
	si el duque Octavio lo enmienda.	190

Vanse todos y salen el Duque Octavio y
Ripio, su criado

Ripio   ¿Tan de mañana, señor,
        te levantas?

Octav.   No hay sosiego
        que pueda apagar el fuego
        que enciende en mi alma amor.
        Porque, como al fin es niño,   195
        no apetece cama blanda,
        entre regalada holanda,
        cubierta de blanco armiño.
        Acuéstase, no sosiega,
        siempre quiere madrugar   200
        por levantarse a jugar,
        que, al fin, como niño, juega.
        Pensamientos de Isabela
        me tienen, amigo, en calma,
        que como vive en el alma   205
        anda el cuerpo siempre en pena,
        guardando ausente y presente
        el castillo del honor.

Ripio   Perdóname, que tu amor
        es amor impertinente.   210

Octav.   ¿Qué dices, necio?

Ripio   Esto digo:
        impertinencia es amar
        como amas; ¿quies escuchar?

Octav.   Ea, prosigue.

Ripio   Ya prosigo.
        ¿Quiérete Isabela a ti?   215

---

193   this raging fire: Tirso presents us here with a delightfully ironic
        picture of the traditional sleepless lover. The irony of Octavio's
        situation stems largely from his preoccupation with Isabela's honour and
        our knowledge that she has none – a good example of our privileged
        position as spectators of the action.

195   love's a child: Cupid. See 175, note.

205   she occupies my very soul: Golden-Age literature is full of allusions to
        lovers whose souls have become the property of the loved one.
        Frequently the lover who is about to depart speaks of leaving his soul
        behind, i.e., with the loved one, for the latter possesses his whole
        being. Thus, in Lope de Vega's *El caballero de Olmedo* (*The Knight*
        From Olmedo), Alonso departs with these words to his beloved Inés:

Perhaps my error won't seem quite the same
If only Octavio will save my name.   190
They leave. The Duke Octavio enters with Ripio, his servant.

Ripio It's early, master; just the crack of dawn.
What gets you out of bed like this?

Octav.   No sleep
Can ever overcome this raging fire
That love has lit and kindled in my breast!
The explanation's simple: love's a child,   195
And for that reason he detests a bed
That's over-soft and made with linen sheets,
Or covered with an eiderdown of ermine.
He goes to bed but cannot settle down.
He's eager to be up when it's still night,   200
To play some game or have a bit of fun.
Who can stop a child acting like a child?
My thoughts are always with sweet Isabela,
The source, Ripio, of all my pain and anguish,
And since she occupies my very soul,   205
Her presence there denies my body rest,
Obliging it to be the constant guardian
Of honour's pure, chaste and sacred fortress.

Ripio Forgive me, master, but it seems to me
Your love's a proper case of lunacy.   210

Octav. You are the lunatic! Shut up!

Ripio   It's true,
Master. To love a woman as you do
Must be lunacy. Shall I say my bit?

Octav. Well, only if you must.

Ripio   Then I'll say it!
How can you be sure the woman loves you?   215

Great is my sorrow. I leave for Olmedo
And leave my soul behind me in Medina.(Act III,2175-76).
For a detailed study of love in Golden-Age literature the reader is
recommended to Otis H. Green, *Spain and the Western Tradition: The
Castilian Mind in Literature from 'El Cid' to Calderón* (Madison, London,
1968), I, 72-300.

213 Shall I say my bit?: in the drama of the Golden Age the common sense
of servants often contrasts with the imprudence of those they serve and
allows the dramatist to underline the moral dimension of the play. It
does not follow from this, however, that the servants are themselves
particularly moral characters, for they are usually susceptible to the
same temptations that they condemn in their masters.

Octav.	¿Eso, necio, has de dudar?	
Ripio	No; mas quiero preguntar:	
	¿y tú, no la quieres?	
Octav.	Sí.	
Ripio	Pues ¿no seré majadero,	
	y de solar conocido,	220
	si pierdo yo mi sentido	
	por quien me quiere y la quiero?	
	Si ella a ti no te quisiera,	
	fuera bien el porfialla,	
	regalalla y adoralla,	225
	y aguardar que se rindiera;	
	mas si los dos os queréis	
	con una mesma igualdad,	
	dime: ¿hay más dificultad	
	de que luego os desposéis?	230
Octav.	Eso fuera, necio, a ser	
	de lacayo o lavandera	
	la boda.	
Ripio	Pues, ¿es quienquiera	
	una lavandriz mujer,	
	lavando y fregatrizando,	235
	defendiendo y ofendiendo,	
	los paños suyos tendiendo,	
	regalando y remedando?	
	Dando dije, porque al dar	
	no hay cosa que se le iguale,	240
	y si no a Isabela dale,	
	a ver si sabe tomar.	

Sale un Criado

Criado	El embajador de España	
	en este punto se apea	
	en el zaguán, y desea,	245
	con ira y fiereza extraña,	
	hablarte, y si no entendí	
	yo mal, entiendo es prisión.	
Octav.	¡Prisión! Pues ¿por qué ocasión?	
	Decid que entre.	

216-17 The literal translation of these lines is:
        OCTAVIO: Can you be in any doubt, you fool?
        RIPIO: No; but I want to ask you a question.
231-42 I have translated these lines fairly freely but in a way which attempts
      to capture the down-to-earth vulgarity of the *gracioso*.
233 <u>Let them get married!</u>: Duke Octavio implies that, unlike commoners,

Octav.	As it's a fact that you're a fool, it's true.	
Ripio	No need to get narked! Answer me this truly!	
	Are you sure that you love her?	
Octav.	Most surely!	
Ripio	Then tell me this: aren't I a proper fool,	
	A first-class chump of the very best school,	220
	If I persist in knocking my brains out,	
	When of her love I've not the slightest doubt?	
	Now if her love for you was not the case,	
	You would be wise to set out on the chase,	
	To give her gifts and praise her to the skies,	225
	To press your case until you win first prize.	
	But if the two of you are so in love,	
	And both of you are like two cooing doves,	
	I've got to say that I can't see the problem.	
	For God's sake make of her an honest woman!	230
Octav.	The argument, fool, might just be relevant	
	To a lackey or to some female servant.	
	Let them get married!	
Ripio	It's plain audacity	
	To call a washer-woman a nobody.	
	I tell you, master, she's superbly clean;	235
	She's always full of energy and steam,	
	Eager to put her linen on display,	
	Anxious to give her all in every way.	
	Her generosity's a precious gift,	
	There's nothing else can ever equal it.	240
	The moral is give it to Isabel.	
	If she rejects it she can go to Hell.	
	A servant enters	
Servant	The ambassador of Spain's arrived, my lord.	
	He's there outside, dismounted in the courtyard.	
	I don't know what's the cause, but he's insisting	245
	On speaking with you in an angry tone	
	Of voice; and if I heard him right, I'm sure	
	The word prison was one that passed his lips.	
Octav.	Why would he speak of prison? There's no reason.	
	Ask him to enter.	

---

people of quality should not rush into marriage but ensure first that the proposed partner is suitable in all senses. While there is no doubt that he and Isabela love each other and intend to be married, their delay in so doing points less to any practical reason than to a self-indulgent delight in the risks and pleasures of a pre-marital relationship.

Entra Don Pedro Tenorio, con guardas

D. Ped.	Quien así	250
	con tanto descuido duerme,	
	limpia tiene la conciencia.	
Octav.	Cuando viene vuexcelencia	
	a honrarme y favorecerme	
	no es justo que duerma yo;	255
	velaré toda mi vida.	
	¿A qué y por qué es la venida?	
D. Ped.	Porque aquí el rey me envió.	
Octav.	Si el rey, mi señor, se acuerda	
	de mí en aquesta ocasión,	260
	será justicia y razón	
	que por él la vida pierda.	
	Decidme, señor, ¿qué dicha	
	o qué estrella me ha guiado,	
	que de mí el rey se ha acordado?	265
D. Ped.	Fué, duque, vuestra desdicha.	
	Embajador del rey soy;	
	dél os traigo una embajada.	
Octav.	Marqués, no me inquieta nada;	
	decid, que aguardando estoy.	270
D. Ped.	A prenderos me ha enviado	
	el rey; no os alborotéis.	
Octav.	¡Vos por el rey me prendéis!	
	Pues ¿en qué he sido culpado?	
D. Ped.	Mejor lo sabéis que yo;	275
	mas, por si acaso me engaño,	
	escuchad el desengaño,	
	y a lo que el rey me envió.	
	Cuando los negros gigantes,	
	plegando funestos toldos,	280
	ya del crepúsculo huyen,	
	tropezando unos con otros,	
	estando yo con su alteza	
	tratando ciertos negocios,	
	porque antipodas del sol	285

---

250   Well, I'd say the man: from the outset Don Pedro, knowing Octavio to be innocent, treats him as though he were guilty. The scene between them is another bravura acting performance on Don Pedro's part, in the course of which he employs sarcasm, the weight of his authority, and a superbly embroidered account of Isabela's seduction to bludgeon Octavio into submission. Once again, though, our privileged position as spectators of the action allows us to observe both Don Pedro's self-interested motives and his disloyalty to the king.

22

Enter Don Pedro Tenorio, with guards

D. Ped.   Well, I'd say the man   250
    Who sleeps so soundly, evidently free
    From care, must surely sleep with easy conscience.

Octav.   When you decide to call on me, my lord,
    Granting me honour and favour by your visit,
    For me to favour sleep would be an insult; 225
    I'd rather spend my entire life awake.
    But tell me: what's the reason for your visit?

D. Ped. I come, my lord, commanded by the King.

Octav.   The King? Why should the King concern himself
    With me, sending you as his emissary? 260
    If this is true, it's only fair and just
    That I for him should sacrifice my life.
    But you can tell me, sir, what kindly fate
    Or friendly constellation smiles on me,
    That I should occupy the King's thoughts now. 265

D. Ped. The King's preoccupation is your misfortune.
    I come, sir, as ambassador to the King,
    Entrusted by him with this special mission.

Octav.   But, Marquis, I've done nothing wrong to merit
    This, so you had better tell me why you've come. 270

D. Ped. The purpose of my visit's to arrest you.
    The King's orders! It's best you don't resist!

Octav.   Is this some foolish joke? To arrest me?
    You'd better tell me what's the accusation.

D. Ped. You'll know the cause of it as well as I. 275
    But if there's some mistake or explanation
    Needed, this is the story I've been told;
    You'll see the action of the King's well-founded.
    When those dark messengers of gloomy night
    Unfurled black canopies across the sky, 280
    And banished swiftly evening's friendly light,
    Their sudden haste the cause of their confusion,
    I was in conversation with the King.
    Matters of state were our preoccupation
    – invariably the enemies of light 285

---

262 sacrifice my life: Octavio's assertion of loyalty and obedience to the
  monarch regardless of self-interest provides the moral context within
  which Don Pedro's actions can be judged.

279 When those dark messengers: a rhetorical flourish which is not
  characteristic of the language of the play in general but which is
  perfectly suited here both to the dramatic tale which Don Pedro is
  about to tell and to the role which he gives himself in it as the King's
  confidante, which in turn is designed to impress on Octavio his own
  hopeless position.

son siempre los poderosos,
voces de mujer oímos
cuyos ecos, menos roncos
por los artesones sacros,
nos repitieron "¡socorro!"   290
A las voces y al ruido
acudió, duque, el rey propio,
halló a Isabela en los brazos
de algún hombre poderoso;
mas quien al cielo se atreve,   295
sin duda es gigante o monstruo.
Mandó el rey que los prendiera;
quedé con el hombre solo;
llegué y quise desarmarlle;
pero pienso que el Demonio   300
en él tomó forma humana,
pues que, vuelto en humo y polvo,
se arrojó por los balcones,
entre los pies de esos olmos
que coronan, del palacio,   305
los chapiteles hermosos.
Hice prender la duquesa,
y en la presencia de todos
dice que es el duque Octavio
el que con mano de esposo   310
la gozó.

Octav.   ¿Qué dices?

D. Ped.   Digo
lo que al mundo es ya notorio
y que tan claro se sabe:
que Isabela por mil modos. . .

Octav.   Dejadme, no me digáis   315
tan gran traición de Isabela.
Mas si fué su amor cautela,
proseguid, ¿por qué calláis?
Mas si veneno me dais,
que a un firme corazón toca,   320
y así a decir me provoca,

---

295   assault the heavens: the allusion is to the Titans of Greek mythology, a
         race of giants who rebelled against the Olympian gods, were defeated
         and condemned to Tartarus. In the same way the 'handsome stranger',
         an intruder in the palace, offends the king.

Are men who wield great influence and power!
Without warning, we heard a woman's voice,
Its echo somewhat muffled and less harsh
In the great vastness of the royal chambers,
But calling out repeatedly for help.   290
The woman's cries and general confusion
Succeeded in attracting the attention
Of the King, and there – would you believe it? –
Was Isabela with a handsome stranger;
Though anyone who dares assault the heavens   295
Is better called a giant or a monster.
The King at once commanded their arrest,
And left me to apprehend the daring fellow.
I did my best, seeking to disarm him,
But I am quite convinced the very devil   300
Had in that person taken human form.
Enveloped in a cloud of smoke and dust,
He flung himself down from the balcony,
And landed at the foot of those great elms
Whose soaring majesty is equalled only   305
By the high towers of the royal palace.
The duchess was arrested on my orders,
And there and then, and overheard by others,
She claimed that Duke Octavio was the man
Who, pretending that he would marry her,   310
Enjoyed her favours.

Octav.   What?

D. Ped.   I just repeat
A fact that's now become quite common knowledge;
Some tittle-tattle that the whole world knows;
For Isabela in one way or another. . .

Octav.   Enough, enough! I'll not hear any more   315
Of Isabela's wicked treachery!
But if this business does involve deception,
You'd better tell me more and not be silent,
Even though you are feeding me with poison
That's strong enough to make a stout heart break.   320
This is a matter that obliges me

---

300   the very devil: see 15, note. Don Pedro's description of Don Juan's
      escape is intended merely to impress upon Octavio the daring of the
      intruder. On the other hand, the diabolical implication is one which,
      taken in conjunction with other images in the play, raises Don Juan to
      a poetic, superhuman plane.

que imita a la comadreja,
que concibe por la oreja
para parir por la boca.
¿Será verdad que Isabela,   325
alma, se olvidó de mí
para darme muerte? Sí,
que el bien suena y el mal vuela.
Ya el pecho nada recela
juzgando si son antojos;   330
que, por darme más enojos,
al entendimiento entró,
y por la oreja escuchó
lo que acreditan los ojos.
Señor marqués, ¿es posible   335
que Isabela me ha engañado,
y que mi amor ha burlado?
¡Parece cosa imposible!
¡Oh, mujer! ¡Ley tan terrible
de honor, a quien me provoco   340
a emprender! Mas ya no toco
en tu honor esta cautela.
¿Anoche con Isabela
hombre en palacio?. . . Estoy loco.

D. Ped. Como es verdad que en los vientos   345
hay aves, en el mar peces,
que participan a veces
de todos cuatro elementos;
como en la gloria hay contentos,
lealtad en el buen amigo,   350
traición en el enemigo,
en la noche escuridad
y en el día claridad,
así es verdad lo que digo.

Octav. Marqués, yo os quiero creer.   355
Ya no hay cosa que me espante,

---

322   To imitate the weasel: Octavio is simply saying, in a rather obscure
      conceit, that he is absorbing Don Pedro's unpleasant news through his
      ears and that its effect is to force him to speak, just as the weasel,
      having conceived through its ear, produced its off-spring through its
      mouth. The story that the weasel gives birth through its mouth goes
      back to classical times. It may be found, for example, in Ovid,
      Metamorphosis, IX, 306-21.
339   honour's obligation!: the fact that Isabela's seduction is now public
      knowledge means that her honour and reputation have been lost and can
      only be restored if her seducer - Octavio himself as far as the world at

To imitate the weasel, who, it's said,
Conceives in some strange manner through its ear,
And then proceeds to give birth through its mouth.
Can it be true of Isabela that she,   325
My very soul, can have forgotten me,
In order to make certain of my death?
The sweetest dreams precede the blackest nightmares.
My heart will fear now no further harm,
Wondering whether this is true or false,   330
For to intensify my sense of anguish,
My fears serve to deepen understanding;
My ears provide the certain confirmation
Of all my eyes unwillingly observed.
Can it really be possible, my lord,   335
That Isabela's so abused my trust,
And made a mockery of my love for her?
How can I believe in such a cruel fate?
Oh, woman! Such is honour's obligation!
And I am now compelled to deal with it!   340
But why should your honour in any way
Concern me, when you are the one's deceived
Me? Discovered in someone else's arms
And in the palace! I daren't think of it!

D. Ped.   There's no one needs persuading that the sky's   345
Of the province of the birds, the sea of fish,
Though all of them partake in some degree
Of all the elements that make the world.
It's certain that the blessed are in Heaven,
That loyalty's the sure sign of friendship,   350
That treachery's the mark of enmity,
Darkness the very quality of night
And clarity the essence of the day.
As that is true, so is my story certain.

Octav.   Marquis, you have convinced me of the truth   355
Of this. There's nothing will now surprise me.

---

large is concerned – marries her. The literature of the Golden Age
contains many examples of women who have been seduced and
abandoned and who subsequently set out in pursuit of the seducer in
order to make him fulfill his obligation to her. Such is the predicament
of Rosaura at the beginning of Calderón's *La vida es sueño* and Dorotea
in Part I of *Don Quixote*. Later in *The Trickster* Isabela, Tisbea and
Aminta all set out in pursuit of Don Juan.

348   all the elements: the world was thought to be composed of the four
elements of earth, air, fire and water. For an interesting exposition of
this topic see E.M.W. Tillyard, *The Elizabethan World Picture* (London,
1952), especially pp. 55–60.

	que la mujer más constante	
	es, en efeto, mujer.	
	No me queda más que ver,	
	pues es patente mi agravio.	360
D. Ped.	Pues que sois prudente y sabio,	
	elegid el mejor medio.	
Octav.	Ausentarme es mi remedio.	
D. Ped.	Pues sea presto, duque Octavio.	
Octav.	Embarcarme quiero a España,	365
	y darle a mis males fin.	
D. Ped.	Por la puerta del jardín,	
	duque, esta prisión se engaña.	
Octav.	¡Ah, veleta! ¡Débil caña!	
	A más furor me provoco,	370
	y extrañas provincias toco	
	huyendo desta cautela.	
	¡Patria, adiós! ¿Con Isabela	
	hombre en palacio? ¡Estoy loco!	

*Vanse todos y sale Tisbea, pescadora, con una
caña de pescar en la mano*

Tisbea	Yo, de cuantas el mar,	375
	pies de jazmín y rosa,	
	en sus riberas besa	
	con fugitivas olas,	
	sola de amor esenta,	
	como en ventura sola,	380

---

376   sweet mixture of jasmine and rose: Tisbea is in social terms an ordinary fisher-girl and in that sense represents a third stratum of society in the play, the other two being the monarchy and the nobility. On the other hand, she belongs very much to the literary tradition of the pastoral novel, so popular in Spain in the sixteenth century. Thus, like the disdainful shepherdess, Tisbea glories in the torments of those admirers whose attentions she rejects. Like them too her language is highly poetic and courtly, much more the language of literature than of life. This long soliloquy contains elements - colourful imagery, involved syntax - which characterize the poetic movement known as *culteranismo* or *gongorismo*, through its association with the poet Luis de Góngora, which developed in Spain in the early part of the seventeenth century and which had subsequently a significant impact on both poetry and drama. The allusion to Tisbea's feet as 'sweet mixture of jasmine and rose' is, of course, one that evokes their colour - white-pink - though it also suggests scent, and is typical of *culteranismo* both in its idealization and in its sensuous character. As far as Tisbea's use of such language is concerned, Tirso clearly wished to draw attention to her pride. She considers herself to be superior to her friends and companions in the sense that she alone has resisted love and maintained

	The woman who is thought to be most constant	
	Is always in the end an ordinary	
	Woman. I need no further proof of this.	
	The degree of my injury's plain to see.	360
D. Ped.	Since you, sir, are a wise and prudent man,	
	It's best you think of some way out of this.	
Octav.	The only way's to get away at once.	
D. Ped.	In that case, Duke Octavio, don't delay.	
Octav.	I'll find a ship whose destination's Spain.	365
	Perhaps there my pain will find some remedy.	
D. Ped.	Best use the door that leads out from the garden,	
	And hurry if you want to escape these chains.	
Octav.	Oh, fickle weather-vane, oh, fragile reed!	
	I'm driven to this act of desperation,	370
	To spend my days in a land that's not my own,	
	As the consequence of your trickery!	
	I leave my country behind me! And you	
	With some other man! The thought drives me mad!	

They leave. Enter Tisbea, a fisher-girl carrying a
fishing rod

Tisbea	Of all the girls who live along this shore,	375
	Whose feet, sweet mixture of jasmine and rose,	
	The waves gently kiss on golden sand,	
	Before attempting to escape and hide,	
	I alone am free from love's harsh tyranny,	
	And only I can boast I'm really happy!	380

---

her independence. Her high-flown language is thus a reflection of her feelings of superiority, for it distinguishes her from the others and gives her certain airs. It is worth drawing attention here too to the soliloquy as a form in Spanish Golden-Age drama. In the *Arte nuevo de hacer comedias* Lope de Vega had spoken of the restlessness of Spanish audiences and of the dramatist's need to retain their attention. In this respect the soliloquy poses problems, given the lack of action and incident that must accompany it, and Lope at one point in the *Arte nuevo* refers to the sonnet as a suitable form for the character who is alone on stage. Nevertheless, in practice Lope's plays often contain quite long soliloquies, as do the plays of other Golden-Age dramatists, notably those of Calderón. In this respect Spanish seventeenth-century drama is rather different from its English counterpart in which, on the whole, soliloquies are shorter and character is revealed through action. Tisbea's soliloquy of one hundred and forty one lines is not unlike an operatic aria. In practice, as the Theatre Clwyd workshop performance indicated, the speech works very well, not least because it falls into three clear sections - Tisbea in relation to her friends (375-434); description of Anfriso's love for her (435-481); description of the ship-wreck (482-516) -, each contrasting in mood and tone with the previous section.

29

tirana me reservo
de sus prisiones locas,
aquí donde el sol pisa
soñolientas las ondas,
alegrando zafiros   385
las que espantaba sombras.
Por la menuda arena,
(unas veces aljófar
y átomos otras veces
del sol que así la adora),   390
oyendo de las aves
las quejas amorosas,
y los combates dulces
del agua entre las rocas;
ya con la sutil caña   395
que al débil peso dobla
del necio pececillo
que el mar salado azota;
o ya con la atarraya
(que en sus moradas hondas   400
prenden cuantos habitan
aposentos de conchas),
segura me entretengo,
que en libertad se goza
el alma que amor áspid   405
no le ofende ponzoña.
En pequeñuelo esquife,
y en compañia de otras,
tal vez al mar le peino
la cabeza espumosa;   410
y cuando más perdidas
querellas de amor forman,
como de todo río,
envidia soy de todas.

---

383   the sun begins its daily journey: the allusion is to Phoebus, who daily
        drives the chariot of the sun across the sky, rising at dawn out of the
        sea. The poet Góngora describes dawn in somewhat similar fashion in
        his great poem, Las soledades, written in 1613-1614. See the Soledad
        primera, 179-181:
                    ... The Sun, emerging from its canopy
                    Of foam, took to its chariot, and its rays
                    Did strike the green obelisk of the cottage.
402   inside their shell: again these lines are reminiscent of a passage in
        Góngora. See the Soledad segunda, 83-84:
                    Of no advantage to the lustful oyster
                    Is the bony armour of its shell...

For I can speak with pride of liberty,
And of my rejection of passion's bonds,
Here where the sun begins its daily journey,
Awakening the sleepy waves from slumber,
And showering the dawn with brightest sapphire   385
To banish the shadows of darkest night.
Whenever I walk on this pleasant sand,
Whose grains have the beauty of tiny pearls,
Or seem like particles of golden sun,
The object of its amorous advance,   390
I am compelled to listen to the birds'
Constant complaining of forsaken love,
And the gentle, persuasive dialogue
Of the water's embracing of the rocks.
Meanwhile, I am devoted to my fishing,   395
The slender rod bent double with the weight
Of foolish fish who gladly take my bait,
And then in desperation seek to escape;
Or, the rod discarding for a net,
I trap in the dark prison of its mesh   400
As many as I can of those who live,
They think, securely, inside their shell.
But I'm the only one who's truly free,
For only I enjoy the liberty
Of that happy person the serpent love   405
Has failed to infect with his fatal poison.
Trusting sometimes to a small, flimsy boat,
And in the company of other girls,
I venture out to sea, our boat a comb
To the ocean's flowing and foamy tresses.   410
The other girls, helpless victims of love,
Voice their constant and desperate complaints,
While I, since I can mock their hopeless plight,
Am the true envy of each and every one.

---

409   our boat a comb: although Tisbea's speech as a whole contains many
        examples of *culteranismo*, this metaphor has a certain *conceptista*
        quality, at least in its association of two otherwise quite disparate
        things. *Conceptismo* was a feature of seventeenth-century prose style
        and is often associated with Francisco de Quevedo y Villegas
        (1580-1645), though its origins lay much further back in time. While
        culteranismo appealed on the whole to the senses and *conceptismo* to the
        intellect, it is true to say, nevertheless, that they often overlapped,
        culteranismo having recourse to *conceptista* figures. Consequently,
        examples of *conceptismo* are to be found in writers who are
        predominantly *culterano*, while exponents of *culteranismo*, like Góngora
        himself, often indulge in *conceptos*.

¡Dichosa yo mil veces,   415
amor, pues me perdonas,
si ya, por ser humilde,
no desprecias mi choza!
Obeliscos de paja
mi edificio coronan,   420
nidos, si no hay cigarras,
a tortolillas locas.
Mi honor conservo en pajas,
como fruta sabrosa,
vidrio guardado en ellas   425
para que no se rompa.
De cuantos pescadores
con fuego Tarragona
de piratas defiende
en la argentada costa,   430
desprecio soy y encanto;
a sus suspiros, sorda;
a sus ruegos, terrible;
a sus promesas, roca.
Anfriso, a quien el cielo   435
con mano poderosa,
prodigio en cuerpo y alma,
dotó de gracias todas,
medido en las palabras,
liberal en las obras,   440
sufrido en los desdenes,
modesto en las congojas,
mis pajizos umbrales,
que heladas noches ronda,
a pesar de los tiempos,   445
las mañanas remoza;
pues con los ramos verdes
que de los olmos corta,
mis pajas amanecen
ceñidas de lisonjas.   450

---

19   obelisk: a four-sided pillar which tapers to a point, usually monumental.
      The roof of Tisbea's cottage is presumably steep.
21   crickets: the sound of the cricket, which is produced by the friction of
      its forewings, is to be heard throughout the Spanish countryside
      during the hot summer months.
22   doves, whose silly and constant cooing: the dove is, of course,
      associated with Venus and thus with love. For this reason their
      presence is a source of annoyance to the disdainful Tisbea.
28   Tarragona: a seaport on the north-east coast of Spain, some sixty-five

Oh, blessed, Love, am I a thousand times   415
When you decide that I shan't be your slave,
Seeing I'm just an ordinary girl
Whose cottage isn't worth a second glance.
Thatch or humble straw's the only obelisk
That crowns my simple, unpretentious dwelling,   420
Making it a refuge not just for crickets
But for doves, whose silly and constant cooing
Drives me mad. But that straw protects my virtue,
A perfect fruit without the slightest blemish,
A piece of glass packed with the utmost care   425
To avoid the risk of damage on the journey.
To all the fishermen along the coast
Of Tarragona, where bright bonfires warn
Of pirates and help us to keep at bay
Those ships which navigate that silver shore,   430
I am an irresistible attraction;
But I reject them all, deaf to their sighs,
Unmoved by the fierce anguish of their cries,
To all their promises a piece of granite.
Amongst them is Anfriso, a young man   435
Who's favoured by the heavens in every way;
In soul and body Nature's prodigy,
Endowed with every possible attraction.
He uses words with utmost moderation;
His actions are so generous and kind;   440
He suffers my disdain without complaint;
His anguish really is quite moderate.
My cottage, this abode of humble straw,
He guards at night, although the nights be freezing,
And, through the different seasons of the year,   445
He brings to each morning a touch of Spring,
For always there are lovely green bouquets,
Cut from the branches of the towering elms,
And placed before my door to greet the day,
To surround me with Nature's flattery.   450

---

miles south of Barcelona. It was one of the earliest Roman settlements
in Spain. Evidence of Roman architecture may still be seen in the older
parts of the city.

429   pirates: the Mediterranean coastline was constantly threatened in the
sixteenth and seventeenth centuries. Raids by Moors from North Africa
were common, while the Turks posed a considerable threat to both
Charles V and Philip II up until their defeat in the Battle of Lepanto in
1571. The approaching danger was announced, as 428 suggests, by the
lighting of bonfires.

Ya con vigüelas dulces
y sutiles zampoñas
músicas me consagra;
y todo no me importa,
porque en tirano imperio   455
vivo, de amor señora;
que hallo gusto en sus penas
y en sus infiernos gloria.
Todas por él se mueren,
y yo, todas las horas,   460
le mato con desdenes:
de amor condición propia,
querer donde aborrecen,
despreciar donde adoran;
que si le alegran, muere,   465
y vive si le oprobian.
En tan alegre día
segura de lisonjas,
mis juveniles años
amor no los malogra;   470
que en edad tan florida,
amor, no es suerte poca
no ver entre estas redes
las tuyas amorosas.
Pero, necio discurso   475
que mi ejercicio estorbas,
en él no me diviertas
en cosa que no importa.
Quiero entregar la caña
al viento, y a la boca   480
del pececillo el cebo.
Pero al agua se arrojan
dos hombres de una nave,
antes que el mar la sorba,
que sobre el agua viene   485
y en un escollo aborda;

---

452   The soft guitar: the instrument referred to in the Spanish text is the
       vihuela, which was in fact an early form of the guitar. The second
       instrument, which I have translated as 'flute', is the _zampoña_, a rustic
       flute or shepherd's pipe.
486   Battered against the rocks: there is evidently a sudden storm at sea
       which drives the boat onto the rocks. This storm is also, of course, as

Sometimes as well he'll offer me sweet music,
The soft guitar, the shepherd's gentle flute,
Their music dedicated just to me.
Despite all this, I'm totally unmoved,
For I am ever mistress of my fate,   455
As far as love's concerned, it's queen and sovreign.
In fact, my greatest pleasure is his pain,
And in his suffering I find my heaven.
The other girls willingly die for him,
While I, at every opportunity,   460
Destroy his eager hopes with my disdain;
But isn't this the proper thing to do
In love's affairs? To love the man who hates
You; likewise, to despise the man who loves?
For if you favour him, you'll kill his love;   465
Despise him and he'll love you all the more.
This is the pleasant way I spend my days,
Assured of every kind of flattery.
No, I'll not waste the precious years of youth
Devoting all my time to love's pursuit.   470
When life's exciting and so full of fun,
It's truly not the greatest of misfortunes
That here amongst these nets of mine there's not
A sign of love's net, set to capture me.
But that's enough of all this foolish talk!   475
It's only interfering with my fishing;
And what's the point of squandering my time
On something that's not worth a second thought?
I'll cast out my line, see how far the wind
Carries it out to sea, so that the fish   480
Into its eager mouth will take my bait.
But what is that? My eyes perceive two men
Who are throwing themselves into the sea
Before the greedy waves swallow their boat.
It's being swept by the incoming tide,   485
Battered against the rocks and smashed to pieces.

---

was often the case in sixteenth and seventeenth-century literature, an
external manifestation of the emotional confusion which Don Juan's
arrival is about to unleash in Tisbea herself, for the girl who has
boasted of resisting love's storms and tempests is on the point of being
overwhelmed by them. This final section of the soliloquy is particularly
effective if it is spoken with a sense of horror and fascination as
Tisbea, rooted to the spot, observes the dramatic events.

como hermoso pavón,
hace las velas cola,
adonde los pilotos
todos los ojos pongan.   490
Las olas va escarbando;
y ya su orgullo y pompa
casi la desvanece.
Agua un costado toma. . .
Hundióse y dejó al viento   495
la gavia, que la escoja
para morada suya,
que un loco en gavias mora.

[Dentro] ¡Que me ahogo!

Un hombre al otro aguarda
que dice que se ahoga.   500
¡Gallarda cortesía!
En los hombros le toma.
Anquises le hace Eneas,
si el mar está hecho Troya.
Ya, nadando, las aguas   505
con valentía corta,
y en la playa no veo
quien le ampare y socorra.
Daré voces. ¡Tirseo,
Anfriso, Alfredo, hola!   510
Pescadores me miran,
¡plega a Dios que me oigan!
Mas milagrosamente
ya tierra los dos toman:
sin aliento el que nada,   515
con vida el que le estorba.

Saca en brazos Catalinón a Don Juan, mojados

---

487   some lovely peacock: Sebastián de Covarrubias, *Tesoro de la lengua castellana o española* (Madrid, 1611), makes the point that the peacock was often seen as a symbol of the proud and beautiful woman who is all too conscious of her beauty. For the writers of the Golden Age, with its strongly religious and moral character, physical beauty was, of course, something essentially fleeting and transcient and in that sense typical of wordly values. Thus, in Góngora's *Soledad primera*, 309-314, the peacock's dazzling beauty cannot save it from death. In Calderón's religious play, *No hay más fortuna que Dios*, the allegorical figure Beauty (Hermosura) falls into a pit and, when rescued by her companions, emerges as a skeleton, stripped of all her good looks. The

Stranded there, it's like some lovely peacock,
The sails in imitation of the tail,
Their beauty and dazzling brightness commanding
The sailors' eyes, ravishing their sight.   490
The movement of the waves plucks at its feathers;
It's loveliness and pride begin to fade,
And all its splendour's slowly stripped away.
The water's ripped a great hole in its side.
Now it's gone under; only its main sail   495
Remains above the waves, so that the wind
May choose, if it so wishes, to dwell there,
A madman locked and howling in a cage.
Cries for help off-stage
One of the men is struggling with the other
Whose head has disappeared beneath the waves.   500
What bravery and courage he displays!
He's trying to lift him onto his shoulders,
The one Aeneas to the other's Anchises,
As though the sea is suddenly Troy's wreckage.
He's striking out now for the shore, the water   505
Making way before this brave show of courage,
Though on the shore there's no one to be seen
Who can provide them with the help they need.
I'll call for help! See if they hear! Tirseo!
Anfriso! Alfredo! Hurry! Come at once!   510
The fishermen all turn in my direction.
I pray to God they will have heard my words!
By some miraculous stroke of luck the two
Swimmers have struggled to the shore at last.
The one who was swimming has now collapsed.   515
The other, clinging to his back, is still breathing.
Catalinón carries Don Juan from the water

---

irony of Tisbea's situation is that she does not associate the shipwreck
with her own fate, but the point would have been clear to a
contemporary audience.

503   The one Aeneas to the other's Anchises: Aeneas was a Trojan hero, son
of Anchises and Venus. After the destruction of Troy by the Greeks,
Aeneas rescued his father. For an account of the story see Virgil's
Aeneid, II, 705-710. The brave and courageous swimmer compared to
Aeneas is, of course, Don Juan who saves his servant, Catalinón, from
drowning (500).

515   The one who was swimming: as the result of his heroic efforts Don Juan
is totally exhausted and Catalinón finally drags him from the water
(516+).

Catal.   ¡Válgame la cananea,
           y qué salado está el mar!
           Aquí puede bien nadar
           el que salvarse desea,   520
           que allá dentro es desatino,
           donde la muerte se fragua;
           donde Dios juntó tanta agua,
           no juntara tanto vino.
           Agua salada: ¡estremada   525
           cosa para quien no pesca!
           Si es mala aun el agua fresca,
           ¿qué será el agua salada?
           ¡Oh, quién hallara una fragua
           de vino, aunque algo encendido!   530
           Si del agua que he bebido
           escapo yo, no más agua.
           Desde hoy abernuncio della,
           que la devoción me quita
           tanto, que aun agua bendita   535
           no pienso ver, por no vella.
           ¡Ah, señor! Helado y frío
           está. ¿Si estará ya muerto?
           Del mar fué este desconcierto,
           y mío este desvarío.   540
           ¡Mal haya aquel que primero
           pinos en la mar sembró,
           y que sus rumbos midió
           con quebradizo madero!
           ¡Maldito sea el vil sastre   545
           que cosió el mar que dibuja
           con astronómica aguja,
           causa de tanto desastre!

---

517   Cana's wine!: the Spanish text contains no reference to wine. Catalinón's words are '¡Válgame la cananea...!' In his footnote to this line in the Clásicos Castellanos edition Américo Castro observes that *cananea* is a corruption of *hacanea*, 'a nag', and that Catalinón, the *gracioso* or comic character of the play, is merely indulging in a ridiculous joke, alluding to himself, since he is bowed down by Don Juan's weight, as a beast of burden. In this case the line might be translated: 'He'd have me for his nag this master of mine!' On the other hand, the allusion to salt water in 518 suggests that there should be a contrast in 517. Christ's transformation of water into wine at Cana is the basis for my suggestion.

524   If he'd used wine: the *gracioso* of Golden-Age plays, like the fool of Elizabethan drama, is essentially a materialist, given to wine, women and song, even though he is fond of giving his master moral advice.

Catal.   Someone give me a swig of Cana's wine!
             All I can taste is the salt of bloody brine!
             This spot is shallow; it's alright to swim
             Here, and get the hang of how to save your skin.   520
             Out there it's deep, a bloody dangerous place,
             With death waiting to look you in the face.
             God's gone and put together all that water.
             If he'd used wine, I'd pray to Him forever!
             But the sea is all salt! That's a fine thing,   525
             I suppose, for someone who's keen on fishing.
             As for me, I hate water of any kind,
             So water full of salt's a sodding bind!
             Oh, can't someone give me a scalding pot
             Of wine? I'd drink it though it's boiling hot!   530
             If the water I've swallowed doesn't stop
             My breath, I'll never touch another drop.
             From this day forth I shall renounce the stuff!
             It's destroyed my reverence! I've had enough!
             I swear in future even holy water   535
             I shall ignore, and that's no laughing matter!
             Oh, master! Frozen stiff and cold as ice!
             A penny to a pound he's left this life!
             It's the sea's responsible for this lot.
             It's gone and put me in a real spot!   540
             I curse the wretch who had the silly notion
             To put trees in the middle of the ocean!
             Who could that fool be, measuring the sea
             With bits of flimsy wood chopped from a tree?
             Who's the fart, the madcap idiot tailor   545
             Who thought the sea's a pattern the sailor
             Could thread by using a needle and stars?
             For all the sea's disasters there's your cause!

Catalinon is a particularly fine example of this traditional comic character.

541   I curse the wretch: Catalinón's attack on sea-faring parallels similar passages in other Golden-Age writers. It has been suggested that Tirso found his inspiration in two odes of Horace, notably *Ode I, iii*, though Lope de Vega's *Isidro* seems a more likely source of inspiration. There is also an extremely powerful attack on sea-faring, voyages of discovery and the ruthless exploitation of countries and peoples associated with them in Góngora's *Soledad primera*, 366-502. In the seventeenth century the theme, part of the more general theme of the increasing materialism and moral emptiness of the so-called civilized world, acquired an added force as a result of the discoveries of Columbus and Vasco da Gama.

547   needle: the sailor's needle is, of course, the compass.

	¡Maldito sea Jasón,	
	y Tifis maldito sea!	550
	Muerto está, no hay quien lo crea;	
	¡mísero Catalinón!	
	¿Qué he de hacer?	
Tisbea	Hombre, ¿qué tienes	
	en desventuras iguales?	
Catal.	Pescadora, muchos males,	555
	y falta de muchos bienes.	
	Veo, por librarme a mí,	
	sin vida a mi señor. Mira	
	si es verdad.	
Tisbea	No, que aun respira.	
Catal.	¿Por dónde? ¿Por aquí?	
Tisbea	Sí;	560
	pues ¿por dónde?	
Catal.	Bien podía	
	respirar por otra parte.	
Tisbea	Necio estás.	
Catal.	Quiero besarte	
	las manos de nieve fría.	
Tisbea	Ve a llamar los pescadores	565
	que en aquella choza están.	
Catal.	Y si los llamo, ¿vernán?	
Tisbea	Vendrán presto. No lo ignores.	
	¿Quién es este caballero?	
Catal.	Es hijo aqueste señor	570
	del camarero mayor	
	del rey, por quien ser espero	
	antes de seis días conde	
	en Sevilla, donde va,	

---

549   Jason: the leader of the Argonauts who in the ship *Argo* sailed to Colchis, a country at the eastern end of the Black Sea, in search of the Golden Fleece.

550   Typhys: pilot of the Argonauts.

571   high chamberlain: Don Juan's father, Don Diego Tenorio, holds a position of high office indeed, for the High Chamberlain attended the king in his quarters and was responsible for the many ceremonial activities that took place in the palace. Mention has been made earlier – see note to 26+ – of the influence acquired by those men close to the King during the reigns of Philip III and Philip IV. The High Chamberlain in 1620, a possible date for *The Trickster's* composition, was, interestingly enough, Pedro Girón, Duke of Osuna (see the Introduction). Clearly, Don Diego Tenorio, portrayed as a good and morally upright man in the play, has the qualities which Pedro Girón lacked and is to be seen as the ideal royal adviser. Tirso embodied Pedro Girón's deficiencies in Don Pedro Tenorio rather than in the High Chamberlain to the King of Castle, but the implications would have been

	As for that Jason, he can go to hell!	
	And that Typhys too, he can go as well!	550
	My poor master's dead, no doubt at all!	
	Oh, Catalinón, you're a wretched mortal!	
	What am I going to do?	
Tisbea	Man, what's the matter	
	With you? Can your trouble be as great as that?	
Catal.	Oh, fishermaid, a great surfeit of problems	555
	Matched only by a total lack of fortune.	
	Through his efforts to save me, you can see	
	My master's done himself in! Look at him!	
	Tell me the truth!	
Tisbea	I'd say your master's breathing.	
Catal.	Where's he breathing? Through here?	
Tisbea	Of course through there!	
	How else would he be breathing?	560
Catal.	Who's to know?	
	That's not the only place the wind comes through!	
Tisbea	Don't be disgusting!	
Catal.	How I'd like to kiss	
	Those hands of yours, as white as whitest snow.	
Tisbea	Just go and call the other fishermen.	565
	You'll find them in that cottage over there!	
Catal.	If I call them, can I be sure they'll come?	
Tisbea	Of course they'll come! Tell them that I sent you.	
	But first tell me who's this fine gentleman.	
Catal.	Oh, this fine, handsome gentleman's the son	570
	Of the most excellent high chamberlain	
	To the King. Through him I'm expecting	
	To be a count before six days are out,	
	In Seville, which city's his destination,	

---

clear to a contemporary audience.

574   Seville: together with Madrid, Seville was an extremely important city during the Golden Age, for it was there that the greatest impact of South American trade was felt. Consequently, in the course of the sixteenth century Seville became one of the largest cities in Europe and continued to enjoy considerable prosperity long after other centres of commerce had declined. By the time Tirso wrote *The Trickster* the economic situation of the country as a whole was very serious, a fall from greatness was accompanied by moral decline, and writers were portraying past greatness as present sleaziness. While Seville remained an important city, Tirso portrays it here as tawdry and immoral, a city of rakes and prostitutes and largely dissolute nobleman. It is a picture of the city also painted by Cervantes in his exemplary short stories, *Rinconete y Cortadillo* and *El celoso extremeño*. Even given that the town-country contrast, so common in Golden-Age literature, had a long tradition, the unfavourable picture of Seville clearly had a basis in reality.

	y adonde su alteza está,	575
	si a mi amistad corresponde.	
Tisbea	¿Cómo se llama?	
Catal.	Don Juan	
	Tenorio.	
Tisbea	Llama mi gente.	
Catal.	Ya voy.	

Coge en el regazo Tisbea a Don Juan

Tisbea	Mancebo excelente,	
	gallardo, noble y galán.	580
	Volved en vos, caballero.	
D. Juan	¿Dónde estoy?	
Tisbea	Ya podéis ver:	
	en brazos de una mujer.	
D. Juan	Vivo en vos, si en el mar muero.	
	Ya perdí todo el recelo,	585
	que me pudiera anegar,	
	pues del infierno del mar	
	salgo a vuestro claro cielo.	
	Un espantoso huracán	
	dió con mi nave al través,	590
	para arrojarme a esos pies	
	que abrigo y puerto me dan.	
	Y en vuestro divino oriente	
	renazco, y no hay que espantar,	
	pues veis que hay de amar a mar	595
	una letra solamente.	
Tisbea	Muy grande aliento tenéis	
	para venir sin aliento,	
	y tras de tanto tormento	
	muy gran contento ofrecéis.	600
	Pero si es tormento el mar	
	y son sus ondas crueles,	
	la fuerza de los cordeles,	
	pienso que os hace hablar.	
	Sin duda que habéis bebido	605
	del mar la oración pasada,	
	pues, por ser de agua salada,	

---

584   To die in the sea: this passage is particularly effective in performance
if spoken quietly, as though Don Juan is waking from a dream. The
language, especially the contrasts involving birth and death and the
allusions to woman's beauty as heavenly, is, of course, the language of
Courtly Love. In *The Trickster*, however, the traditional theme of love
as something that ennobles is used largely for ironic effect. On the one
hand, Don Juan himself is far removed from the traditional,

	And where his majesty's in residence,	575
	That is, if I've not lost his confidence!	
Tisbea	What name does he go by?	
Catal.	Don Juan Tenorio's	
	My master's name.	
Tisbea	Then go and call my friends.	
Catal.	I'm on my way!	

Tisbea places Don Juan's head in her lap

Tisbea	What a fine man this is!	
	Oh, what a noble, handsome, dashing fellow!	580
	You must recover your senses, sir! Speak up!	
D. Juan	Where am I?	
Tisbea	Can't you tell where you are, sir?	
	Don't you know when you're in a woman's arms?	
D. Juan	To die in the sea and be born again	
	To your beauty! And to set aside	585
	The fear of death that almost destroyed me!	
	For from the depths of the sea's darkest hell	
	I'm rescued by the beauty of your heaven!	
	A whirlwind, frightening in its sheer fury,	
	Set upon my ship and overturned it,	590
	In order to wash me up at your feet,	
	Making them a safe refuge from the storm,	
	And so in the light of your lovely dawn	
	I swear I'm born again and fear nothing.	
	To tell the truth, from ocean to devotion	595
	The distance must be reckoned very small.	
Tisbea	My goodness, sir, but you've a lot of breath	
	For someone who just now was almost breathless!	
	And after all the danger you've been through,	
	I can't believe that you can be so cheerful!	600
	But if the sea's an instrument of torture	
	Whose waves are full of hate and cruelty,	
	Then it will be their battering of you	
	That's forcing you to speak to me like this.	
	Apart from that, it's true you will have swallowed	605
	All those fine words on swallowing the water,	
	For since the ocean's water is so sharp,	

---

long-suffering courtly lover who gladly endures the torments of love, while Tisbea, as her reply to him suggests – 597–620 –, is hardly the kind of woman worthy of being placed on a pedestal. In a sense Tirso treats the situation as mockingly as does Cervantes in the Quixote-Dulcinea episodes of *Don Quixote*, though Don Juan, it has to be said, is himself lacking in the virtues – devotion, selflessness, fidelity – exemplified by Don Quixote.

	con tan grande sal ha sido.	
	Mucho habláis cuando no habláis,	
	y cuando muerto venís	610
	mucho al parecer sentís;	
	¡plega a Dios que no mintáis!	
	Parecéis caballo griego	
	que el mar a mis pies desagua,	
	pues venís formado de agua,	615
	y estáis preñado de fuego.	
	Y si mojado abrasáis,	
	estando enjuto, ¿qué haréis?	
	Mucho fuego prometéis;	
	¡plega a Dios que no mintáis!	620
D. Juan	A Dios, zagala, plugiera	
	que en el agua me anegara	
	para que cuerdo acabara	
	y loco en vos no muriera;	
	que el mar pudiera anegarme	625
	entre sus olas de plata	
	que sus límites desata;	
	mas no pudiera abrasarme.	
	Gran parte del sol mostráis,	
	pues que el sol os da licencia,	630
	pues sólo con la apariencia,	
	siendo de nieve abrasáis.	
Tisbea	Por más helado que estáis,	
	tanto fuego en vos tenéis,	
	que en este mío os ardéis.	635
	¡Plega a Dios que no mintáis!	

Salen Catalinón, Coridón y Anfriso, pescadores

Catal.	Ya vienen todos aquí.
Tisbea	Y ya está tu dueño vivo.
D. Juan	Con tu presencia recibo

---

613   Trojan horse: the wooden horse in which the Greeks concealed
        themselves in order to enter Troy. Allusions to Troy are frequent in
        relation to Tisbea. She has already spoken in 503 of Don Juan's rescue
        of Catalinón in terms of Aeneas carrying his father from the burning
        city. Suspecting now that Don Juan's flattery is merely intended to
        deceive her, she alludes once more to Troy in a manner which evokes
        not heroism but deception. While the image was a literary commonplace
        and its meaning clear, it does serve to indicate here that Tisbea is no
        fool, which in turn underlines the irony of her subsequent seduction.

615   water: Tisbea responds to Don Juan's conceits with conceits of her own
        which are both teasing and provocative. They are clearly more earthy
        than the flowery conceits which marked the opening of her soliloquy,
        for now her interest in Don Juan is increasingly sexual. Tisbea

	Your words are sharp too, sir, and full of wit.	
	You speak a lot when you can barely speak,	
	And though you seem half dead, it's pretty clear	610
	That there's a lot of life still left in you.	
	Please God you aren't a trickster and a liar!	
	There's something tells me you're a Trojan horse	
	The sea's washed up here at my very feet.	
	And though you've gone and swallowed all that water,	615
	When I touch you, you seem to be on fire!	
	So if you burn when you are soaking wet,	
	Heaven knows what you'll be up to when you're dry!	
	It's my opinion you've got lots of fire.	
	Please God you aren't a trickster and a liar!	620

D. Juan If only God, sweet fishergirl, had let
The ocean take away this precious life,
Had let me leave this life with all my senses,
He'd have spared me the madness of this passion.
The waves would have embraced me, swallowed me 625
Completely in their limitless expanse,
Ranging as far as any eye can see,
But even they would not have dared burn me.
Your beauty has the power of the sun,
Enjoying its supreme authority. 630
To gaze upon it is for any man,
Though it be white as snow, to be consumed.

Tisbea You're still as cold as ice itself, my lord,
And yet there's still sufficient spark in you
To catch fire from the flame that burns in me! 635
Please God you aren't a trickster and a liar!

Enter Catalinón, Córidon and Anfriso, fishermen

Catal. They came at once in answer to my call.

Tisbea And here's your master, as good as ever was.

D. Juan Your presence has restored to me the gift

---

evidently delights here in a teasing game whose dangers she does not recognize. She is indeed 'playing with fire', and although the fire-love image is a purely conventional one, it points to the danger that lies ahead.

632 snow: her skin is as white as snow but to gaze upon it kindles the fires of love in any man. This is a typical Gongoristic paradox.

635 flame: in the course of her soliloquy Tisbea has boasted of her coldness and lack of feeling for her many suitors. Now the flame of love begins to burn in her. Indeed, in performance touch should play an important part, for from 616, where Tisbea refers to touching Don Juan, there should be an increasing emphasis on physical contact between them. At first - 579 - Tisbea simply places Don Juan's head in her lap. By 636 she is on the point of kissing him but is interrupted by the arrival of the fishermen.

	el aliento que perdí.	640
Corid.	¿Qué nos mandas?	
Tisbea	Coridón,	
	Anfriso, amigos. . .	
Corid.	Todos	
	buscamos por varios modos	
	esta dichosa ocasión.	
	Di que nos mandas, Tisbea,	645
	que por labios de clavel	
	no lo habrás mandado a aquel	
	que idolatrarte desea,	
	apenas, cuando al momento,	
	sin cesar, en llano o sierra,	650
	surque el mar, tale la tierra,	
	pise el fuego, y pare el viento.	
Tisbea	[Ap.] ¡Oh, qué mal me parecían	
	estas lisonjas ayer,	
	y hoy echo en ellas de ver	655
	que sus labios no mentían!	
	Estando, amigos, pescando	
	sobre este peñasco, vi	
	hundirse una nave allí,	
	y entre las olas nadando	660
	dos hombres; y compasiva,	
	di voces, y nadie oyó;	
	y en tanta aflicción, llegó	
	libre de la furia esquiva	
	del mar, sin vida a la arena,	665
	déste en los hombres cargado,	
	un hidalgo ya anegado,	
	y envuelta en tan triste pena	
	a llamaros envié.	
Anfriso	Pues aquí todos estamos,	670
	manda que tu gusto hagamos,	
	lo que pensando no fué.	
Tisbea	Que a mi choza los llevemos	
	quiero, donde, agradecidos,	

---

644   to serve you: the notion of serving a lady with devotion, without expectation of reward, is central to the philosophy of Courtly Love and thus to the pastoral novel whose characters, far from being real shepherds and shepherdesses, owe much to the courtly love tradition. Tisbea's attitude to her suitors, as revealed in her soliloquy, is, as we have seen, in the tradition of the disdainful shepherdess of pastoral literature, but it would seem too that her suitors have something of the unrequited lovers of the pastoral novel.

	Of life that I considered lost forever. 640
Corid.	*[To Tisbea]* Your wish is our command.
Tisbea	Thanks, Coridón,

Anfriso, loyal friends. . .

Corid.   Each one of us
Looks only for the opportunity
And happy chance to serve you as he can.
Tell us, Tisbea, what you'd have us do,   645
For orders given by those lips of yours,
Sweet as the sweet carnation, are most precious
Gifts to the man who idolizes you.
No sooner given, your command's his will,
He'll set his mind to it without delay,   650
Though his task be to plough the sea, submerge
The land, to walk on fire or stop the wind.

Tisbea   *[Aside]* Why, only yesterday such flattery
Seemed painful to me, more than I could bear!
But now I see there's more to it than that.   655
I fancy that their words proclaim the truth.
[Aloud] My friends, it's just that I was fishing here,
Sitting upon this rock, when suddenly
I saw a ship capsize far out to sea
And two men thrown into the water, fighting   660
For their lives. Moved by their sorry plight,
I called for help, but no one heard my cries.
Imagine my bewilderment! But then,
As though freed from the fury of the sea,
There landed at my feet upon the sand,   665
Borne on the shoulders of this valiant man,
This other handsome gentleman, half-dead.
It was a sight that filled my heart with pity,
And so I sent the servant off for help.

Anfriso   And so we came in answer to your call.   670
Just tell us what you wish. It will be done.
Not often do we get a chance like this.

Tisbea   My wish is that you take them to my cottage.
For there, in payment for the honour they

---

674   the honour: the fisherfolk are honoured by the mere presence of a
nobleman and by the opportunity of serving him. The corollary to this
is that the nobleman should respect them and not take advantage of his
superior social position. The theme of the individual's right to honour
and respect became the subject of many Golden-Age plays, amongst
which Lope de Vega's *Peribáñez y el Comendador de Ocaña* and
Fuenteovejuna, as well as Calderón's *El alcalde de Zalamea*, can be
singled out. In a sense these plays can be regarded as the dramatists'
advocacy of a greater democratic spirit in a society characterized by its
strict social divisions. Don Juan, of course, abuses nobleman and
peasant alike.

	reparemos sus vestidos,	675
	y allí los regalaremos;	
	que mi padre gusta mucho	
	desta debida piedad.	
Catal.	¡Estremada es su beldad!	
D. Juan	Escucha aparte.	
Catal.	Ya escucho.	680
D. Juan	Si te pregunta quién soy,	
	di que no sabes.	
Catal.	¡A mí. . .	
	quieres advertirme a mí	
	lo que he de hacer!	
D. Juan	Muerto voy	
	por la hermosa pescadora.	685
	Esta noche he de gozalla.	
Catal.	¿De qué suerte?	
D. Juan	Ven y calla.	
Corid.	Anfriso: dentro de una hora	
	los pescadores prevén	
	que canten y bailen.	
Anfriso	Vamos,	690
	y esta noche nos hagamos	
	rajas y palos también.	
D. Juan	Muerto soy.	
Tisbea	¿Cómo, si andáis?	
D. Juan	Ando en pena, como veis.	
Tisbea	Mucho habláis.	
D. Juan	Mucho entendéis.	695
Tisbea	¡Plega a Dios que no mintáis!	

*Vanse todos y salen Don Gonzalo de Ulloa y
el Rey Don Alfonso de Castilla*

Rey	¿Cómo os ha sucedido en la embajada,
	comendador mayor?
D. Gon.	Hallé en Lisboa

---

682   you don't know my name!: Catalinón has in fact already informed Tisbea
      – 570-576 – both of his master's name and position.

685   Has got me hooked!: this is my own free rendering of Don Juan's
      'Muerto voy/por la hermosa pescadora', 'I'm dying for the lovely
      fishergirl'. It seems perfectly appropriate to Don Juan's character.

693   I'm dying: there is a strong element of teasing and banter between Don
      Juan and Tisbea. Thus he utters 695 – 'You know what I desire' –
      with a laugh. On the other hand, Tisbea's suspicions and fears are
      genuine enough, as 696 suggests.

	Bestow on us, we'll mend their damaged clothes,	675
	And see if we can give them entertainment.	
	My father loves to give a helping hand.	
	It's something that will always warm his heart.	
Catal.	I swear this fishergirl's a real beauty!	
D. Juan	Come here, my friend! Listen!	
Catal.	I'm listening.	680
D. Juan	If anyone should ask you who I am,	
	Tell them that you don't know my name!	
Catal.	Me tell	
	Them that? No need for you to tell me that.	
	I know exactly what to say.	
D. Juan	The girl	
	Has got me hooked! Her beauty is outstanding	685
	Tonight I plan to have her for myself.	
Catal.	How will you do that?	
D. Juan	Come, and not a word!	
Corid.	Anfriso! In an hour from now our friends	
	The fishermen should be prepared to sing	
	And dance in honour of our guests.	
Anfriso	Let's go.	690
	Tonight's the night we'll all go celebrate,	
	Slices of lemon, grapes fresh from the vine!	
D. Juan	I'm dying, Tisbea!	
Tisbea	You're on your feet!	
D. Juan	But in the direst pain, as you can see.	
Tisbea	You've breath enough!	
D. Juan	You know what I desire!	695
Tisbea	Please God you aren't a trickster and a liar!	

*They exit. Enter Don Gonzalo de Ulloa and the King
Don Alfonso of Castile*

King	I trust your royal embassy went well,	
	My lord Commander?	
D. Gon.	In Lisbon I encountered	

696+   Don Alfonso of Castile: as has already been indicated, the king in question is Alfonso XI who died in 1350.

698   My lord Commander?: the reference is to the Grand Commander of the order of Calatrava – see Act II, 65–66 –, one of the semi-military, semi-religious orders which were of great importance in Spain in the Middle Ages. The order of Calatrava was founded in 1158, those of Alcántara and Santiago in 1166 and 1170. They lost much of their actual power at the end of the fifteenth century but continued to have great social prestige throughout the Golden Age. The position of grand Commander was second in rank to that of Grand Master.

	al rey don Juan, tu primo, previniendo	
	treinta naves de armada.	
Rey	¿Y para dónde?	700
D. Gon.	Para Goa me dijo; mas yo entiendo	
	que a otra empresa más fácil apercibe.	
	A Ceuta o Tánger pienso que pretende	
	cercar este verano.	
Rey	Dios le ayude,	
	y premie el celo de aumentar su gloria.	705
	¿Qué es lo que concertasteis?	
D. Gon.	Señor, pide	
	a Serpa y Mora, y Olivencia y Toro;	
	y por eso te vuelve a Villaverde,	
	al Almendral, a Mértola y Herrera	
	entre Castilla y Portugal.	
Rey	Al punto	710
	se firmen los conciertos, don Gonzalo.	
	Mas decidme primero cómo ha ido	
	en el camino, que vendréis cansado	
	y alcanzado también.	
D. Gon.	Para serviros,	
	nunca, señor, me canso.	
Rey	¿Es buena tierra	715
	Lisboa?	
D. Gon.	La mayor ciudad de España;	
	y si mandas que diga lo que he visto	
	de lo exterior y célebre en un punto	
	en tu presencia te pondré un retrato.	
Rey	Yo gustaré de oíllo. Dadme silla.	720
D. Gon.	Es Lisboa una otava maravilla.	

---

699   His majesty, your cousin John:the king in question is King John I, who was indeed a cousin of Alfonso XI, but he did not become king until 1385, thirty five years after Alfonso's death.

701   Goa: the capital of those territories acquired by Portugal in India, though it did not fall into Portuguese hands until the sixteenth century. This is yet another of the many anachronisms in the play.

703   Ceuta or Tangier: seaports on the coast of what is now Morocco from which Moorish raiders frequently invaded Spanish territory. John I is said by some historians to have captured Ceuta in 1415, the first part of Africa to be taken by any Spanish or Portuguese king.

707   Serpa, Mora, Toro: although these three towns, and those mentioned subsequently, existed and were located on the Spanish-Portuguese border, the exchange alluded to here has no historical basis.

717   The largest city: Lisbon was not a part of Spain during the reign of Alfonso XI. It did not become so until 1580 when Philip II of Spain acquired Portugal. In 1578 the young Portuguese king, Sebastian, had been killed in a foolish campaign in North Africa, leaving Philip in the direct line of succession.

	His majesty, your cousin John, busily	
	Preparing thirty ships.	
King	With what in mind?	700
D. Gon.	En route for Goa, I was told. I think,	
	Though, they're intended for some easier task.	
	To lay seige to Ceuta or Tangier	
	This coming Summer.	
King	May God assist his cause	
	And thus reward his servant's dedication.	705
	What was the outcome of your conversations?	
D. Gon.	My lord, he asks for Serpa, Mora, Toro	
	And Olivenza, in return for which	
	he'll give you Villaverde, Almendral	
	Herrera and Mertola, districts each	710
	Of them between Castile and Portugal.	
King	Then have the contract signed. But tell me now	
	About your journey. You'll be tired and out	
	Of pocket, I'm quite sure.	
D. Gon.	I never tire	
	In your service, your majesty.	
King	What kind	715
	Of place is Lisbon?	
D. Gon.	In the whole of Spain	
	The largest city. If you wish to listen,	
	I'll set before your eyes a verbal picture	
	Of all the sights from which it draws its fame.	
King	In readiness, Gonzalo, I'll sit down.	720
D. Gon.	That city is undoubtedly the world's	

---

721   That city: the ensuing description of Lisbon contains a great deal of accurate detail and suggests first-hand knowledge of the city. The point has been made by Blanca de los Ríos, *Tirso de Molina. Obras dramáticas completas* (Madrid, 1946-1958), II, 854a, that Tirso may have visited Galicia and Portugal in 1619, while it is certainly true that a number of his plays have a Portuguese setting and, as in the case of *Doña Beatriz de Silva*, point to a familiarity with Lisbon. The very different question of the relevance of this passage to the play as a whole is one that has been discussed by several critics. The emphasis on the religious character of Lisbon is very clear and suggests a deliberate contrast to the corrupt life of Seville and the immorality of Court life which is embodied there. Thus, the dramatist uses the Lisbon speech, significantly given to Don Gonzalo de Ulloa, a good and virtuous man, to attack the moral condition of Spain, exemplified in one of its principal cities, Seville, and, of course, in its most infamous son, Don Juan. See J.E. Varey, 'Social Criticism in *El burlador de Sevilla*', *Theatre Research International* and Robert Ter Horst, 'The *loa* of Lisbon and the Mythical Substructure of *El burlador de Sevilla*',

De las entrañas de España,
que son las tierras de Cuenca,
nace el caudaloso Tajo,
que media España atraviesa.   725
Entra en el mar Oceano,
en las sagradas riberas
de esta ciudad, por la parte
del sur; mas antes que pierda
su curso y su claro nombre,   730
hace un puerto entre dos sierras,
donde están de todo el orbe
barcas, naves, carabelas.
Hay galeras y saetías
tantas, que desde la tierra   735
parece una gran ciudad
adonde Neptuno reina.
A la parte del poniente
guardan del puerto dos fuerzas
de Cascaes y San Gian,   740
las más fuertes de la tierra.
Está, desta gran ciudad,
poco más de media legua,
Belén, convento del santo
conocido por la piedra,   745
y por el león de guarda,
donde los reyes y reinas
católicos y cristianos
tienen sus casas perpetuas.
Luego esta máquina insigne,   750
desde Alcántara comienza
una gran legua a tenderse
al convento de Jabregas.
En medio está el valle hermoso
coronado de tres cuestas,   755

Bulletin of Hispanic Studies, **L** (1973), 147–65. Varey argues that the speech is also important 'as a bridge scene allowing for the passage of time between Tisbea's coming upon the shipwrecked Don Juan and his subsequent seduction of her. . .' (p.199). In practice the bridge proves to be far too long and was finally cut in the Theatre Clwyd performance.

724 The Tagus: this major river has its source in the mountains of Cuenca, less than one hundred miles from Spain's east coast, flows in a south-westerly direction across Spain and Portugal and enters the Atlantic at Lisbon.

740 Cascais and Saint Julian: Cascais is situated some sixteen miles to the west of Lisbon on the bay of Cascais. Saint Julian is the name of a fort

Eighth wonder. In the very heart of Spain,
That is to say the region known as Cuenca,
The Tagus has its source, that mighty river
Which in its course divides our land in two.   725
The point where finally it meets the sea
Is on the hallowed banks of this fine city,
But somewhat to the southern side of it.
And there, before it makes the sacrifice
Of both its name and its identity,   730
It forms a harbour set between two hills:
A port in which are found from all the world's
Great oceans ships and vessels of all kinds:
Galleons and caravels in such abundance
That from the shore this teeming harbour seems   735
To be a city, a great capital
Where Neptune proudly rules and holds his Court.
On Lisbon's western side, where the sun sets,
Two fortresses are built to give protection
To the harbour, Cascais and Saint Julian   740
By name, by far the strongest in the land.
Outside the city, half a mile away
Or more, there stands the convent of Belem,
In honour of our blessed Saint Jerome,
The saint whose trusted guardian was a lion,   745
Whose sinfulness was punished with a stone.
There nowadays the royal family,
True fountainhead of Catholic belief
And Christianity, is laid to rest.
Then, having left this wondrous place behind,   750
You must proceed at least another league,
And there beyond Alcántara's stream you'll find
Another convent, called this time *Jabregas*.
It fills the centre of a lovely valley
And is surrounded on all three sides by hills   755

---

	some eight miles to the west of the city, constructed by Philip II.
743	Belem: the name of the Hieronymite convent built in the sixteenth century.
745	a lion: after Saint Jerome removed a thorn from the paw of a lion, the beast protected the monks of the convent.
746	punished with a stone: it was Saint Jerome's practice to atone for his sins by striking himself on the chest with a stone.
749	is laid to rest: a reference to the royal tombs situated in one of the monastery buildings.
752	Alcántara's stream: the stream separates Lisbon and the convent of Belem.
753	Jabregas: the Franciscan convent of Jabregas, founded in 1508.

que quedara corto Apeles
cuando pintarlas quisiera;
porque, miradas de lejos,
parecen piñas de perlas
que están pendientes del cielo,   760
en cuya grandeza inmensa
se ven diez Romas cifradas
en conventos y en iglesias,
en edificios y calles,
en solares y encomiendas,   765
en las letras y en las armas,
en la justicia tan recta,
y en una Misericordia
que está honrando su ribera,
y pudiera honrar a España   770
y aun enseñar a tenerla.
Y en lo que yo más alabo
desta máquina soberbia,
es que del mismo castillo
en distancia de seis leguas,   775
se ven sesenta lugares
que llega el mar a sus puertas,
uno de los cuales es
el convento de Odivelas,
en el cual vi por mis ojos   780
seiscientas y treinta celdas,
y entre monjas y beatas
pasan de mil y doscientas.
Tiene desde allí Lisboa,
en distancia muy pequeña,   785
mil y ciento y treinta quintas,
que en nuestra provincia Bética
llaman cortijos, y todas
con sus huertos y alamedas.
En medio de la ciudad   790
hay una plaza soberbia

---

756   Apelles: a Greek painter of the fourth century B.C.
770   Misericordia: completed in 1534, the 'Casa de Misericordia' ('House of
      Mercy') was a temple and hospital. In 1755 it was almost completely
      destroyed by an earthquake.
774   castle: the reference appears to be to the Saint George's Castle, an
      ancient Moorish citadel situated on a hill dominating the eastern part of
      Lisbon.
779   Odivelas: a Cistercian convent built in 1305, situated some five miles

Before whose dazzling beauty even Apelles,
Prince amongst painters, must admit defeat.
Looked at from far away this is a city
That seems a cluster of the finest pearls
Whose lovely beauty's balanced in the sky,   760
And in whose greatness even Rome itself
Could be contained at least a dozen times.
Beyond belief the number of its churches,
While convents too, and mansions and great houses
Adorn the streets that are themselves beyond   765
Compare, matched only by this city's fame
In learning, in the exercise of arms,
And in the application of true justice.
Her greatest building, though, is one that's called
Misericordia, source of inspiration   770
To true pity, and envy of all Spain.
Another feature of this city calls
For praise, in this case more than any other,
For from the battlements of its great castle
A distance of six leagues can be perceived,   775
And sixty towns scattered throughout the region,
Each one of them within the sea's embrace.
One of these has a special claim to fame:
This is the convent known as Odivelas,
For there I swear that my own eyes beheld   780
Six hundred cells and more, and all of them
Inhabited by nuns, at least twelve hundred,
Their lives to our blessed Lord devoted.
Within its boundaries Lisbon contains
Some fifteen hundred country villas, each   785
With its fine garden and its avenues
Of poplar trees, the kind of house that those
Of us familiar with the South of Spain,
The land of Andalusia, call cortijos,
The city has too at its very centre   790
A square whose splendour is beyond belief

---

northwest of Lisbon. It contained the remains of the famous Portuguese
monarch, King Denis (1279–1325).

782   twelve hundred: the number seems to be an exaggeration, for evidence
        suggests that there were four hundred nuns at this convent in 1608
        and six hundred in 1620, the approximate year of the play's
        composition.

789   'cortijos': the Diccionario de Autoridades defines cortijo as a farmhouse,
        the word being particularly associated with Andalusia.

que se llama del Rucio,
grande, hermosa y bien dispuesta,
que habrá cien años y aun más
que el mar bañaba su arena,   795
y ahora della a la mar
hay treinta mil casas hechas,
que, perdiendo el mar su curso,
se tendió a partes diversas.
Tiene una calle que llaman   800
rua Nova o calle Nueva,
donde se cifra el Oriente
en grandezas y riquezas;
tanto, que el rey me contó
que hay un mercader en ella   805
que, por no poder contarlo,
mide el dinero a fanegas.
El terrero, donde tiene
Portugal su casa regia,
tiene infinitos navíos,   810
varados siempre en la tierra,
de sólo cebada y trigo
de Francia y Ingalaterra.
Pues el palacio real,
que el Tajo sus manos besa,   815
es edificio de Ulises,
que basta para grandeza,
de quien toma la ciudad
nombre en la latina lengua,
llamándose Ulisbona.   820
cuyas armas son la esfera,
por pedestal de las llagas
que en la batalla sangrienta
al rey don Alfonso Enríquez
dió la Majestad Inmensa.   825

---

792   Rossío: the square, situated in the older part of the city, is still
referred to by this name, though its official name is *Praça de Dom
Pedro Quarto*.

802   the treasures of the East: an allusion to the riches brought to Lisbon
from Portuguese territories in the East.

808   Terreiro: this is the *Terreiro do Paço*, the square in front of the royal
palace which faces the Tagus. The square was destroyed by the
earthquake of 1755 but was subsequently rebuilt and called the *Praça
do Commercio*.

816   fashioned by Ulysses' hand: the story of the foundation of Lisbon by
Ulysses has no basis.

820   Ulisbona: the ancient name of Lisbon was *Olisipiom*, which was also
written as *Ulyssipo*, clearly deriving from the myth which stated that
Ulysses had founded a city in Iberia.

And which is called *Rossío*, great in size,
A pleasure to the eye, and well arranged.
A hundred years ago, so it is said,
The ocean lapped that very spot where now   795
The square is to be found, and there as well
Some thirty thousand houses stand and force
The raging sea to turn its back on them
And vent its anger on some other shore.
This district of the city has a street   800
Called *Rua Nova*, in our language New
Street, where the treasures of the East in all
Their grandeur and wealth are now contained.
According to the King, a merchant there
Has such excessive wealth he cannot count   805
In coins, so is obliged to weigh his money
And measure it, apparently, in bushels.
Terreiro, as the place is called, is where
The royal family of Portugal
Resides, and from the house ships can be seen,   810
A great armada anchored in the port,
A fleet that bears great quantities of wheat
And barley all the way from France and England.
Such is the splendour of the royal palace,
The mighty Tagus comes to pay it homage,   815
For it was fashioned by Ulysses' hand,
A name whose very synonym is greatness
And after whom the city once was called,
For in the Latin language Lisbon bore
The celebrated name of *Ulisbona*.
The royal court of arms have for their base
A sphere in celebration of the wounds
Which in a battle fought against the Moors
The King Alfonso Enriquez gladly suffered
In order to proclaim God's glorious name.   825

---

824   King Alfonso Enríquez: the battle fought against the Moors took place at
       Ourique in 1139. The Portuguese coat of arms, said here to be given to
       the victorious king by God, consisted according to tradition of five
       small shields which form a cross on a larger shield. In the battle King
       Alfonso Enríquez received five wounds, corresponding to the five
       wounds of Christ on the cross, which became the five shields of the
       coat of arms. In another play, *Las quinas de Portugal*, Tirso has
       Christ addressing King Alfonso in the following manner:
                 This court of arms which Portugal receives
                 From me, in token of my gratitude,
                 Consists of five small shields, their colour blue,
                 Their number corresponding to my wounds,
                 And as a cross arranged. . .   (Act I.)

Tiene en su gran tarazana
diversas naves, y entre ellas,
las naves de la conquista,
tan grandes, que de la tierra
miradas, juzgan los hombres   830
que tocan en las estrellas.
Y lo que desta ciudad
te cuento por excelencia
es, que estando sus vecinos
comiendo, desde las mesas   835
ven los copos del pescado
que junto a sus puertas pescan,
que, bullendo entre las redes,
vienen a entrarse por ellas;
y sobre todo, el llegar   840
cada tarde a su ribera
más de mil barcos cargados
de mercancías diversas,
y de sustento ordinario:
pan, aceite, vino y leña,   845
frutas de infinita suerte,
nieve de Sierra de Estrella
que por las calles a gritos,
puestas sobre las cabezas,
las venden. Mas, ¿qué me canso?   850
porque es contar las estrellas
querer contar una parte
de la ciudad opulenta.
Ciento y treinta mil vecinos
tiene, gran señor, por cuenta,   855
y por no cansarte más,
un rey que tus manos besa.

Rey   Más estimo, don Gonzalo,
escuchar de vuestra lengua
esa relación sucinta,   860
que haber visto su grandeza.
¿Tenéis hijos?

D. Gon.   Gran señor,
una hija hermosa y bella,

---

846   Ice: for the purpose of cooling drinks. The Serra da Estrela is a
       mountain range situated some one hundred and thirty five miles
       northeast of Lisbon.
855   one hundred and thirty thousand people: the population of Lisbon in
       1620 was indeed approximately this. See Öliveyra's *Livro das grandezas
       de Lisboa* (Lisbon, 1620).

The harbour too impresses in its size,
An anchorage for ships of different kinds,
And there you'll find the mighty 'men o'war',
So massive in their size that, looked at from
The land, they have the appearance of giants   830
That seem to reach up to the stars themselves.
Above all, what I found most pleasing there
Is that the citizens, in the course of
Their eating can, when seated at their tables,
Look out upon a fleet of fishing boats   835
And watch them fishing there so close to home
That, in their struggle to escape the nets,
The fish leap from the sea only to meet
Their end instead, stranded on the shore.
They have the opportunity to see   840
There too, arriving every evening,
More than a thousand vessels, fully laden
With every kind of rare and common goods:
Bread, oil, wine, wood, and such variety
Of fruit the mind can scarcely entertain.   845
Ice too brought from the Serra da Estrela,
And sold by women in the city's streets,
The nature of their wares loudly proclaimed
And borne in baskets balanced on their heads.
But why attempt to tell you any more?   850
To try to paint a picture of a fraction
Of Lisbon's opulence is just as vain
As if I were to try to count the stars.
It has, your majesty, a population
Of one hundred and thirty thousand people.   855
And to conclude, and tire you no further,
A King who through me pays you loyal homage.

King   I'm more than grateful to you, Don Gonzalo,
For that brief summary. It's almost better,
Coming from your own mouth, than if I'd gone   860
To Lisbon and observed it for myself.
Do you have any children?

D. Gon.   Yes, my lord,
A daughter blessed with such outstanding beauty,

---

859   that brief summary: although Don Gonzalo is presented in general as a
good and virtuous man, he is initially very conventional and extremely
boring, as the king's ironic comment suggests. Tirso seems to be
exposing in the course of the play not merely the corruption of the
Spanish court – though Don Gonzalo is an exception to this – but also
its stiffness and pomposity.

	en cuyo rostro divino	
	se esmeró naturaleza.	865
Rey	Pues yo os la quiero casar	
	de mi mano.	
D. Gon.	Como sea	
	tu gusto, digo, señor,	
	que yo lo acepto por ella.	
	Pero ¿quién es el esposo?	870
Rey	Aunque no está en esta tierra,	
	es de Sevilla, y se llama	
	don Juan Tenorio.	
D. Gon.	Las nuevas	
	voy a llevar a doña Ana.	

....

Rey	Id en buen hora, y volved,
	Gonzalo, con la respuesta.

Vanse y salen Don Juan Tenorio y Catalinón

D. Juan	Esas dos yeguas prevén,	
	pues acomodadas son.	
Catal.	Aunque soy Catalinón,	
	soy, señor, hombre de bien;	880
	que no se dijo por mí:	
	"Catalinón es el hombre";	
	que sabes que aquese nombre	
	me asienta al revés a mí.	
D. Juan	Mientras que los pescadores	885
	van de regocijo y fiesta,	
	tú las dos yeguas apresta,	
	que de sus pies voladores	
	sólo nuestro engaño fío.	

___

867   to arrange her marriage: in many Golden-Age plays the monarch is portrayed in an idealized light, the representative on earth of divine justice, the source of a country's health and harmony. In one sense Don Alfonso of Castile is precisely this, for he is constantly trying to patch up the havoc created by Don Juan. He is certainly more favourably portrayed than the King of Naples who prefers to close his eyes to problems in his court. On the other hand, it has to be said that Tirso would have been unwise to have presented his audience with an ostensibly unfavourable picture of the Spanish king. What he does very effectively is show us a man who is always a step behind events and who, in consequence, is ever looking for solutions and rarely finding them. Thus, when he arranges Ana's marriage to Don Juan, we know that Isabela's seduction makes the marriage impossible. The King will have to change his mind. In short, Tirso's portrayal of Alfonso is one that points to inefficiency and hasty pragmatism. The Crown is shown to be out of touch with events.

879   My name's Catalinón: the precise meaning of the name is difficult to ascertain, though it may well be derived from *catalina*, an Andalusian

	Nature surpassed itself in the formation	
	And true perfection of her lovely face.	865
King	In that case it will be a privilege	
	For me to arrange her marriage.	
D. Gon.	If that, sir,	
	Is your wish, I'm happy to accept	
	On her behalf, as she'll be happy too.	
	But who, your majesty, is the lucky man?	870

King Unfortunately, he's away at present,
But he's a native of Seville, his name
Don Juan Tenorio.

D. Gon.   In that case I shall
Ensure that Doña Ana is informed.

King Then go at once, Gonzalo, inform your daughter, 875
And let me know her wishes in this matter.

They exit. Enter Don Juan and Catalinón

D. Juan Quick as you can, get the two horses ready.
They'll guarantee a swift escape for us.

Catal. My name's Catalinón, that's true enough,
Master. It means a 'shit', but I'm no 'shit'. 880
There's not a man could ever say to me:
'Catalinón, your name's appropriate'.
They gave me my name quite improperly.
They should have known there are no flies on me!

D. Juan The fishermen are having a fine time, 885
So while they're wholly occupied with wine
And feasting, you will saddle up the horses.
Remember the success of this deception,
Depends upon the fleetness of their feet.

---

colloquialism meaning 'excrement'. There is also the word, *catalicón*, a vulgar form of *diacatalicón* which means a purgative. The *gracioso* or comic character of Golden-Age plays is usually someone lacking in any kind of virtue, and his name often epitomises his failings. Thus, Clarín, the *gracioso* of Calderón's *La vida es sueño*, is a self-interested individual whose name – meaning 'bugle' or 'trumpet' – points to his willingness to inform on others, to betray confidences, in order to advance himself.

884 no flies on me!: there is no basis for this joke in the Spanish text, but it seems appropriate to the character.

887 saddle up the horses: the galloping horse suggests, of course, the unbridled nature of passion and may be related both to Don Juan and to Tisbea whose head is now ruled by her heart. As far as Don Juan is concerned, the swift movement of the horse links with other allusions to speed and impetuosity – as in 303 where Don Pedro describes his leap from the balcony – and combines with them to create an impression of a sweeping and irresistible force.

Catal.	Al fin ¿pretendes gozar	890
	a Tisbea?	
D. Juan	Si burlar	
	es hábito antiguo mío,	
	¿qué me preguntas, sabiendo	
	mi condición?	
Catal.	Ya sé que eres	
	castigo de las mujeres.	895
D. Juan	Por Tisbea estoy muriendo,	
	que es buena moza.	
Catal.	¡Buen pago	
	a su hospedaje deseas!	
D. Juan	Necio, lo mismo hizo Eneas	
	con la reina de Cartago.	900
Catal.	Los que fingís y engañáis	
	las mujeres de esa suerte	
	lo pagaréis con la muerte.	
D. Juan	¡Qué largo me lo fiáis!	
	Catalinón con razón	905
	te llaman.	
Catal.	Tus pareceres	
	sigue, que en burlar mujeres	
	quiero ser Catalinón.	
	Ya viene la desdichada.	
D. Juan	Vete, y las yeguas prevén.	910
Catal.	¡Pobre mujer! Harto bien	
	te pagamos la posada.	

Sale Catalinón y entra Tisbea

Tisbea	El rato que sin ti estoy	
	estoy ajena de mí.	
D. Juan	Por lo que finges ansí,	915
	ningún crédito te doy.	
Tisbea	¿Por qué?	

---

895   the scourge of women: the literal translation of the Spanish phrase is
'the punishment of women', and it is a curious fact of the play that, as
has already been suggested in Isabela's case, the women who suffer are
all themselves guilty of wrongdoing. That Don Juan should be the
instrument of their punishment and the punishment more serious than
their offence is undoubtedly ironic, but irony and ambiguity are two of
the play's most interesting features.

898   all her hospitality!: see 90, note. Again the servant is used to comment
on his master's moral shortcomings.

899   Aeneas: after his flight from Troy he encountered Dido, the reputed
founder of Carthage and its beautiful queen. She fell in love with him
and committed suicide when he abandoned her. The story is recounted
in Virgil's *Aeneid*, Book IV.

Catal.	Your mind's made up, then, master, to deceive Tisbea?	890
D. Juan	What do you expect of me? Seduction is the habit of a lifetime. If you already know it's in my nature, Why ask the question?	
Catal.	What I know for sure, Master, is that you are the scourge of women.	895
D. Juan	Oh, I can hardly wait to have Tisbea! What a fine body of a girl!	
Catal.	A fine Reward for all her hospitality!	
D. Juan	Don't be a bore! This was the way Aeneas Acted towards the lovely Queen of Carthage.	900
Catal.	What sort of man is it that takes advantage Of these poor women? But you'll pay the price For it one day. I hope you'll rot in Hell!	
D. Juan	Plenty of time for me to pay that debt! Whoever gave you your name was right. Catalinón, he's always got the runs!	905
Catal.	You run your way. In matters of deceiving Honest women I prefer to run away. Here comes the wretched girl. I pity her!	
D. Juan	You just make sure the horses are prepared.	910
Catal.	Poor girl! Her loss is our benefit. Such is the way we pay for board and lodge!	

Exit Catalinón. Enter Tisbea

Tisbea	I've hardly been away from you, and yet It's just as if I'd left my soul behind.	
D. Juan	I fancy you are teasing me, Tisbea, And so I won't believe a word you say.	915
Tisbea	Why won't you?	

---

904   Plenty of time for me to pay that debt!: the phrase '¡Qué largo me lo fiáis!' was, in the slightly different form of *Tan largo me lo fiáis*, the title of an earlier version of *The Trickster* (see the Introduction). It is used by Don Juan on a number of occasions in the play to express his scorn for the conventional fear of death and the day of reckoning. As a young man, he wishes only to enjoy the pleasures of life and forget what lies ahead, but in so doing he closes his eyes to the fact that the pleasures of the world are fleeting and pass quickly by. The themes of the brevity of human life and the importance of placing one's faith in those values that are spiritual and eternal were central to the literature of seventeenth-century Spain and were powerfully expressed in the work of such writers as Quevedo, Góngora and Calderón.

914   my soul: once again Tisbea expresses herself in the language of Courtly Love. See Octavio's allusion to his love for Isabela, 205, note.

D. Juan	Porque, si me amaras,
	mi alma favorecieras.
Tisbea	Tuya soy.
D. Juan	Pues di, ¿qué esperas,
	o en qué, señora, reparas?	920
Tisbea	Reparo en que fué castigo
	de amor el que he hallado en ti.
D. Juan	Si vivo, mi bien, en ti
	a cualquier cosa me obligo.
	Aunque yo sepa perder	925
	en tu servicio la vida,
	la diera por bien perdida,
	y te prometo de ser
	tu esposo.
Tisbea	Soy desigual
	a tu ser.	930
D. Juan	Amor es rey
	que iguala con justa ley
	la seda con el sayal.
Tisbea	Casi te quiero creer;
	mas sois los hombres traidores.	935
D. Juan	¿Posible es, mi bien, que ignores
	mi amoroso proceder?
	Hoy prendes con tus cabellos
	mi alma.
Tisbea	Yo a ti me allano
	bajo la palabra y mano	940
	de esposo.
D. Juan	Juro, ojos bellos,
	que mirando me matáis,
	de ser vuestro esposo.

---

929   I'm unworthy: Tisbea is well aware of the fact that the social divide between herself and Don Juan is very great indeed. In the play as a whole the social hierarchy of monarchy, nobility and peasants is suggested very clearly, as well as the divisions between the classes. Thus Isabela and Octavio, Ana and Mota are suited to each other in terms of class and marriage prospects, for all of them are nobles. Similarly, Tisbea is suited to the fisherman, Anfriso, whom she rejects, and the peasants, Batricio and Aminta, are made for each other. In contrast, although she has pretensions and aspirations to higher things, Tisbea is totally unsuited to Don Juan and can only bring trouble upon herself in trying to surmount the class barriers. In Golden-Age literature in general the rigid, hierarchical nature of society and the social and moral disorder attendant on its disruption are common themes. One of the best examples of a member of the lower orders who attempts to rise socially and comes to grief is Pablos, the protagonist of Quevedo's picaresque novel of 1626, *Historia de la vida*

D. Juan	Because, if you really loved
	Me, you would ease this anguish in my soul.
Tisbea	I do love you.
D. Juan	Then why wait any longer?
	I think there must be something on your mind.	920
Tisbea	What makes me hesitate's the thought that my
	Love for you is a punishment on me.
D. Juan	How can that be when from this moment on
	My life is dedicated to your cause?
	Why, though my life be lost in your service,	925
	The loss is one that, given the reward,
	Makes such a sacrifice appear quite small!
	In any case, I've given you my word
	That we'll be joined in marriage.
Tisbea	I'm unworthy
	Of your status.
D. Juan	Love's a king supreme,	930
	According to whose law there's no distinction
	Between the finest silk or roughest sackcloth.
Tisbea	I'm tempted to believe your argument,
	But it's a fact that men are cheats and liars.
D. Juan	How can it be, my love, that you are deaf	935
	To pleas inspired by my true devotion?
	Such is the beauty of your lovely hair,
	It has ensnared my soul.
Tisbea	And you, my lord,
	Command me. I accept your word and hand
	In holy matrimony.
D. Juan	The perfection	940
	Of your eyes is such that they destroy
	Me with their gaze. I swear we shall be married.

---

del buscón. While the literature of the time examines these issues, it is nevertheless true to say that in reality the degree of social movement upwards was somewhat greater.

941   your eyes: Don Juan speaks to Tisbea in the manner of a courtly lover, for whom, as Otis Green observes – *Spain and the Western Tradition: The Castilian Mind in Literature from 'El Cid' to Calderón*. . . I, p.255-, '. . .love is born of beauty, and the eyes are the instruments of its communication'. See too Sebastián de Covarrubias, *Tesoro de la lengua castellana o española*, in which eyes are described as 'the most precious part of the body. . ., the windows where the soul reveals itself, providing us with evidence of its passions and affections. . ., the messengers of the heart, the advocates of what is concealed deeply in our hearts. . .' Needless to say, Don Juan is merely giving a performance, though a highly convincing one. Throughout the play the idea of individuals giving a performance, in particular the nobility, points to the facade and the superficiality of Court life.

Tisbea	Advierte,
	mi bien, que hay Dios y que hay muerte.
D. Juan	¡Qué largo me lo fiáis!
	Y mientras Dios me dé vida, 945
	yo vuestro esclavo seré.
	Esta es mi mano y mi fe.
Tisbea	No seré en pagarte esquiva.
D. Juan	Ya en mí mismo no sosiego.
Tisbea	Ven, y será la cabaña 950
	del amor que me acompaña
	tálamo de nuestro fuego.
	Entre estas cañas te esconde
	hasta que tenga lugar.
D. Juan	¿Por dónde tengo de entrar? 955
Tisbea	Ven y te diré por dónde.
D. Juan	Gloria al alma, mi bien, dais.
Tisbea	Esa voluntad te obligue,
	y si no, Dios te castigue.
D. Juan	¡Qué largo me lo fiáis! 960

Vanse y salen Coridón, Anfriso, Belisa y
Músicos

Corid.	Ea, llamad a Tisbea,
	y los zagales llamad
	para que en la soledad
	el huésped la corte vea.
Anfriso	¡Tisbea, Usindra, Atandria! 965
	No vi cosa más cruel.
	¡Triste y mísero de aquel
	que en su fuego es salamandria!

---

947   And here's my hand: the motif of the hand, associated with a promise solemnly given, occurs in various forms throughout the play. For the most part the promise is made to Don Juan's female victims and is broken. Later the hand motif is reintroduced in the case of the promise made to the stone guest, and the promise is kept. The stone guest also extends his hand to Don Juan in a gesture of goodwill and proceeds to crush him, deceiving him as he has deceived others. The deceiver is thus deceived, the 'burlador burlado', the title of the play turned on its head.

954   an opportunity to enter: the literal meaning of Tisbea's words does not conceal a powerful sexual quality, reinforced by 956. By the end of Act I she is very different indeed from the woman who earlier gloated over the sufferings of the men she delighted in rejecting. According to Jung, *Psychology and Alchemy* (London, 1953), 72, a door symbolises female virginity. There is a very interesting discussion of this topic in relation to Spanish ballads and traditional poetry by J.M. Aguirre, 'Moraima y el prisionero: ensayo de interpretación', in *Studies of the Spanish and Portuguese Ballad*, ed. N.D. Shergold (London, 1972),

Tisbea	Do not forget God's punishment for men Who break their promises is death.
D. Juan	I trust Death's still a long way off, but while I've life 945 My promise is I'll be your loyal slave. And here's my hand, in token of my faith.
Tisbea	In payment of your faith my coldness melts.
D. Juan	With your acceptance my heart's all ablaze.
Tisbea	Our love we'll celebrate in this, my humble 950 Cottage, and there we'll consummate our passion. My bedroom shall be our bridal chamber. But first wait here among the reeds, until You have an opportunity to enter.
D. Juan	But how shall I get in and not be seen? 955
Tisbea	I'll show you. Look! This is the best way in.
D. Juan	Already it's as if my soul were blessed.
Tisbea	Don't forget your obligation to me! If you forget it, may God take revenge!
D. Juan	A debt I'm not obliged to pay as yet! 960

They exit. Enter Coridón, Anfriso, Belisa and Musicians

Corid.	Go call Tisbea and bid her come at once. Bid all our good companions hurry too, So that our honoured guest in this secluded Spot may feast his eyes on our company.
Anfriso	Tisbea, Usindra, Atandria! Join us here! 965 No other girl can match her cruelty! Pity the man who falls in love with her! For like the salamander, he'll dwell in fire.

53-72. Aguirre gives as a pertinent example the conversation between a young girl and her lover in the ballad *El enamorado y la muerte*:

'Open the door to me, my dove
Open the door to me, my love.'
'How can I open the door to you
When circumstance forbids I do?
My father's home, for goodness sake,
And mother is still wide awake.'

In Act II of *The Trickster* Don Juan tells the Marquis of Mota that Doña Ana's door will be open from eleven o'clock at night. He, of course, intends entering it before Mota.

968   the salamander: a kind of lizard which, according to legend, was capable of surviving in fire. Allusions of this kind abound in Golden Age literature in relation to the fires of love. Cf. Don Alonso in Lope de Vega's *El caballero de Olmedo*:

...... for if I were to find myself
Where I would gaze forever on Inés,
Then would my soul be like the salamander.   (Act II, 912-14)

	Antes que el baile empecemos	
	a Tisbea prevengamos.	970
Belisa	Vamos a llamarla.	
Corid.	Vamos.	
Belisa	A su cabaña lleguemos.	
Corid.	¿No ves que estará ocupada	
	con los huéspedes dichosos,	
	de quien hay mil envidiosos?	975
Anfriso	Siempre es Tisbea envidiada.	
Belisa	Cantad algo mientras viene,	
	porque queremos bailar.	
Anfriso	¿Cómo podrá descansar	
	cuidado que celos tiene?	980

    Cantan :

A pescar salió la niña
tendiendo redes;
y, en lugar de peces,
las almas prende.

  Sale Tisbea

Tisbea	¡Fuego, fuego, que me quemo,	985
	que mi cabaña se abrasa!	
	Repicad a fuego, amigos,	
	que ya dan mis ojos agua.	
	Mi pobre edificio queda	
	hecho otro Troya en las llamas,	990
	que después que faltan Troyas	
	quiere amor quemar cabañas.	
	Mas si amor abrasa peñas	
	con gran ira y fuerza extraña,	
	mal podrán de su rigor	995
	reservarse humildes pajas.	
	¡Fuego, zagales, fuego, agua, agua!	
	¡Amor, clemencia, que se abrasa el alma!	
	¡Ay, choza, vil instrumento	
	de mi deshonra y mi infamia!	1000

---

985   My cottage is ablaze: some critics believe that Tisbea's cottage is not on fire and that the allusion is merely to her anger, passion and frustration. Thus Gerald L. Wade, *El burlador de Sevilla y convidado de piedra* (New York, 1969), 191, note to 986-1045: 'Tisbea's cry of *fuego* in 986, and repeated hereafter at intervals, has on occasion been mistakenly thought to be a call for aid for her burning cabin. This would indicate Don Juan's attempt at arson after her seduction. Rather, her cry is one of desperation at his deceit, now that he has fled, and her cabin is burning only figuratively as a result of her own intense fire of thwarted love. . .' The end of the Act is clearly much more

	My friends, we'll wait a moment to begin	
	The dance until Tisbea joins us here.	970
Belisa	We'll go and fetch her.	
Corid.	Yes, we'll go at once!	
Belisa	We'll find her in her cottage. Let's go there!	
Corid.	We'd better not! She'll be preoccupied	
	In entertaining our noble guests!	
	How envious we are of their good fortune!	975
Anfriso	Tisbea's always the one who's envied most.	
Belisa	Until she comes we'll entertain ourselves	
	In song, and straight away begin the dance.	
Anfriso	How can the lover rest whose heart is heavy	
	And torn in two by cruel jealousy?	980

They sing

'The fishergirl went out to fish,
But all the fish swam by in shoals,
When she returned, she had no fish,
Her net was full of lovers' souls.'

Enter Tisbea

Tisbea	Help me, my friends! My cottage is ablaze,	985
	Burning, and I too am consumed by flames!	
	Sound the alarm! Bring water too as quickly	
	As you can, for my tears are not enough	
	To quench these flames! My cottage has become	
	Another Troy, destroyed by flame and fire!	990
	As though, having burnt all the other Troys,	
	Love's flame consumes the humblest cottage too.	
	But if love's fire is such that its assault	
	Reduces to mere ash the hardest stone,	
	What chance of escape from its fierce ardour	995
	Can straw have, when fragility's its nature?	
	My friends, the fire spreads! Bring water quickly!	
	My soul's on fire too! It burns! Have pity!	
	My own cottage, the vile and treacherous source	
	Of my disgrace and infamous dishonour!	1000

---

dramatic if the fire is real. If it were, it would parallel the flames of the torches in Act II, 579, and the fire that fills the chapel in Act III, 976. In purely practical terms, setting fire to Tisbea's cottage provides Don Juan with a better opportunity to escape, for the blaze occupies the fishermen's attention and thus creates a timely diversion.

990   Another Troy: cf. 613.

996   straw: Tisbea has alluded earlier to the straw roof of her cottage which protects her unblemished virtue in the same way that straw protects glass-ware. Don Juan's blazing passion has now consumed and destroyed her honour just as the flames destroy the brittle roof of the cottage.

¡Cueva de ladrones fiera,
que mis agravios ampara!
Rayos de ardientes estrellas
en tus cabelleras caigan,
porque abrasadas estén,   1005
si del viento mal peinadas.
¡Ah, falso huésped, que dejas
una mujer deshonrada!
Nube que del mar salió
para anegar mis entrañas.   1010
¡Fuego, fuego, zagales, agua, agua!
¡Amor, clemencia, que se abrasa el alma!
Yo soy la que hacía siempre
de los hombres burla tanta;
que siempre las que hacen burla,   1015
vienen a quedar burladas.
Engañóme el caballero
debajo de fe y palabra
de marido, y profanó
mi honestidad y mi cama.   1020
Gozóme al fin, y yo propia
le di a su rigor las alas
en dos yeguas que crié,
con que me burló y se escapa.
Seguilde todos, seguilde.   1025
Mas no importa que se vaya,
que en la presencia del rey
tengo de pedir venganza.
¡Fuego, fuego, zagales, agua, agua!
¡Amor, clemencia, que se abrasa el alma! 1030

Vase Tisbea

Corid.   Seguid al vil caballero.
Anfriso   ¡Triste del que pena y calla!
Mas ¡vive el cielo! que en él,
me he de vengar desta ingrata.
Vamos tras ella nosotros.   1035
porque va desesperada,
y podrá ser que ella vaya
buscando mayor desgracia.

1009   A cloud emerging from the sea: reference has already been made to the
four elements of which the world was thought to be composed. See 348,
note. A cloud's natural element was, of course, air and not water, but
Tisbea refers here to a cloud emerging from water. In short, this
confusion of elements points to the confusion and chaos which Don Juan
has brought into her previously peaceful life. The whole of Tisbea's

70

A lair and hiding-place for cruel thieves,
For those two architects of my offence.
Let blazing sparks, hot as the hottest star,
Fall on your head and set your hair on fire;
Let flames consume, destroy it totally,   1005
And the wind comb whatever ruin's left!
False guest, that you should act so treacherously
Towards a woman's hospitality!
A cloud emerging from the sea to drown
And overwhelm me, to destroy my being!   1010
My friends, the fire spreads! Bring water quickly!
My soul's on fire too. It burns. Have pity!
I am the one who always mocked all men
And took delight in all their suffering.
The truth is those who think they fool all others   1015
Are in the end the ones who fool themselves.
The nobleman's the source of my deception,
For he's betrayed the promise of his hand
In marriage, abused me, profaned my bed
And robbed me of my honesty and virtue.   1020
For he's the one's seduced me. I'm the one
Who's favoured his escape by giving him
The wings of horses to facilitate
His trickery and make a fool of me.
I beg you, follow him and track him down.   1025
The fact that he's escaped won't help him much.
I'll seek an audience with the King and beg him
To intervene and guarantee me vengeance.
My friends, the fire spreads! Bring water quickly!
My soul's on fire too. It burns. Have pity!   1030

Exit Tisbea

Corid. We'll all pursue this treacherous nobleman.
Anfriso Pity the man who loves in vain!
But even so I swear that Heaven through him
Gives me my vengeance for her faithlessness.
We'd better go at once and look for her;   1035
Her state of mind is desperate; we'd best
Make sure she doesn't, in her desperation,
Add further to the sum of her misfortunes.

---

speech, as well as its physical action, underline this idea, for throughout the allusions to the contrasting elements of fire and water mingle, while at the end of the act Tisbea herself, burning with passion, wades into the sea.

1023 The wings of horses: presumably a reference to Pegasus, the winged horse of Greek mythology.

71

Corid.	Tal fin la soberbia tiene.
	¡Su locura y confianza	1040
	paró en esto!

[Dice Tisbea dentro] ¡Fuego, fuego!

Anfriso	Al mar se arroja.
Corid.	Tisbea, detente y para.
Tisbea	¡Fuego, fuego, zagales, agua, agua!
	¡Amor, clemencia, que se abrasa el alma!

Corid.   How true it is: pride always comes before
           A fall. Such was her over-confidence,   1040
           Such is its consequence.
       Tisbea's cries off-stage: My soul's on fire!
Anfriso   She's in the water!
Corid.   Tisbea! Wait! Come back! Go out no further!
Tisbea   My friends, the fire spreads! Bring water quickly!
           My soul's on fire too! It burns! Have pity!

JORNADA SEGUNDA

Salen el Rey Don Alonso y Don Diego Tenorio,
de barba

Rey	¿Qué me dices?
D.Diego	Señor, la verdad digo.

Por esta carta estoy del caso cierto,
que es de tu embajador y de mi hermano:
halláronle en la cuadra del rey mismo
con una hermosa dama de palacio.   5

Rey	¿Qué calidad?
D.Diego	Señor, es la duquesa

Isabela.

Rey	¿Isabela?
D.Diego	Por lo menos. . .
Rey	¡Atrevimiento temerario! ¿Y dónde

ahora está?

D.Diego	Señor, a vuestra alteza

no he de encubrille la verdad: anoche   10
a Sevilla llegó con un criado.

Rey:
Ya conocéis, Tenorio, que os estimo,
y al rey informaré del caso luego,
casando a ese rapaz con Isabela,
volviendo a su sosiego al duque Octavio,   15
que inocente padece; y luego al punto
haced que don Juan salga desterrado.

D.Diego	¿Adónde, mi señor?
Rey	Mi enojo vea

en el destierro de Sevilla; salga
a Lebrija esta noche, y agradezca   20
sólo al merecimiento de su padre. . .
Pero, decid, don Diego, ¿qué diremos
a Gonzalo de Ulloa, sin que erremos?
Caséle con su hija, y no sé cómo
lo puedo ahora remediar.

D.Diego	Pues mira, 25

gran señor, qué mandas que yo haga

---

1   Don Diego: in the earlier version of the play entitled *Tan largo me lo*
     fidis – see Introduction – Don Juan's father is called Don Juan Tenorio,
     viejo. In this respect see Act II, 669 of *The Trickster* where Gaseno
     clearly thinks that the father's name is also Don Juan Tenorio.

3   your ambassador: of Don Alfonso of Castile, sent by him to Naples. Don
     Diego, we recall, is High Chamberlain to King Alfonso.

7   Isabela!: it is not clear how the King of Castile would have known quite
     so well a particular lady of the Court of Naples. In reality, as has been

ACT II

Enter the King, Don Alfonso and Don Diego Tenorio,
bearded

King   What are you saying?

D. Diego   Nothing but the truth,
My lord. This letter makes the matter clear.
It's signed by your ambassador, my brother.
They found him in the King's own royal chamber,
And with him there a lady of the Court.   5

King   What rank was she?

D. Diego   None other than the Duchess
Isabela!

King   The Duchess Isabela?
What bare-faced boldness! Where's the rascal now?

D. Diego   Your majesty, I am an honest man.
I'll not conceal the truth from you. Last night   10
He reached Seville, accompanied by his servant.

King   You know, Tenorio, I esteem you highly.
I'll see the King of Naples is informed
Of this. The rogue must marry Isabela.
We must restore Octavio's peace of mind.   15
He suffers in all innocence. As well
As that, Don Juan is exiled from this moment!

D. Diego   Where shall he go, your majesty?

King   My anger's
Such, that he's now banished from Seville.
Lebrija'll be his home, and he can thank   20
His father that his sentence is so light. . .
But now, Don Diego, what are we to say
To Don Gonzalo de Ulloa when I've
Arranged his daughter's marriage to your son?
What are we now to do?

D. Diego   My only wish,   25
Your majesty, whatever you command,

---

stated previously, there were no political links between Castile and
Naples at the time of the play's action. Even if there had been, King
Alfonso would have been unlikely to respond to Isabela's plight in this
way. Tirso invented and heightened relationships for greater dramatic
effect.

20   Lebrija: the town of Lebrija is situated some thirty-five miles south of
Seville and was mentioned by Roman writers.

75

```
                que esté bien al honor de esta señora,
                hija de un padre tal.
Rey                                  Un medio tomo,
                con que absolvello del enojo entiendo:
                mayordomo mayor pretendo hacelle.          30
        Sale un Criado
Criado      Un caballero llega de camino,
                y dice, señor, que es el duque Octavio.
Rey         ¿El duque Octavio?
Criado                              Sí, señor.
Rey                                          Sin duda
                que supo de don Juan el desatino,
                y que viene, incitado a la venganza,       35
                a pedir que le otorgue desafío.
D.Diego     Gran señor, en tus heroicas manos
                está mi vida, que mi vida propia
                es la vida de un hijo inobediente;
                que, aunque mozo, gallardo y valeroso,     40
                y le llaman los mozos de su tiempo
                el Héctor de Sevilla, porque ha hecho
                tantas y tan extrañas mocedades,
                la razón puede mucho. No permitas
                el desafío, si es posible.
Rey                                  Basta.                 45
                Ya os entiendo, Tenorio: honor de padre.
                Entre el duque.
D.Diego                          Señor, dame esas plantas.
                ¿Cómo podré pagar mercedes tantas?
        Sale el Duque Octavio, de camino
Octav.      A esos pies, gran señor, un peregrino,
                mísero y desterrado, ofrece el labio,      50
                juzgando por más fácil el camino
                en vuestra gran presencia.
Rey                                  Duque Octavio...
Octav.      Huyendo vengo el fiero desatino
```

---

30   major-domo: Don Gonzalo de Ulloa is, as we have seen, the Grand
      Commander of the order of Calatrava. See Act I, 698. The position of
      major-domo involved living in the palace, assuming responsibility for the
      palace keys at night, arranging official functions, attending the king at
      ceremonies in public, and commanding the palace guard. Clearly, King
      Alfonso sees the promotion of Don Gonzalo in terms of a sop to offended
      pride. Once more he is seen to be a step behind events as they occur,
      attempting to behave pragmatically in order to resolve them but in the
      process revealing himself to be a monarch who is somewhat hasty and
      inefficient. See Act I, 867, note.

42   the Hector of Seville: in Homer's *Iliad* Hector, son of Priam and Hecuba,

	Is that the lady's honour be considered.	
	Her father is a worthy man.	
King	My plan	
	To overcome his wrath should prove sufficient.	
	I'll make him major-domo of the palace.	30

A servant enters

Servant	A nobleman's arrived, your majesty,	
	From Italy. His name is Duke Octavio.	
King	The Duke Octavio?	
Servant	Yes, your majesty.	
King	No doubt he's learned of Don Juan's treachery	
	And comes inflamed with thoughts of vengeance, bent	35
	On seeking my permission for a duel.	
D.Diego	Your majesty, my life is in your hands,	
	A father's name and reputation tied	
	Inexorably to a disobedient	
	Son, young, handsome and bold, who by his friends	40
	Throughout the length and breadth of this our city	
	Is called the Hector of Seville, because	
	His deeds appear to defy the mortal.	
	But reason can achieve great things, my lord.	
	I beg of you, forbid they fight a duel.	45
King	I understand, Tenorio, what a father's	
	Honour means to him. Bid the Duke come in.	
D.Diego	Your majesty, I am forever grateful.	

Enter Duke Octavio, dressed as a traveller

Octav.	I kneel before you, your great majesty,	
	And pay you homage, the misery of exile,	50
	My long and tedious journey now transformed	
	By your noble presence.	
King	Duke Octavio. . .	
Octav.	A woman's senseless folly and the actions	

---

is portrayed as the Trojan hero during the seige of Troy. This kind of heroism is evidently not that for which Don Juan is best known in Seville, but Don Diego, though aware of his son's shortcomings, is anxious that the King should see him in the most favourable light possible.

47   Honour: the implication seems to be that a duel at Octavio's request would require an accusation against Don Juan which would make his seduction of and treachery towards Isabela public knowledge, thereby dragging the Tenorio name through the mud.

48+   dressed as a traveller: Octavio is probably wearing the traditional costume of coloured cloth, a hat with plumes and boots with spurs.

	de una mujer, el no pensado agravio	
	de un caballero que la causa ha sido	55
	de que así a vuestros pies haya venido.	
Rey	Ya, duque Octavio, sé vuestra inocencia.	
	Yo al rey escribiré que os restituya	
	en vuestro estado, puesto que el ausencia	
	que hicisteis algún daño os atribuya.	60
	Yo os casaré en Sevilla con licencia	
	y también con perdón y gracia suya,	
	que puesto que Isabela un ángel sea,	
	mirando la que os doy, ha de ser fea.	
	Comendador mayor de Calatrava	65
	es Gonzalo de Ulloa, un caballero	
	a quien el moro por temor alaba,	
	que siempre es el cobarde lisonjero.	
	Este tiene una hija en quien bastaba	
	en dote la virtud, que considero,	70
	después de la beldad, que es maravilla;	
	y es sol de las estrellas de Sevilla.	
	Esta quiero que sea vuestra esposa.	
Octav.	Cuando este viaje le emprendiera	
	a sólo esto, mi suerte era dichosa	75
	sabiendo yo que vuestro gusto fuera.	
Rey	Hospedaréis al duque, sin que cosa	
	en su regalo falte.	
Octav.	Quien espera	
	en vos, señor, saldrá de premios lleno.	
	Primero Alfonso sois, siendo el onceno.	80

Vanse el Rey y Don Diego, y sale Ripio

Ripio	¿Qué ha sucedido?
Octav.	Que he dado
	el trabajo recebido,

---

67   Whose reputation terrifies the Moors: since the action of the play is set in the first half of the fourteenth century, the Reconquest of Spain by the Christians still had more than a century left for its completion. The orders of Calatrava, Alcántara and Santiago, all founded in the twelfth century, had, as has been stated – Act I, 698, note –, both a military and religious character and were responsible for defence at important points along the frontier between the Christian and Moorish territories, wherever that happened to be at any given time between the second half of the twelfth century and the final defeat of the Moors in 1492.

72   she is the sun: just as the world was thought to consist of the four elements – see Act I, 348, note–, so everything had its alloted place in the great chain of being, the sun reigning supreme amongst the planets. The medieval and post-medieval habit of thinking in terms of

	Of a nobleman are the cause of my	
	Departure and the reason why I now	55
	Appear before you and implore your help.	
King	I know, Octavio, you are innocent.	
	Your king shall be informed of this; his favour	
	You shall enjoy once more, lest it be thought	
	Your absence is the proof of your guilt.	60
	A marriage in Seville I shall arrange	
	For you, with his permission and agreement,	
	To a lady who in her beauty far	
	Exceeds Isabela. Her father's Don	
	Gonzalo de Ulloa, the commander	65
	Of Calatrava, nobleman and soldier,	
	Whose reputation terrifies the Moors	
	And out of fear generates their praise.	
	His daughter's virtue is itself sufficient	
	As a dowry, matched only by her beauty	70
	Which is itself a second miracle.	
	Amongst Seville's bright stars she is the sun,	
	The lovely bride that I intend for you.	
Octav.	Were this, your majesty, the only purpose	
	Of my journey, I would be happy indeed	75
	In the knowledge that this is your pleasure.	
King	[To Don Diego]	
	Accommodate the Duke and make quite sure	
	He's not deprived of anything.	
Octav.	How wise	
	Are we who place our faith in King Alfonso,	
	Eleventh in line but first in generosity!	80

Exit the King and Don Diego. Enter Ripio

Ripio	What did he say?
Octav.	The troubles that have plagued
	Me, Ripio, are now nothing when compared

---

correspondences between man and the world in which he lived led too to
analogies and images of the kind we have here: the supreme beauty of
Don Gonzalo's daughter expressed in terms of the sun, the supreme
planet.

80   Eleventh in line but first in generosity: from the moment of his arrival
at Alfonso's court, Octavio is all humility and gratitude. His difficulties
are, as we have seen, considerable, involving not only the loss of
Isabela but also the disfavour of his king, and it is therefore
understandable that he should express himself as he does. On the other
hand, it is clear that Tirso's ironic portrayal of Octavio, evident in Act
I, continues here. His earlier distress over Isabela's treachery vanishes
with the promise of a new bride, even though he has not set eyes on
her. Self-interest appears to motivate him as much as it does all the
other characters of the play.

	conforme me ha sucedido,	
	desde hoy por bien empleado.	
	Hablé al rey, vióme y honróme.	85
	César con el César fuí,	
	pues vi, peleé y vencí;	
	y hace que esposa tome	
	de su mano, y se prefiere	
	a desenojar al rey	90
	en la fulminada ley.	
Ripio	Con razón el nombre adquiere	
	de generoso en Castilla.	
	Al fin, ¿te llegó a ofrecer	
	mujer?	
Octav.	Sí, amigo, mujer	95
	de Sevilla, que Sevilla	
	da, si averiguallo quieres,	
	porque de oíllo te asombres,	
	si fuertes y airosos hombres,	
	también gallardas mujeres.	100
	Un manto tapado, un brío,	
	donde un puro sol se esconde,	
	si no es en Sevilla, ¿adónde	
	se admite? El contento mío	
	es tal que ya me consuela	105
	en mi mal.	

Salen Don Juan y Catalinón

Catal.	Señor: detente,	
	que aqui está el duque, inocente	
	Sagitario de Isabela,	
	aunque mejor le diré	
	Capricornio.	
D. Juan	Disimula.	110
Catal.	Cuando le vende la adula.	

---

87   I came, I saw, and even conquered too!: Tirso's mockery of a man
      capable of uttering such absurdities in the full flush of his own
      success, yet blind to that absurdity, is very clear here.

105   my anguish has become my joy!: no sooner are Octavio's fortunes
      transformed for the better than he is confronted by the author of his
      original misfortune, though he is as yet unaware of Don Juan's part in
      it. Nevertheless, the apparently episodic and loose structure of the
      play is often, as in this case, used for ironic effect. Don Juan's casual
      appearance already sets before us the prospect of Octavio's losing the
      bride he has not yet seen, of the bubble of self-congratulatory
      complacency about to be pricked. In the light of this possibility
      Octavio's fulsome praise of Don Juan renders him even more comic,
      while Don Juan's blatant flattery of Octavio ensures that we warm to
      the rogue.

	To the good fortune I've been favoured with	
	Today. I'd say the wheel has come full-circle.	
	The audience with the King has honoured me,	85
	Caesar favoured by yet another Ceasar;	
	I came, I saw, and even conquered too!	
	The King has chosen to arrange my marriage	
	By his own hand, and promised he will speak	
	On my behalf to our King in Naples.	90
	The law that exiles me will be repealed.	
Ripio	My word, my lord! He's famous in Castile	
	For generosity. It's well deserved!	
	Do you mean to say he offered you a wife	
	As well?	
Octav.	He did, Ripio. He told me she	95
	Is from Seville, and as I understand	
	It – and if you wish, you can confirm this truth	
	If you have little faith in this assertion –,	
	Seville boasts of its strong and handsome men	
	And also of the beauty of its women.	100
	A veil conceals a face, a lively spirit,	
	Hiding the dazzling beauty of the sun!	
	Where else but in Seville can that be true?	
	In short, the happiness confered on me	
	Is such, my anguish has become my joy!	105

Enter Don Juan and Catalinon

Catal.	Hold your horses, master! Look who's here!	
	The Duke himself, in all his innocence,	
	The Sagittarius to your Isabela,	
	Though I'd prefer to call him Capricorn!	
D. Juan	You hold your tongue! Pretend that nothing's happened!	
Catal.	Flatter him well, before you turn the knife!	

---

108   Sagittarius: the ninth sign of the zodiac. The constellation is portrayed as a centaur shooting an arrow. The classical story relates to Chiron, the wise centaur, who was accidentally wounded by Heracles and subsequently placed by Zeus among the stars as Sagittarius. Catalinón refers to Octavio as Sagittarius because he has been wounded by Isabela's treachery and exiled on account of her.

109   Capricorn!: the tenth sign of the zodiac. In classical mythology Capricorn was in fact the god Pan who changed himself into a goat through fear of the giant, Typhon. As a constellation Capricorn was represented with goat's feet and horns. For the seventeenth century horns suggested infidelity and cuckoldry, and for Catalinón, therefore, Octavio is not only a Sagittarius, a man betrayed, but a Capricorn, a cuckold.

D. Juan	Como a Nápoles dejé
	por enviarme a llamar
	con tanta priesa mi rey,
	y como su gusto es ley,	115
	no tuve, Octavio, lugar
	de despedirme de vos
	de ningún modo.
Octav.	Por eso,
	don Juan, amigo os confieso:
	que hoy nos juntamos los dos	120
	en Sevilla.
D. Juan	¡Quién pensara,
	duque, que en Sevilla os viera
	para que en ella os sirviera,
	como yo lo deseaba!
	¿Vos Puzol, vos la ribera	125
	dejáis? Mas aunque es lugar
	Nápoles tan excelente,
	por Sevilla solamente
	se puede, amigo, dejar.
Octav.	Si en Nápoles os oyera	130
	y no en la parte que estoy,
	del crédito que ahora os doy
	sospecho que me riera.
	Mas llegándola a habitar
	es, por lo mucho que alcanza,	135
	corta cualquiera alabanza
	que a Sevilla queréis dar.
	¿Quién es el que viene allí?
D. Juan	El que viene es el marqués
	de la Mota. Descortés	140
	es fuerza ser.
Octav.	Si de mí
	algo hubiereis menester,
	aquí espada y brazo está.
Catal.	[Ap.] Y si importa gozará
	en su nombre otra mujer;	145
	que tiene buena opinión.

---

121   A coincidence, Octavio: a good example of Don Juan's ironic mocking tone and of the way in which, during the first half of the play in particular, he makes the audience a sympathetic party to his mockery of others.

125   Pozzuoli: a town near Naples, distinguished for its beautiful sandy bay.

144   In that case you won't mind if your name: the asides of Catalinón provide an additional mocking, deflating element in the play, here in relation to Octavio's chivalrous offer to Don Juan. Golden-Age literature

D. Juan	Octavio, my apologies! I left
	Naples with what must seem unseemly haste.
	The King's orders, you understand, so blame
	Him for my not taking my leave of you.	115
	He sent for me quite unexpectedly.
	I couldn't disobey but neither could
	I say goodbye to you. You will forgive
	My disrespect now won't you?
Octav.	There's no need
	To forgive when now we renew our friendship	120
	In Seville.
D. Juan	A coincidence, Octavio,
	Beyond belief! Who would have guessed I'd see
	You once again and in Seville, where I
	Can serve you, place myself at your disposal.
	How could you bring yourself to leave Pozzuoli,	125
	That sandy shore? And Naples too? The world
	Acclaims it as a city unsurpassed,
	Except by Seville, which, to tell the truth,
	Cannot be matched by any other place.
Octav.	If we were still in Naples, my dear friend,	130
	And not in Seville, I would hardly give
	The slightest credence to such lavish praise.
	It's much more likely that I'd laugh at it.
	But now I've had a chance to see the place,
	I'd even say that such extravagance	135
	As yours falls short of any approbation
	That this most beautiful of cities merits.
	But who's this man that now approaches us?
D. Juan	His name's the marquis of Mota, a friend
	Of mine. You'll understand that if I speak	140
	To him, it's no discourtesy to you.
Octav.	My sword's at your disposal if you need
	It. Your wish, Don Juan, is my command.
Catal.	[Aside] In that case you won't mind if your name
	Will help my master, give him half a chance,	145
	To fool some other girl – with your permission!

---

abounds in such mockery, often realized through the juxtaposition of opposites. Thus, Sancho Panza's earthy good sense constantly pierces Don Quixote's inspiring idealism, while in the drama especially the down-to-earth, sometimes crude observations of the *graciosos* explode all manner of high-flown rhetoric on matters such as love and honour. In a sense it is a pointer to the growing disillusionment of the seventeenth century, of a much more sceptical attitude to the high ideals of the Renaissance. And it is certainly an indication of the greater complexity of the age.

D. Juan	De vos estoy satisfecho.	
Catal.	Si fuere de algún provecho,	
	señores, Catalinón,	
	vuarcedes continuamente	150
	me hallarán para servillos.	
Ripio	¿Y dónde?	
Catal.	En los Pajarillos,	
	tabernáculo excelente.	

*Vanse Octavio y Ripio, y sale el Marqués
de la Mota*

Mota	Todo hoy os ando buscando,	
	y no os he podido hallar.	155
	¿Vos, don Juan, en el lugar,	
	y vuestro amigo penando	
	en vuestra ausencia?	
D. Juan	¡Por Dios,	
	amigo, que me debéis	
	esa merced que me hacéis!	160
Catal.	*[Ap.]* Como no le entreguéis vos	
	moza o cosa que lo valga,	
	bien podéis fiaros dél;	
	que en cuanto en esto es cruel,	
	tiene condición hidalga.	165
D. Juan	¿Qué hay de Sevilla?	
Mota	Está ya	
	toda esta corte mudada.	
D. Juan	¿Mujeres?	
Mota	Cosa juzgada.	
D. Juan	¿Inés?	
Mota	A Vejel se va.	

---

153   'The Duck and Drake'!: this is a free rendering of the Spanish text in which the name of the inn is given as 'Pajarillos', 'Little Birds'. The two servants here imitate mockingly the earlier exchanges between Don Juan and Octavio, a common device in Golden Age drama aimed in part, no doubt, at raising a laugh amongst the servants in the audience who would have been situated in the standing area immediately in front of the stage.

159   A gesture of friendship: just as Don Juan has mocked Octavio with affirmations of loyalty and friendship, so he now mocks Mota, once more carrying with him the sympathies of the spectator. Mota, like Don Juan, represents the Spanish nobility but is shown by Tirso to have little nobility about him. Throughout Act II he is presented as an individual distinguished above all by a double standard of sexual morality, as Catalinón observes in 165.

168   Any worthwhile women?: the women alluded to in the ensuing conversation are, of course, prostitutes, and the picture of Seville which emerges is of an extremely corrupt and immoral place. At the

D. Juan	Glad to have seen you once again, Octavio!	
Catal.	If any of you gentlemen would like	
	To have me at your disposal, I'd be glad	
	To wait on you. You'll find me always ready	150
	And willing to provide the best of service.	
Ripio	I need a lackey! Where would you serve me?	
Catal.	'The Duck and Drake'! A very fine hostelry!	

Exit Octavio and Ripio. Enter the Marquis of Mota

Mota	My friend, I've spent the whole day scouring	
	The city looking for you! Here and there,	155
	Up and down, in and out, and not a scrap	
	Of care or concern for a dear friend	
	Who's broken-hearted because he can't find	
	You!	
D. Juan	A gesture of friendship matching my	
	Affection for you! How can you complain?	160
Catal.	*[Aside]* As long as you don't offer him something	
	Valuable, such as your best girl-friend,	
	You can be sure he's a gentleman.	
	But when it comes to girls, it's something else!	
	He just behaves like all these gentlemen!	165
D. Juan	What news in Seville since I went away?	
Mota	The place has changed. Barely recognizable.	
D. Juan	Any worthwhile women?	
Mota	Not much to shout	
	About.	
D. Juan	What about Inés? She still here?	
Mota	She's gone. To Vejel.	

---

time of the play's composition Seville was – see Act I, 574, note – one of Spain's most important cities and felt the greatest impact of South American trade. Reference has been made to the portrayal of Sevillian 'low-life' in such writers as Cervantes, and this picture is clearly reinforced by contemporary accounts of a more factual nature. Thus, an apparent contemporary of Tirso, the *licenciado* Porras de la Cámara, writing to the Archbishop of Seville, draw attention to the city's immorality, its adulterers, murderers, swindlers, idlers, usurers, its 300 gambling houses and its 3000 brothels. See *Revista de Archivos Bibliotecas y Museos*, IV (1900), 550–54. The point has been made already that the description of Seville, with its evident criticism of the Spanish Court, contrasts with the earlier praise of Lisbon – see Act I, 721, note.

169   Vejel: this is Vejel de la Frontera, a city in the province of Cadiz, but in the Spanish text there is also a joke which cannot be suggested in English, for Vejel brings to mind the Spanish word for old age, 'vejez', which Inés is quickly travelling towards.

D. Juan	Buen lugar para vivir	170
	la que tan dama nació.	
Mota	El tiempo la desterró	
	a Vejel.	
D. Juan	Irá a morir.	
	¿Constanza?	
Mota	Es lástima vella	
	lampiña de frente y ceja.	175
	Llámale el portugués vieja,	
	y ella imagina que bella.	
D. Juan	Sí, que velha en portugués	
	suena vieja en castellano.	
	¿Y Teodora?	
Mota	Este verano	180
	se escapó del mal francés	
	por un río de sudores;	
	y está tan tierna y reciente,	
	que anteayer me arrojó un diente	
	envuelto entre muchas flores.	185
D. Juan	¿Julia, la del Candilejo?	
Mota	Ya con sus afeites lucha.	
D. Juan	¿Véndese siempre por trucha?	
Mota	Ya se da por abadejo.	
D. Juan	El barrio de Cantarranas,	190
	¿tiene buena población?	
Mota	Ranas las más dellas son.	
D. Juan	¿Y viven las dos hermanas?	
Mota	Y la mona de Tolú	
	de su madre Celestina	195
	que les enseña dotrina.	
D. Juan	¡Oh, vieja de Bercebú!	
	¿Cómo la mayor está?	

---

176   Her hair's dropped out: no doubt her loss of hair is a symptom of venereal disease.
179   In Portuguese: the Portuguese word for 'old' is *velha*, the Spanish for 'pretty' *bella*. As in the case of 169, the joke cannot be translated.
182   She sweated over that: sweating was one of the traditional treatments for venereal disease. In Cervantes's short story, *El casamiento engañoso*, the protagonist, Campuzano, emerges from the Hospital de la Resurrección in Valladolid where he has been treated for syphilis and made to sweat profusely twice a day for twenty days.
186   flowers: the literal translation of the Spanish here is 'wrapped in many flowers'. It is not clear whether the flowers are real or whether the word *flores* is being used in the sense of 'compliment'.
187   Lamp Street?: the street was apparently known by this name from as early as 1492, the name deriving from a story connected with Pedro I

86

D. Juan	A fine place to live	170
	For a woman of such distinguished birth.	
Mota	It's time that marched her there, and not before	
	Time!	
D. Juan	Sounds as if her only future bed–	
	Fellow is death! And any news of Constance?	
Mota	I'm sorry to say she's a sorry sight.	175
	Her hair's dropped out, her eyebrows too. A chap	
	I knew – a Portuguese – called her a hag.	
	She thought the poor fellow'd called her pretty!	
D. Juan	In Portuguese the Spanish word for pretty	
	Does mean old! A nice mistake! How's Theodora?	180
Mota	A narrow escape this summer from the pox.	
	She sweated over that and now she's cured,	
	A tender piece of ham, so appetising!	
	She gave me a nice present yesterday:	
	A tooth of hers she's cut quite recently,	185
	And with it a beautiful bunch of flowers.	
D. Juan	What about Julia, she lives in Lamp Street?	
Mota	Gets on your wick! She's just a painted tart!	
D. Juan	And passing herself off as tasty trout?	
Mota	A piece of cod gone off! Just have a sniff?	190
D. Juan	The district Cantarranas. What's that like?	
Mota	As you'd expect! It means the Singing Frogs,	
	It's full of them.	
D. Juan	Are those two sisters still	
	Around?	
Mota	Yes, and the monkey from Tolú,	
	The old procuress teaching them her tricks.	195
D. Juan	Yes, that's the one! Truly a hag from Hell.	
	The elder of the girls, what's she like now?	

(the Cruel), King of Castile from 1350 to 1369. Seeing Pedro killing a man in a duel, an old woman, overcome by fright, dropped a lamp from her window.

189   tasty trout?: the allusions to these women as trout, cod and frogs, in descending order of tastiness, are common enough in the literature of the Golden Age.

191   Cantarranas: the meaning of the name is 'the singing frogs'. It has been suggested that the district was so called on account of an area of swampy ground which contained many frogs. Santiago Montoto, *Las calles de Sevilla* (Seville, 1940), p.245, suggests that the name was applied not to a district but to a street, now named Gravina, and that the name derived from the fact that the street contained the outlet drains for the city.

194   Tolú: a town on the coast of Colombia from which monkeys were dispatched to Europe.

Mota	Blanca, sin blanca ninguna;
	tiene un santo a quien ayuna.	200
D. Juan	¿Agora en vigilias da?
Mota	Es firme y santa mujer.
D. Juan	¿Y esotra?
Mota	Mejor principio
	tiene; no desecha ripio.
D. Juan	Buen albañir quiere ser.	205
	Marqués: ¿qué hay de perros muertos?
Mota	Yo y don Pedro de Esquivel
	dimos anoche un cruel,
	y esta noche tengo ciertos
	otros dos.
D. Juan	Iré con vos,	210
	que también recorreré
	cierto nido que dejé
	en güevos para los dos.
	¿Qué hay de terrero?
Mota	No muero
	en terrero, que en-terrado	215
	me tiene mayor cuidado.
D. Juan	¿Cómo?
Mota	Un imposible quiero.
D. Juan	Pues ¿no os corresponde?
Mota	Sí,
	me favorece y estima.
D. Juan	¿Quién es?
Mota	Doña Ana, mi prima,	220
	que es recién llegada aqui.
D. Juan	Pues ¿dónde ha estado?
Mota	En Lisboa,
	con su padre en la embajada.
D. Juan	¿Es hermosa?
Mota	Es estremada,
	porque en doña Ana de Ulloa	225
	se estremó naturaleza.
D. Juan	¿Tan bella es esa mujer?

---

198   If you mean Penny: the Spanish line reads: 'Blanca, sin blanca ninguna'. There is a play on words, *Blanca* being the name of the girl, *sin blanca* meaning 'without a penny'. To retain the joke in English requires changing the girl's name.

Mota	If you mean Penny, she's quite penniless!
	But pure with it! A good and honest man
	Suffers on her behalf.
D. Juan	And she abstains
	On his account?
Mota	Oh, she's become a true
	And constant woman. No chance there for you!
D. Juan	The other one?
Mota	Now she's more promising.
	Show her a good hand and she'll come up trumps!
D. Juan	That sounds more like it! But what about the tarts
	You've tricked, done business with and left them empty-
	Handed?
Mota	Last night Pedro Esquivel and I
	Plucked all the feathers from a lovely bird.
	Two more are certain to be plucked tonight.
D. Juan	In that case you won't mind if I come too.
	There's a little love-nest I'd like to find.
	A little plot I'd like to hatch. What about
	Courting ladies at their windows from
	The terrace below?
Mota	Don't mention below.
	Below ground's where I'll find myself quite soon.
	Believe me. I'm a sick man, doomed to die.
D. Juan	But what is your affliction?
Mota	Hopeless love!
D. Juan	You mean she doesn't favour you at all?
Mota	She does! She loves me, thinks the world of me.
D. Juan	Who is she?
Mota	She's my cousin, Doña Ana!
	It's only recently she's come to live
	Here in Seville.
D. Juan	Where was she?
Mota	Lived in Lisbon
	With her father. He was ambassador.
D. Juan	Good looking girl?
Mota	No, more than that. Outstanding!
	When nature fashioned Ana de Ulloa,
	It must have been amazed by its achievement.
D. Juan	No woman is as beautiful as that!

Line numbers in right margin: 200 (at "And she abstains"), 205 (at "That sounds more like it! But what about the tarts"), 210 (at "In that case you won't mind if I come too."), 215 (at "Below ground's where I'll find myself quite soon."), 220 (at "She's my cousin, Doña Ana!"), 225 (at "When nature fashioned Ana de Ulloa,").

---

207   Pedro Esquivel: Gerald E. Wade, *El burlador de Sevilla y convidado de piedra* (New York, 1969), p.197, observes that the Esquivel family 'was well known in Sevilla' and cites various works of reference as evidence. He concludes: 'Although we cannot identify exactly the Pedro Esquivel of our text, we do not doubt his reality as a person of Tirso's time. .'

	¡Vive Dios que la he de ver!	
Mota	Veréis la mayor belleza	
	que los ojos del rey ven.	230
D. Juan	Casaos, pues es estremada.	
Mota	El rey la tiene casada,	
	y no se sabe con quién.	
D. Juan	¿No os favorece?	
Mota	Y me escribe.	
Catal.	[Ap.] No prosigas, que te engaña	235
	el gran burlador de España.	
D. Juan	Quien tan satisfecho vive	
	de su amor, ¿desdichas teme?	
	Sacalda, solicitalda,	
	escribilda y engañalda,	240
	y el mundo se abrase y queme.	
Mota	Agora estoy aguardando	
	la postrer resolución.	
D. Juan	Pues no perdáis la ocasíon,	
	que aqui estoy aguardando.	245
Mota	Ya vuelvo.	

Vanse el Marqués y el Criado

Catal.	Señor Cuadrado	
	o señor Redondo, adiós,	
Criado	Adiós.	
D. Juan	Pues solos los dos,	
	amigo, habemos quedado,	
	síguele el paso al marqués,	250
	que en el palacio se entró.	

Vase Catalinón. Habla por una reja una Mujer

Mujer	Ce, ¿a quién digo?	
D. Juan	¿Quién llamó?	
Mujer	Pues sois prudente y cortés	

---

232   I can't. The King has just arranged her marriage: the King has, in fact, arranged a marriage for Doña Ana on two occasions: firstly, in Act I he informs her father, Don Gonzalo, that she shall be married to Don Juan; secondly, in Act II, having been informed of Don Juan's seduction of Isabela, Alfonso banishes him from Seville and promises Ana to Octavio. Mota's words indicate that neither marriage has been announced publicly.

235   If he says any more: Don Juan has skilfully elicited from Mota all the information he requires. As well as being a man of extremely dubious morality, Mota is portrayed by Tirso as being highly gullible. If he is so well acquainted with Don Juan's inclinations, the very last thing he should do is offer him information about his own beloved. No doubt Mota's feelings for Ana blind him to the danger. At all events Tirso exploits fully the comic and ironic possibilities of the situation.

	You prove it to me! I'll have to see her!	
Mota	See her and you will see the greatest beauty	
	Any king could hope to cast his eyes on.	230
D. Juan	Well, why not marry her if she's so pretty?	
Mota	I can't. The King has just arranged her marriage.	
	But no one knows who she's supposed to marry.	
D. Juan	And yet she loves you?	
Mota	Writes me daily too!	
Catal.	[Aside] If he says any more, it serves him right!	
	Spain's greatest trickster's got her in his sights!	
D. Juan	A man can have such faith in a woman's	
	Love and fear still some terrible misfortune?	
	You ought to show her off, be more forthcoming,	
	Bombard her with your letters, lead her up	240
	The garden-path and stuff the world's opinion.	
Mota	The only reason why I'm here's to find	
	Out what decision's taken on the girl.	
D. Juan	Then don't waste time! Go and find out! I'll wait	
	Here for you. Come and tell me what they've done!	245
Mota	Alright! You wait for me! I'll be back soon.	

Mota and his servant exit

Catal.	Farewell then, Mister Square or Mister Round.	
Servant	Farewell.	
D. Juan	Well since we're on our own again,	
	My friend, here's what you have to do for me.	
	Just keep an eye on Mota! Follow him	250
	Closely. Go after him into the palace!	

*Exit Catalinón. A woman calls to Don Juan through the
bars of her window*

Woman	You there! Who are you?	
D. Juan	Did someone call me?	
Woman	You seem a good and honest gentleman,	

---

247   Mister Square or Mister Round: Mota's servant is evidently known by one of these names, in Spanish *Señor Cuadrado* and *Señor Redondo* respectively. There is an element of joke here, which may have to do with the physical shape of the actor who played the part. An actor with the name of Juan Quadrado died in 1636, but there is no evidence that such a person had a role in *The Trickster*. It is a well-known fact that Tirso liked to tease friends by introducing their names into his plays and it seems quite possible that it may be the case here. A certain Fray Alonso Redondo is, for instance, said to have been a friend of Tirso's, though there is not other information about him.

251+   through the bars of her window: the *reja* or iron framework which traditionally covered the windows of Spanish houses on the outside, protecting the house against intruders. It was also here that lovers would meet, the man speaking to the woman through the bars.

	y su amigo, dalde luego	
	al marqués este papel;	255
	mirad que consiste en él	
	de una señora el sosiego.	
D. Juan	Digo que se lo daré:	
	soy su amigo y caballero.	
Mujer	Basta, señor forastero.	260
	Adiós.	

Vase

D. Juan	Ya la voz se fué.	
	¿No parece encantamiento	
	esto que agora ha pasado?	
	A mí el papel ha llegado	
	por la estafeta del viento.	265
	Sin duda que es de la dama	
	que el marqués me ha encarecido:	
	venturoso en esto he sido.	
	Sevilla a voces me llama	
	el Burlador, y el mayor	270
	gusto que en mí puede haber	
	es burlar una mujer	
	y dejalla sin honor.	
	¡Vive Dios, que le he de abrir,	
	pues salí de la plazuela!	275
	Mas, ¿si hubiese otra cautela?. . .	
	Gana me da de reír.	
	Ya está abierto el tal papel;	
	y que es suyo es cosa llana,	
	porque firma doña Ana.	280
	Dice así : "Mi padre infiel	
	en secreto me ha casado	
	sin poderme resistir;	
	no sé si podré vivir,	
	porque la muerte me ha dado.	285

---

258   I give my word, madam: another example of a promise made by Don
Juan which he has no intention of keeping. See Act I, 90, note; 947,
note. On this occasion the lady places her trust in Don Juan, having
seen that he is a friend of Mota. Don Juan abuses both that trust and
Mota's friendship. He refers to himself in 259 as a 'gentleman', a
'caballero', the implication being that he possess all the qualities of
chivalry, valour and honour associated with such a person. What Tirso
is showing us very clearly is that in the society of his day, notably in
the Spanish Court, the old values have lost their meaning. A.A.
Parker, *The Approach to the Spanish Drama of the Golden Age*,
Diamante, VI (London, 1957), p. 13, observes: 'Because Don Juan is the

A friend of the Marquis. Give him this letter!
I beg of you, please place it in his hands!   255
The only other thing I need to say,
My friend, is a lady's life depends on it.
D. Juan   I give my word, madam. You have my promise.
In me you find both friend and gentleman
Combined.
Woman   My thanks, sir. I appreciate   260
Your kindness. Fare you well!
   The woman withdraws
D. Juan   She's disappeared.
Was that a vision, a fantastic dream
That seemed so magical but also real?
I swear this letter reached me as though it
Were transported by the wind or air!   265
I wonder if the woman is the one
Whose beauty our friend Mota's just been praising
To the skies! If so, it's a piece of luck
I'll not despise! Not for nothing am I
Labelled the greatest trickster of Seville.   270
My very favourite pastime, my delight's
To trick a woman, steal away her honour,
Deprive her of her treasured reputation.
As for this letter, now I've left the square,
I'm sorry, but I'll have to open it.   275
Could be there's yet another trick in this
For me. Already it gives me good cause
To laugh. Let's have a look. At least I know
That Ana de Ulloa is the sender.
Here, clearly written, is her signature.   280
And this is what it says: 'My love, my father
Has betrayed me. Secretly he's arranged
That I be married. It's impossible
For me to disobey. I have no say
In it. I don't know how I'll go on living.   285

---

negation of "caballerosidad" in every respect, he disrupts all social
ties, and society itself will fall apart and disappear if his anarchism is
allowed to prevail.'
282   Has betrayed me: the fact is, of course, that Ana is deceiving her
father by conducting a secret affair with Mota which compromises both
her own honour and that of the family. Since Mota is a nobleman, there
is presumably no obstacle to his marriage to Ana and Don Gonzalo would
not oppose it. As in the case of Isabela and Octavio, the lovers appear
to enjoy the vicarious thrill of a secret courtship and in that sense
behave both recklessly and dishonourably.

Si estimas, como es razón,
mi amor y mi voluntad,
y si tu amor fué verdad,
muéstralo en esta ocasión.
Por que veas que te estimo,   290
ven esta noche a la puerta,
que estará a las once abierta,
donde tu esperanza, primo,
goces, y el fin de tu amor.
Traerás, mi gloria, por señas   295
de Leonorilla y las dueñas,
una capa de color.
Mi amor todo de ti fío,
y adiós." ¡Desdichado amante!
¿Hay suceso semejante?   300
Ya de la burla me río.
Gozárela, ¡vive Dios!,
con el engaño y cautela
que en Nápoles a Isabela.

      Sale Catalinón

Catal.   Ya el marqués viene.
D. Juan   Los dos   305
aquesta noche tenemos
que hacer.
Catal.   ¿Hay engaño nuevo?
D. Juan   Estremado.
Catal.   No lo apruebo.
Tú pretendes que escapemos
una·vez, señor, burlados;   310
que el que vive de burlar
burlado habrá de escapar
pagando tantos pecados
de una vez.

---

292   You'll find the door already open: see Act I, 954, note. The sexual
implications of Ana's message are very clear. It is hardly surprising that
Don Juan should react to the content of the letter with such relish and
anticipation.

297   A cloak – crimson: at night men generally wore coloured clothing but
Mota's crimson cloak is to be for the purposes of identification. Red is
also a colour associated with passion and in that sense can be linked to
other distinctive metaphors of passion in the play, notably fire.

301   This trick delights: the word *burla*, 'trick', links with the title of the
play, *El burlador de Sevilla*, *The Trickster of Seville*, and underlines
the point that it is not only the seduction and the enjoyment of a
woman which appeal to Don Juan but the cunning and ingenuity with

I'm certain this will bring about my death.
If you, as I am sure you do, esteem
My love and know my will, I beg of you,
In honour of our love, do what I ask.
I'll prove to you the depth of my affection.   290
Come to my door at eleven o'clock tonight.
You'll find the door already open. Come
Inside and there, cousin, your love for me
And all your deepest hopes will be fulfilled.
My maids will need to know you by your dress.   295
So for their benefit it's best you wear
A cloak – crimson would be most suitable.
My love, my fate's entirely in your hands.
Farewell.' Farewell to love's appropriate,
I think, given these happy circumstances!   300
This trick delights me even as I think
Of how I'll see it through! I'll have this girl
With all the ingenuity with which
The Duchess Isabela succumbed in Naples!

Enter Catalinón

Catal.   Here comes the Marquis, master!

D. Juan   Both of us   305
Have pressing business to attend to, designed
To occupy us half the night!

Catal.   Executors
Of some new trick!

D. Juan   The best of all! You'll see!

Catal.   Not me! I don't approve of it. Besides,
The way you're going you are bound to get   310
Your fingers burnt, and mine. I'm telling you,
The man who spends his time deceiving others
Is in the end deceived and comes off second
Best. Live now and pay later! On the day
Of reckoning!

---

which the seduction is achieved. Thus, Daniel Rogers observes of him in *Tirso de Molina. El burlador de Sevilla*. Critical Guides to Spanish Texts (London, 1977), p.36: '. . . the truly distinctive thing about him is that he adopts the pretence for fun . . . not just for the fulfilment of his physical desires, but for the malicious pleasure of deceit. . .'

313   <u>Is in the end deceived</u>: this piece of advice from Catalinón encapsulates one of the central themes of the play, the idea of the *burlador burlado*, 'the trickster tricked'. The notion of poetic justice, of man reaping the harvest of his deeds and actions, is deeply embedded in the literature of the Golden Age, reflecting, of course, the predominantly religious character of the time.

D. Juan	¿Predicador	
	te vuelves, impertinente?	315
Catal.	La razón hace al valiente.	
D. Juan	Y al cobarde hace el temor.	
	El que se pone a servir	
	voluntad no ha de tener,	
	y todo ha de ser hacer,	320
	y nada de ser decir.	
	Sirviendo, jugando estás,	
	y si quieres ganar luego,	
	haz siempre, porque en el juego,	
	quien más hace gana más.	325
Catal.	Y también quien hace y dice	
	pierde por la mayor parte.	
D. Juan	Esta vez quiero avisarte,	
	porque otra vez no te avise.	
Catal.	Digo que de aquí adelante	330
	lo que me mandas haré,	
	y a tu lado forzaré	
	un tigre y un elefante.	
	Guárdese de mí un prior,	
	que si me mandas que calle	335
	y le fuerce, he de forzalle	
	sin réplica, mi señor.	
D. Juan	Calla, que viene el marqués.	
Catal.	Pues, ¿ha de ser el forzado?	

Sale el Marqués de la Mota

D. Juan	Para vos, marqués, me han dado	340
	un recaudo harto cortés	
	por esa reja, sin ver	
	el que me lo daba allí;	
	sólo en la voz conocí	
	que me lo daba mujer.	345
	Dícete al fin que a las doce	
	vayas secreto a la puerta	
	(que estará a las once abierta),	
	donde tu esperanza goce	
	la posesión de tu amor;	350

---

315   a boring preacher: the play is indeed a dramatic sermon, though a
highly entertaining one. The moral lesson, often in the form of
warnings or advice, is placed in the mouths of many characters and is
given more and more emphasis as the action unfolds, though in this
respect Catalinón undoubtedly has pride of place.

337   and not a word I'll speak!: the point has been made previously that
although the servants in Golden-Age plays give moral advice, they are

D. Juan	You are a boring preacher,	315
	And you've become too forward for a servant!	
Catal.	Wisdom and reason make a brave man, sir!	
D. Juan	And fear makes a coward! Some men, fool,	
	Are born to serve, not born for bravery!	
	A servant has no will to call his own!	320
	Does everything he's told and bites his tongue!	
	A servant's like a man who's playing cards.	
	To profit from the game he has to work,	
	The more he works the more he always wins.	
	You work and shut your mouth you'll be a winner!	325
Catal.	Wise words, master! Many's the man who's lost	
	At cards through opening his mouth too soon!	
D. Juan	Make sure you learn the lesson. Don't forget	
	It. I don't want to have to teach you more!	
Catal.	I promise, master. Seen and never heard	330
	I'll be! Obedient to your every word,	
	That's me! At your side my loyalty	
	Will force an elephant or fierce tiger	
	To its knees. And as for any blabbing preacher,	
	He'd best look out! Give me the order, sir,	335
	To shut him up, I'll do it silently,	
	To good effect, and not a word I'll speak!	
D. Juan	Be silent! The Marquis is coming back!	
Catal.	Is he the one whose mouth I have to shut?	

Enter the Marquis of Mota

D. Juan	A message for you, Marquis, that someone's	340
	Just this minute asked me to give to you.	
	The message was delivered through this window,	
	And though the speaker wasn't visible,	
	The voice was unmistakably a woman's;	
	Of that there's not the slightest doubt at all.	345
	She asks that you at twelve o'clock tonight	
	Proceed with all discretion to her door	
	(She says she'll leave it open from eleven),	
	Where all your fondest hopes and steadfast love	
	Will have their just reward and satisfaction.	350

---

not themselves particularly moral characters and are more often than
not motivated by self-interest. What seems to make Catalinón a distictive
comic character is the fact that, as here, he has the capacity to
ridicule his own shortcomings.

348   open from eleven: by revealing this piece of information Don Juan is
clearly delighting in advance in what he believes will be Mota's helpless
rage when he learns of Ana's seduction.

	y que llevases por señas	
	de Leonorilla y las dueñas	
	una capa de color.	
Mota	¿Qué dices?	
D. Juan	Que este recaudo	355
	de una ventana me dieron,	
	sin ver quién.	
Mota	Con él pusieron	
	sosiego en tanto cuidado.	
	¡Ay amigo! Sólo en ti	
	mi esperanza renaciera.	
	Dame esos pies.	
D. Juan	Considera	360
	que no está tu prima en mí.	
	Eres tú quien ha de ser	
	quien la tiene de gozar,	
	¿y me llegas a abrazar	
	los pies?	
Mota	Es tal el placer,	365
	que me ha sacado de mí.	
	¡Oh sol!, apresura el paso.	
D. Juan	Ya el sol camina al ocaso.	
Mota	Vamos, amigos, de aquí,	
	y de noche nos pondremos.	370
	¡Loco voy!	
D. Juan	[Ap.] Bien se conoce;	
	mas yo bien sé que a las doce	
	harás mayores estremos.	
Mota	¡Ay, prima del alma, prima,	
	que quieres premiar mi fe!	375
Catal.	[Ap.] ¡Vive Cristo, que no dé	
	una blanca por su prima!	

Vase el Marqués y sale Don Diego

D. Dieg.	¿Don Juan?	
Catal.	Tu padre te llama.	
D. Juan	¿Qué manda vueseñoría?	
D. Diego	Verte más cuerdo quería,	380
	más bueno y con mejor fama.	
	¿Es posible que procuras	
	todas las horas mi muerte?	
D. Juan	¿Por qué vienes desa suerte?	

---

356   Oh, my friend!: Mota behaves towards Don Juan just as Octavio did
       previously – see Act II, 120. Once more the gullibility of someone who

	To avoid confusion and make recognition	
	By the maids more certain, ensure you wear	
	A crimson cloak.	
Mota	Are you quite sure?	
D. Juan	As sure	
	As I'm your loyal friend! The message came	
	From that window, and every word was clear,	355
	But not the speaker.	
Mota	Oh, my friend! The message	
	Has given me new hope where there was none!	
	What proof of friendship! You, my dear friend,	
	Bear all responsibility for my	
	Rebirth! How can I show my gratitude?	360
D. Juan	Remeber, friend, I'm not your lovely cousin!	
	Your obligation, as I understand	
	It, is to show your love for her, not me!	
	I fancy your embraces would be better	
	Spent on your lover!	
Mota	Oh, my pleasure's such,	365
	I'm quite beside myself! How can I wait!	
	Oh, sun, I beg of you, quicken your pace!	
D. Juan	The sun's already sinking in the west.	
Mota	Let's go quickly! We must prepare ourselves	
	And dress in preparation for tonight.	370
	I'm quite beside myself!	
D. Juan	[Aside] That's pretty plain	
	To anyone. At twelve o'clock tonight	
	It's not beside himself, more out of his mind	
	He'll be!	
Mota	Oh, cousin dear to my soul!	
	That you reward me for my loyalty!	375
Catal.	[Aside] By God, look at the way this fellow prances!	
	Who'd give a farthing for his cousin's chances?	

Exit the Marquis. Enter Don Diego

D. Diego	Don Juan! Where are you?	
Catal.	It's your old father!	
D. Juan	I'm here, my lord. Command me as you wish!	
D. Diego	I wish you were a bit more sensible,	380
	More honest, and a better reputation!	
	I can't believe your every deed's designed	
	Deliberately with my death in mind!	
D. Juan	Oh, father! What is it makes you so angry?	

---

is himself fond of deceiving others becomes a source of comic irony.

370   <u>And dress in preparation</u>: see 297, note.

99

D. Diego	Por tu trato y tus locuras.	385
	Al fin el rey me ha mandado	
	que te eche de la ciudad,	
	porque está de una maldad	
	con justa causa indignado.	
	Que, aunque me lo has encubierto,	390
	ya en Sevilla el rey lo sabe,	
	cuyo delito es tan grave,	
	que a decírtelo no acierto.	
	¿En el palacio real	
	traición y con un amigo?	395
	Traidor, Dios te dé el castigo	
	que pide delito igual.	
	Mira que, aunque al parecer	
	Dios te consiente y aguarda,	
	su castigo no se tarda,	400
	y que castigo ha de haber	
	para los que profanáis	
	su nombre, que es jüez fuerte	
	Dios en la muerte.	
D. Juan	¿En la muerte?	
	¿Tan largo me lo fiáis?	405
	De aquí allá hay gran jornada.	
D. Diego	Breve te ha de parecer.	
D. Juan	Y la que tengo de hacer,	
	pues a su alteza le agrada,	
	agora, ¿es larga también?	410
D. Diego	Hasta que el injusto agravio	
	satisfaga el duque Octavio,	
	y apaciguados estén	
	en Nápoles de Isabela	
	los sucesos que has causado,	415
	en Lebrija retirado	

---

393   Force myself to speak!: for someone who can barely force himself to speak, Don Diego has plenty to say. The effect, even given that Don Diego is a good man, is comic, contributing further to the ironic tone that suffuses the play as a whole. In a sense the irascible old man is the 'babbling preacher' alluded to by Catalinón in Act II, 334.

396   A punishment appropriate to your crime!: see A.A. Parker, *The Approach to the Spanish Drama of the Golden Age*: '. . . in literature it was, in seventeenth-century Spain, considered fitting that wrongdoing should not go unpunished and that virtue should not remain unrewarded . . . . The most severe punishment is damnation, consignment to hell. This is rare, but it occurs in two famous plays by Tirso de Molina, *El burlador de Sevilla* and *El condenado por desconfiado*. It indicates, of course, that the evil in question has been

D. Diego	Your own stupidity! Tomfoolery!	385
	The King's just told me he's commanded you	
	Be exiled from the city, thrown right out	
	On account of a certain misdemeanour	
	Of yours that with good cause has angered him.	
	Although you hid the truth from me, the King	390
	Has been informed of it here in Seville.	
	A crime so serious, hideously offensive,	
	That I can barely force myself to speak!	
	Such terrible behaviour in the palace!	
	Such treachery, committed in the name	395
	Of friendship! Traitor! May God seek of you	
	A punishment appropriate to your crime!	
	And take note now that though it seems that God	
	Gives you permission for the things you do,	
	The day of judgement's never far behind.	400
	The one thing that is absolutely sure	
	Is punishment for those who take His name	
	In vain. There's no judge more severe than God	
	In matters after death!	
D. Juan	Why speak of death?	
	Plenty of time for me to pay that debt!	405
	In any case, who's ready for it yet?	
D. Diego	My boy, the journey's shorter than you think.	
D. Juan	And what about this journey I'm to make	
	To save my skin and satisfy the King?	
	You'll tell me next that journey has no end!	410
D. Diego	Until you satisfy the grave offence	
	Against Octavio, who is a Duke no less,	
	And give sufficient time for all the scandal	
	To die down in Naples over that affair	
	With Isabela, the King's command is this:	415
	You're exiled to Lebrija where you'll pay	

---

so great and so deliberate that there are no extenuating circumstances to redeem it . . .' (p.7). Don Juan's greatest offence is his presumption that God's mercy can be taken for granted and will be available to him whenever he wishes to repent and it is for this that he is finally punished. Theologians and moralists of the Golden Age often preached of the perils of procrastination in relation to repentance. See, for example, Fray Luis de Granada, *Guía de los pecadores* (1556).

406   who's ready for it yet?: Don Juan exemplifies in a sense the Renaissance zest for life and enjoyment of life's pleasures which by the seventeenth century had given way to Baroque *desengaño*, the sense of the transience of worldly things which is communicated to Don Juan by so many of the characters and embodied finally in the figure of the stone man.

416   Lebrija: see Act II, 20, note.

	por tu traición y cautela,	
	quiere el rey que estés agora:	
	pena a tu maldad ligera.	
Catal.	[Aparte.] Si el caso también supiera	420
	de la pobre pescadora,	
	más se enojara el buen viejo.	
D.Diego	Pues no te vence castigo	
	con cuanto hago y cuanto digo,	
	a Dios tu castigo dejo.	

Vase

Catal.	Fuese el viejo enternecido.	
D. Juan	Luego las lágrimas copia,	
	condición de viejo propia.	
	Vamos, pues ha anochecido,	
	a buscar al marqués.	
Catal.	Vamos,	430
	y al fin gozarás su dama.	
D. Juan	Ha de ser burla de fama.	
Catal.	Ruego al cielo que salgamos	
	della en paz.	
D. Juan	¡Catalinón,	
	en fin!	
Catal.	Y tú, señor, eres	435
	langosta de las mujeres,	
	y con público pregón,	
	porque de ti se guardara	
	cuando a noticia viniera	
	de la que doncella fuera,	440
	fuera bien se pregonara:	
	"Guárdense todos de un hombre	
	que a las mujeres engaña,	
	y es el burlador de España,"	
D. Juan	Tú me has dado gentil nombre.	445

*Sale el Marqués, de noche, con Músicos, y
pasea el tablado, y se entran cantando*

Músic.	El que un bien gozar espera,	
	cuanto espera desespera.	

---

422   choleric!: choler was, with melancholy, phlegm and blood, one of the humours or liquid substances in the body, created in the liver and acting as the body's life-giving moisture. A choleric man was someone in whom choler, a hot and dry humour, gained ascendancy over the others, be it a temporary or permanent ascendancy.

425   I recommend your punishment to God!: in his advice on the writing of plays Lope de Vega had indicated that mid-way through the action of a play some crucial incident should occur, or a key moment should be reached, from which the remainder of the action springs. Don Diego's

	For all your cunning and your treachery.	
	The King thinks such a punishment is just.	
	As far as I'm concerned, it's far too light!	
Catal.	*[Aside]* If only the old man knew how his son	420
	Had fooled the fishergirl, I'm sure that trick	
	Would let you see him even more choleric!	
D. Diego	In that case, seeing that my good advice	
	And prudent admonition are quite useless,	
	I recommend your punishment to God!	425

Exit Don Diego

Catal.	Look what you've done! The old man's left in tears!	
D. Juan	Don't tell me you're about to join him too,	
	Though tears are quite appropriate to dotage!	
	Come on! It's dark already! I must find	
	The Marquis.	
Catal.	Yes. Come on! Let's go and seek	430
	An opportunity to fool his girl!	
D. Juan	And this, you'll see, will be the best trick yet!	
Catal.	Please God, I pray that you watch over me	
	And save your servant from catastrophe!	
D. Juan	True to your name, a man who runs away!	435
Catal.	And you, master, a locust to all women!	
	There ought to be a public proclamation,	
	A timely warning of your destination	
	Delivered to all virgins everywhere:	
	'Beware this locust and this plague embodied	440
	In a man! Take the greatest care with him,	
	Or he will rob you of your treasured harvest.	
	This man deceives all women as he will,	
	He is, no less, the trickster of Seville'.	
D. Juan	Congratulations! What a fine description!	445

*Enter the Marquis, with musicians. He is dressed for
the night. He crosses the stage. They exit singing*

Musicians	*[Sing]*
	'For him who's waiting in anticipation,
	Passing time's a source of desperation.'

---

abandonment of his son to the judgement of God constitutes that
moment, and the second half of the play moves inevitably into the more
sinister area of Don Juan's confrontation with the supernatural.

432   the best trick yet!: see Act II, 301, note.

436   a locust to all woman!: this is clearly an evocation of those locusts and
plagues which, according to the Old Testament, were sent by God to
punish the sins of nations and tribes. Similarly, each of Don Juan's
victims is in some way guilty of wrongdoing and Don Juan the
instrument of retribution.

D. Juan	¿Qué es esto?
Catal.	Música es.
Mota	Parece que habla conmigo
	el poeta. ¿Quién va?
D. Juan	Amigo. 450
Mota	¿Es don Juan?
D. Juan	¿Es el marqués?
Mota	¿Quién puede ser sino yo?
D. Juan	Luego que la capa vi,
	que érades vos conocí.
Mota	Cantad, pues don Juan llegó. 455
Músic.	*Cantan*
	El que un bien gozar espera,
	cuanto espera desespera.
D. Juan	¿Qué casa es la que miráis?
Mota	De don Gonzalo de Ulloa.
D. Juan	¿Dónde iremos?
Mota	A Lisboa. 460
D. Juan.	¿Cómo, si en Sevilla estáis?
Mota	Pues ¿aqueso os maravilla?
	¿No vive, con gusto igual,
	lo peor de Portugal
	en lo mejor de Castilla? 465
D. Juan	¿Dónde viven?
Mota	En la calle
	de la Sierpe, donde ves,
	a Adán vuelto en portugués;
	que en aqueste amargo valle
	con bocados solicitan 470
	mil Evas que, aunque dorados,
	en efecto, son bocados
	con que el dinero nos quitan.
Catal.	Ir de noche no quisiera
	por esa calle cruel, 475
	pues lo que de día es miel
	entonces lo dan en cera.

---

460   Destination Lisbon!: the meaning of the phrase is clarified in the following lines. There was not in fact a district or street in Seville known as Lisbon, nor does it seem that Portuguese prostitutes were sufficiently abundant in the city to give Portugal a bad name.

467   Serpent Street: Santiago Montoto, *Las calles de Sevilla. . .*, p.424, notes that the street now known as *Sierpes* was indeed called *La calle de la Sierpe* at an earlier date. It acquired this name because it contained an inn which had hanging on its frontage the jawbone of a serpent. In the fifteenth century the street was also known as the *Calle*

D. Juan	What is that racket?	
Catal.	Only music, master!	
Mota	As though the muse addresses me, creating	
	Poetry of inspiration! Who goes there?	450
D. Juan	A friend!	
Mota	Are you Don Juan?	
D. Juan	Are you Mota?	
Mota	Who else could it possibly be but I?	
D. Juan	Of course! As soon as I saw your crimson	
	Cape, I knew it was you and no mistake.	
Mota	Musicians, sing! My friend Don Juan's arrived!	455
Musicians	[Sing]	
	'For him who's waiting in anticipation,	
	Passing time's a source of desperation'.	
D. Juan	Tell me, what house is this that takes your fancy?	
Mota	The house of Don Gonzalo de Ulloa.	
D. Juan	Where are we going?	
Mota	Destination Lisbon!	460
D. Juan	How can that be when we're here in Seville?	
Mota	I am surprised that that surprises you!	
	Is it not possible the very worst	
	Of Portugal may live quite happily	
	Here in Castille, the best that Spain can offer?	465
D. Juan	And where would that be?	
Mota	It's a street they call	
	Serpent Street. Walk through there and you will see	
	Adam transformed into a Portuguese.	
	That street's a dark and sinful alleyway	
	Where lurk a thousand Eves who offer pleasure,	470
	Invite us to enjoy the taste of lips	
	That promise honey but, as we partake,	
	Serve merely to divest us of our money.	
Catal.	I'll tell you one thing. You won't find me there	
	After dark! No, the place is far too dangerous!	475
	Go there by day, they shower you with honey.	
	Go there by night, they shower you with shit!	

---

de los Espaderos after the swordsmiths who lived there. At no stage, however, was the street noted for its prostitutes.

468   Adam transformed into a Portuguese: the reputation of Portuguese men was that they were extremely amorous and prone, therefore, to be tempted by modern-day Eves.

477   they shower you with shit!: under cover of darkness chamber-pots were emptied from bedroom windows into the street below, to the obvious discomfort of passers-by.

	Una noche, por mi mal,	
	la vi sobre mí vertida,	
	y hallé que era corrompida	480
	la cera de Portugal.	
D. Juan	Mientras a la calle vais,	
	yo dar un perro quisiera.	
Mota	Pues cerca de aquí me espera	
	un bravo.	
D. Juan	Si me dejáis,	485
	señor marqués, vos veréis	
	cómo de mí no se escapa.	
Mota	Vamos, y poneos mi capa,	
	para que mejor lo deis.	
D. Juan	Bien habéis dicho. Venid,	490
	y me enseñaréis la casa.	
Mota	Mientras el suceso pasa,	
	la voz y el habla fingid.	
	¿Veis aquella celosía?	
D. Juan	Ya la veo.	
Mota	Pues llegad	495
	y decid: "Beatriz", y entrad.	
D. Juan	¿Qué mujer?	
Mota	Rosada y fría.	
Catal	Será mujer cantimplora.	
Mota	En Gradas os aguardamos.	
D. Juan	Adiós, marqués.	
Catal.	¿Dónde vamos?	500
D. Juan	Calla, necio, calla agora;	
	adonde la burla mía	
	ejecute.	
Catal.	No se escapa	
	nadie de ti.	
D. Juan	El trueque adoro.	
Catal.	Echaste la capa al toro.	505
D. Juan	No, el toro me echó la capa.	

Vanse Don Juan y Catalinón

---

483   a trick that's much more daring: Mota is planning a trick of his own here and Don Juan, as a means of obtaining Mota's cloak for the planned seduction of Ana, offers to trick another girl, Beatrix, whom Mota has also had in his sights.

498   water-bottle: the water-bottle referred to here is that which was used in the summer to keep water cool. It was often made of porous clay rather than metal and was thus reddish in colour, a fact which allows for the joke about a pink and cold woman.

	It happened to me once, trust my bad luck!	
	Came down on me from up above, as though	
	Heaven sent. But if you want to know the truth,	480
	That dung from Portugal was far from heavenly!	
D. Juan	Mota, while you are visiting that place,	
	My own plan's for a trick that's much more daring.	
Mota	There's one not far from here I've had in mind.	
	It's far from easy.	
D. Juan	I'll do it for you,	485
	Marquis. Let me do it and you'll be sure	
	The trick will give us double satisfaction.	
Mota	Done! Tell you what! You'd better take my cape.	
	Wear it and it will guarantee success.	
D. Juan	An excellent idea! All I need now	490
	Is to know the house. You'd better show me where	
	It is.	
Mota	Another thing. Use all your cunning.	
	Put on another voice! Disguise your speech!	
	You see that window? That one over there?	
D. Juan	I see the one.	
Mota	Well go right up to it,	495
	Call out the name of Beatrix and go	
	Inside.	
D. Juan	What sort of girl?	
Mota	She's pink and cold.	
Catal.	More like a water-bottle than a woman!	
Mota	Afterwards go to Gradas. We'll be there.	
D. Juan	Farewell, Marquis.	
Catal.	Where are we going now?	500
D. Juan	Shut up, you fool! Just try to hold your tongue!	
	Where else but where I'll have the chance to play	
	My trick.	
Catal.	There's no one in the world escapes	
	From you, master!	
D. Juan	Oh, how I love deception!	
Catal.	A neat pass of the cape to fool the bull	505
	Back there!	
D. Juan	He's given me his cape instead!	

Exit Don Juan and Catalinón

---

499   Gradas: the allusion is to an area around the Cathedral, raised above street-level to a height of some four feet, ringed on its outer edge by strong chains.

505   the bull: a mocking reference to Mota, whom Don Juan will deceive with his own cloak. Mota doubtless thinks of himself as a bull in a sexual sense, but Catalinón's thoughts are much more focused on the bull's horns, synonymous with cuckoldry.

Mota	La mujer ha de pensar
	que soy él.
Músic.	¡Qué gentil perro!
Mota	Esto es acertar por yerro.
Músic.	Todo este mundo es errar. 510
	Cantan
	El que un bien gozar espera,
	cuanto espera desespera.

Vanse, y dice Doña Ana dentro

Ana	¡Falso!, no eres el marqués,
	que me has engañado.
D. Juan	Digo.
	que lo soy.
Ana	¡Fiero enemigo, 515
	mientes, mientes!

Sale Don Gonzalo con la espada desnuda

D. Gon.	La voz es
	de doña Ana la que siento.
Ana	[Dentro.] ¿No hay quien mate este traidor,
	homicida de mi honor?
D. Gon.	¿Hay tan grande atrevimiento? 520
	muerto honor, dijo, ¡ay de mí!,
	y es su lengua tan liviana
	que aquí sirve de campana.
Ana	Matalde.

Salen Don Juan y Catalinón con las espadas desnudas

D. Juan	¿Quién está aqui?
D. Gon.	La barbacana caída 525
	de la torre de mi honor,
	echaste en tierra, traidor,
	donde era alcaide la vida.
D. Juan	Déjame pasar.
D. Gon.	¿Pasar?
	Por la punta desta espada. 530
D. Juan	Morirás.
D. Gon.	No importa nada.
D. Juan	Mira que te he de matar.

---

513 You traitor!: Don Juan does not in fact seduce Ana, a fact which he
himself acknowledges in Act III, 962-65. Her father, Don Gonzalo,
evidently believes that she has been seduced, for he refers in 521 to
'honour lost' and in 523 to 'all our shame'.

527 its central fortress: not only has Don Juan found his way into Don

Mota	The girl is bound to think, when she sees me,
	I'm him.
Musicians	Oh, what a wonderful deception!
Mota	This is to take advantage of confusion!
Musicians	What makes the world go round but men's delusions? 510
	[They sing]
	'For him who's waiting in anticipation,
	Passing time's a source of desperation.'

They exit. Doña Ana's voice, off-stage

Ana	You traitor! Pretending to be the Marquis!
	Trying to trick me!
D. Juan	Won't you believe me?
	I am the Marquis!
Ana	Nothing but a liar! 515
	Your every word a lie!

Enter Don Gonzalo. Sword drawn

D. Gon.	My daughter's voice!
	I'm sure it's hers!
Ana	*[Off-stage]* Is there no one who'll kill
	This traitor on my behalf, this treacherous
	Assassin of my honour? Will no one help?
D. Gon.	What man could be so bold and arrogant? 520
	Did she not speak of honour lost, of honour
	Murdered? Her tongue, voicing such things aloud,
	Is like a bell, proclaiming all our shame!
Ana	Kill him!

Enter Don Juan and Catalinón, with swords drawn

D. Juan	Who's there? Reveal yourself! Speak up!
D. Gon.	You, sir, have broken through the strong defences 525
	Of my honour and made your treacherous
	Assault upon its central fortress where
	My life itself was sovereign.
D. Juan	Let me pass.
	You block my path.
D. Gon.	If you, sir, wish to pass,
	You'll have to find your way past this sharp steel. 530
D. Juan	Stand in my way, you'll die.
D. Gon.	To me it matters
	Not!
D. Juan	In that case, fool, you will have to die!

Gonzalo's house and his daughter's bedroom, he has also, as Gonzalo
sees it, made an assault on his honour at that point where honour
needs to be most staunchly defended - Ana herself. Golden-Age drama
is full of fathers, husbands and brothers who see their women-folk as
vulnerable and in need of constant watchfulness. See Act I, 153, note.

D. Gon.	¡Muere, traidor!	
D. Juan	Desta suerte	
	muero.	
Catal.	Si escapo de aquesta,	
	no más burlas, no más fiesta.	535
D. Gon.	¡Ay, que me has dado la muerte!	
D. Juan	Tú la vida te quitaste.	
D. Gon.	¿De qué la vida servía?	
D. Juan	Huye.	

Vanse Don Juan y Catalinón

D. Gon.	Aguarda que es sangría,	
	con que el valor aumentaste.	540
	Muerto soy; no hay quien aguarde.	
	Seguiráte mi furor;	
	que es traidor, y el que es traidor	
	es traidor porque es cobarde.	

*Entran muerto a Don Gonzalo, y salen el Marqués
de la Mota y Músicos*

Mota	Presto las doce darán,	545
	y mucho don Juan se tarda:	
	¡fiera prisión del que aguarda!	

Salen Don Juan y Catalinón

D. Juan.	¿Es el marqués?	
Mota	¿Es don Juan?	
D. Juan	Yo soy; tomad vuestra capa.	
Mota	¿Y el perro?	
D. Juan	Funesto ha sido.	550
	Al fin, marqués, muerto ha habido.	
Catal.	Señor, del muerto te escapa.	
Mota	¿Búrlaste, amigo? ¿Qué haré?	
Catal.	[Aparte.] También vos sois el burlado.	
D. Juan	Cara la burla ha costado.	555
Mota	Yo, don Juan, lo pagaré,	
	porque estará la mujer	
	quejosa de mí.	
D. Juan	Las doce	
	darán.	
Mota	Como mi bien goce,	
	nunca llegue a amanecer.	560
D. Juan	Adiós, marqués.	

---

540   serves only to increase my fury: in earlier centuries blood-letting was considered to be a remedy for specific ills. Don Gonzalo is suggesting here that his outrage has been insufficient and that the loss of blood is therefore a cure for his deficiency in that regard.

D. Gon.	You die like this!
D. Juan	A death that any man Would welcome!
Catal.	I'm dying to save my skin! From hereon in I shall renounce this trickster's 535 Tricks!
D. Gon.	Traitor! You've mortally wounded me!
D. Juan	You, sir, have brought upon yourself your death.
D. Gon.	What use was life to me to end like this?
D. Juan	Come on! Quickly!

Exit Don Juan and Catalinón

D. Gon.	Each drop of precious blood That's lost serves only to increase my fury. 540 I am dying; no one can help me now. But you, traitor, will not escape my vengeance. Treachery's the province of the man who runs, The coward who's afraid to stand his ground.

*The body of Don Gonzalo is taken away. Enter the Marquis
of Mota and musicians*

Mota	It's almost twelve! It's just about to strike! 545 No sign of Don Juan! Why is he so late? How hard it is on him who has to wait!

Don Juan and Catalinón enter

D. Juan	Psst! Marquis! Is that you?
Mota	Is that Don Juan?
D. Juan	Of course it's me! Here! Take your blessed cape!
Mota	And what about the trick?
D. Juan	A pretty deadly Trick, Marquis, as things turned out in the end.
Catal.	Master, forget the trick. Quickly. Let's go.
Mota	Are you joking, my friend? What shall I do?
Catal.	*[Aside]* Acknowledge that the real joke's on you!
D. Juan	A pretty price we had to pay for that! 555
Mota	Leave it to me, Don Juan. I'll settle up And pay the debt, for I'm the one the girl You've fooled will want to get.
D. Juan	The clock strikes twelve.
Mota	If I strike lucky, let the night be endless, Keep dawn at bay, prolong my happiness! 560
D. Juan	Farewell, Marquis.

---

545   It's almost twelve!: an excellent example of the way in which the
dialogue of Golden-Age drama locates the action. Here, is addition, the
allusion to the time prepares us for Mota's reaction when he discovers
what has happened, though even here there is, as we soon learn, an
unexpected twist to events.

Catal.	Muy buen lance	
	el desdichado hallará.	
D. Juan	Huyamos.	
Catal.	Señor, no habrá	
	aguilita que me alcance.	

Vanse D. Juan y Catalinón

Mota	Vosotros os podéis ir	565
	todos a casa, que yo	
	he de ir solo.	
Criados	Dios crió	
	las noches para dormir.	

Vanse y queda el Marqués de la Mota

	[Dentro.] ¿Vióse desdicha mayor,	
	y vióse mayor desgracia?	570
Mota	¡Válgame Dios! Voces siento	
	en la plaza del Alcázar.	
	¿Qué puede ser a estas horas?	
	Un hielo el pecho me arraiga.	
	Desde aquí parece todo	575
	una Troya que se abrasa,	
	porque tantas luces juntas	
	hacen gigantes de llamas.	
	Un grande escuadrón de hachas	
	se acerca a mí; ¿porqué anda	580
	el fuego emulando estrellas,	
	dividiéndose en escuadras?	
	Quiero saber la ocasión.	

Sale Don Diego Tenorio y la Guardia con hachas

D.Diego	¿Qué gente?	
Mota	Gente que aguarda	
	saber de aqueste ruído	585
	el alboroto y la causa.	
D.Diego	Prendeldo.	
Mota	¿Prenderme a mí?	

[Mete mano a la espada.]

D.Diego	Volved la espada a la vaina,	
	que la mayor valentía	
	es no tratar de las armas.	590

---

576   a Troy consumed by flames: the square is ablaze with flaming torches as Don Tenorio and the guards hunt for the murderer of Don Gonzalo. While Mota uses the Trojan metaphor simply to suggest that the whole city seems to be on fire, it does also link this episode to the ending of Act I. In both instances Don Juan has, in a manner reminiscent of the Trojan horse, succeeded in entering the abode of a lady, deceiving her in relation to his identity and his intentions.

Catal.	Farewell, and lots of fun!
	Oh, what a treat awaits this simpleton!

D. Juan   Let's go!

Catal.   Oh, master, I can guarantee
There's not an eagle can keep up with me.

Exit Don Juan and Catalinón

Mota   All of you can go now! Back to your homes!   565
Such is the nature of my task, I must
Go on alone!

Servants   God in his wisdom made
The night so we can sleep away our cares.

The servants leave. Mota is alone

Voices off Whoever saw a deed as black as this?
Whoever such a crime as this shall witness?   570

Mota   May God protect me! Voices raised and shouting
There in the middle of the castle square?
What can it be at this hour of the night?
A sudden fear turns my heart to ice.
And there, before my eyes, the whole world seems   575
To be ablaze, a Troy consumed by flames
That leap up to the sky, a blaze of torches
That giant-like assaults the very heavens!
A regiment of flares, a mighty army
Approaching, step by step, as though their fire   580
Envied and sought to emulate the stars.
In serried ranks the blazing flames advance.
What can the explanation be for this?

Enter Don Diego Tenorio and guards bearing torches

D. Diego Who goes there?

Mota   Someone who would like to know
The cause of this disturbance, and the reason   585
Why there's such confusion.

D. Diego   Arrest this man!

Mota   Arrest me? Why arrest me? I've done nothing!

[Mota attempts to draw his sword]

D. Diego Don't be a fool! Don't try to draw your sword!
Much more courageous to resist the foolish
Urge to try to overcome such odds!   590

---

578   giant-like: another reference to the Titans of Greek mythology who
       rebelled against the gods. See Act I, 295, note.

581   sought to emulate the stars: the flames of the torches leap towards the
       sky, as though they are attempting to be stars. Of the four elements –
       see Act I, 348, note – both air and fire had a natural tendency to move
       upwards towards their source, the source of fire being the sun and the
       stars.

Mota	¿Cómo al marqués de la Mota
	hablan ansí?
D. Diego	Dad la espada,
	que el rey os manda prender.
Mota	¡Vive Dios!

Salen el Rey y acompañamiento

Rey	En toda España	
	no ha de caber, ni tampoco	595
	en Italia, si va a Italia.	
D. Diego	Señor, aquí está el marqués.	
Mota	¿Vuestra alteza a mí me manda	
	prender?	
Rey	Llevalde y ponelde	
	la cabeza en una escarpia.	600
	¿En mi presencia te pones?	
Mota	¡Ah, glorias de amor tiranas,	
	siempre en el pasar ligeras,	
	como en el vivir pesadas!	
	Bien dijo un sabio que había	605
	entre la boca y la taza	
	peligro; mas el enojo	
	del rey me admira y espanta.	
	No sé por lo que voy preso.	
D. Diego	¿Quién mejor sabrá la causa	610
	que vueseñoría?	
Mota	¿Yo?	
D. Diego	Vamos.	
Mota	¡Confusión extraña!	
Rey	Fulmínesele el proceso	
	al marqués luego, y mañana	
	le cortarán la cabeza.	615
	Y al comendador, con cuanta	
	solenidad y grandeza	
	se da a las personas sacras	
	y reales, el entierro	
	se haga; en bronce y piedras varias	620
	un sepulcro con un bulto	
	le ofrezcan, donde en mosaicas	
	labores, góticas letras	

---

599   Take him away!: it is not so much a question of the King acting hastily
here. His conviction that Mota is the murderer of Don Gonzalo springs
from the fact that someone has glimpsed a figure in a red cloak

Mota	I am the Marquis of Mota! You dare
	To speak to me like this?
D. Diego	Give me your sword.
	At once, Marquis! His majesty's command!
Mota	In God's name!

Enter the King and his attendants

King	In the whole of Spain no hiding	
	Place for him! If he makes for Italy,	595
	He'll find there's no security for him	
	There either.	
D. Diego	Your majesty, the Marquis!	
Mota	Your highness, I am told you order my	
	Arrest.	
King	Take him away! Display his head	
	On an iron spike! Do you dare to show	600
	Yourself to me, his royal majesty?	
Mota	Oh, how love's pleasure soon becomes its chains!	
	Oh, how love's estasy's as swift in passing	
	As in our lives it is our constant pain!	
	How wisely spoke the wise-man who declared	605
	That many is the slip 'tween cup and lip!	
	As for the anger of the King, its cause	
	Is both a source of fright and mystery.	
	What crime is it makes me his prisoner?	
D. Diego	I fancy you, my lord, will know the answer	610
	To that question.	
Mota	I, sir, am totally	
	Bemused.	
D. Diego	I'm sure!	
Mota	And hopelessly confused.	
King	End his confusion, hurry up his trial,	
	Tomorrow morning this fine fellow'll lose	
	His head! The Commander's a different matter.	615
	A man of his nobility and worth	
	Deserves a burial that in all its pomp	
	And ceremony's worthy of a royal	
	Personage. See to it and make his funeral	
	Appropriate to his person. A sepulchre	620
	Of bronze and stone shall be his resting place,	
	And there a fine statue in his memory	
	Shall be placed, and on it an inscription	

---

escaping from the scene of the crime.
615   The Commander's a different matter: on Don Gonzalo de Ulloa's
standing, see Act I, 698, note.

	den lenguas a sus venganzas.	
	Y entierro, bulto y sepulcro	625
	quiero que a mi costa se haga.	
	¿Dónde doña Ana se fué?	
D. Diego	Fuese al sagrado, doña Ana,	
	de mi señora la reina.	
Rey	Ha de sentir esta falta	630
	Castilla; tal capitán	
	ha de llorar Calatrava.	

Vanse todos
Sale Batricio, desposado con Aminta; Gaseno,
viejo; Belisa y Pastores músicos
   Cantan

	Lindo sale el sol de abril	
	con trébol y torongil,	
	y aunque le sirva de estrella,	635
	Aminta sale más bella.	
Batric.	Sobre esta alfombra florida,	
	adonde, en campos de escarcha,	
	el sol sin aliento marcha	
	con su luz recién nacida,	640
	os sentad, pues nos convida	
	al tálamo el sitio hermoso.	
Aminta	Cantalde a mi dulce esposo	
	favores de mil en mil.	

   Cantan

	Lindo sale el sol de abril	645
	con trébol y torongil,	
	y aunque le sirva de estrella,	
	Aminta sale más bella.	
Gaseno	Muy bien lo habéis solfeado;	
	no hay más sones en el kiries.	650

---

628 **She's taken sanctuary:** the reason for Ana's seeking sanctuary is not specifically stated. She has obviously fled in the general confusion that follows her cries for help – 517 – and is presumably unaware of her father's death. Conscious of the dishonour she may have brought upon the family name, she appears to be afraid that Don Gonzalo will take vengeance on her. Her desperate seeking for a safe place to hide parallels the behaviour of many dishonoured women in Golden Age plays.

632 **Calatrava:** see Act I, 698, note.

633 **April's sun is warm and bright:** there are several songs in the course of the play, as there are in Golden-Age drama in general. Theatre companies of the time generally included both musicians and singers. In *The Trickster* most of the songs are ironic, contrasting with what is actually happening. In this particular case, though, the song's purpose

	Boldly written, announcing to the world	
	His vengeance. The cost of burial, tomb	625
	And statue the royal treasury shall meet.	
	But what about the whereabouts of Ana?	
D.Diego	She's taken sanctuary, your majesty,	
	In the safety of the Queen's royal chapel.	
King	This loss is one, my friend, that all Castile	630
	Will surely feel. This man, this great Commander	
	The whole of Calatrava now shall weep.	

Exit all

Enter Batricio, betrothed to Aminta; Gaseno, an old man; Belisa and shepherd musicians

Musicians	*[Sing]*	
	'April's sun is warm and bright,	
	With orange flower and lovely clover.	
	Aminta to the sun's a star,	635
	But she is warm and bright all over'.	
Batric.	Upon this lovely carpet, green and full	
	Of flowers, but white still with the hoary frost,	
	And where the sun steps out, still bleary-eyed	
	But warming slowly to his daily task,	640
	Sit you all down! The beauty of the place	
	Invites us all to make this spot our bed.	
Aminta	I beg you all, bestow your songs and favours	
	On Batricio. To him I'll soon be wed.	
Musicians	*[Sing]*	
	'April's sun is warm and bright,	645
	With orange flower and lovely clover.	
	Aminta to the sun's a star,	
	But she is warm and bright all over'.	
Gaseno	A fine song, lads, a joy to all our ears.	
	Much better than the choir we have in church!	650

---

is to establish an idyllic mood and to contrast the beauty and harmony of the countryside with the corruption of the Court, whose values have been embodied in the scene just ended. Praise of the countryside and of country people is an important topic in Golden-Age literature in general. While the town-country contrast had its origins in classical literature, Horace's *Beatus ille* being a notable influence, the seventeenth century was itself marked by a growing awareness of the hollowness of urban life – a feeling which grew throughout the period as towns and cities grew and became more corrupt in all kinds of ways. In the drama country people are often shown to be morally superior to sophisticated courtiers, as Calderón's *El alcalde de Zalamea* and Lope de Vega's *Peribáñez* both suggest, though the matter is not quite as simple in *The Trickster*. For a general study of the theme see Noël Salomon, *Recherches sur le thème paysan dans la 'comedia' au temps de Lope de Vega* (Bordeaux, 1965).

Batric.	Cuando con sus labios tiries	
	vuelve en púrpura los labios	
	saldrán, aunque vergonzosas,	
	afrentando el sol de abril.	
Aminta	Batricio, yo lo agradezco;	655
	falso y lisonjero estás;	
	mas si tus rayos me das,	
	por ti ser luna merezco;	
	tú eres el sol por quien crezco	
	después de salir menguante.	660
	Para que el alba te cante	
	la salva en tono sutil,	

Cantan

lindo sale el sol, etc.

      Sale Catalinón, de camino

Catal.	Señores, el desposorio	
	huéspedes ha de tener.	665
Gaseno	A todo el mundo ha de ser	
	este contento notorio.	
	¿Quién viene?	
Catal.	Don Juan Tenorio.	
Gaseno	¿El viejo?	
Catal.	No ese don Juan.	
Belisa	Será su hijo galán.	670
Batric.	Téngolo por mal agüero,	
	que galán y caballero	
	quitan gusto y celos dan.	
	Pues ¿quién noticia les dió	
	de mis bodas?	
Catal.	De camino	675
	pasa a Lebrija.	
Batric.	Imagino	
	que el demonio le envió.	
	Mas, ¿de qué me aflijo yo?	
	Vengan a mis dulces bodas	
	del mundo las gentes todas.	680
	Mas, con todo, un caballero	
	en mis bodas, ¡mal agüero!	

---

657   the bright sun in my blue heaven: see Act II, 72, note. As the sun rules supreme amongst the planets, so Batricio reigns supreme in Aminta's life.

662   add its harmony: The relationship of Aminta and Batricio is here presented as harmonious and it is also placed within the context of Nature's harmony, of which the singing of the birds is one example. For the seventeenth century the perfect music of the spheres, evidence

Batric.	The sun, Aminta, wakes and fills its lips
	And cheeks with brightest red, a dazzling hue;
	And yet, no sooner does it dare peep out,
	It's all ablush with shame, for it sees you!
Aminta	Batricio, your words are very pleasing, 655
	Though I believe that you are teasing me.
	Still, you are the bright sun in my blue heaven,
	So I to your sun will be your moon.
	As your warmth and brightness shines on me,
	So my light glows and shines out silvery. 660
	Let the dawn greet you! Let its gentle music
	Add its harmony to your majesty.
Musicians	[Sing]
	'April's sun is warm and bright, etc.,. . . .'
	Enter Catalinón, dressed as a traveller
Catal.	Ah, gentlemen, this wedding's to be honoured
	Further by another special guest. 665
Gaseno	My friend, the whole world has our invitation,
	So everyone may share our celebration!
	Who is the newcomer?
Catal.	Don Juan Tenorio.
Gaseno	The old one would that be?
Catal.	The other one.
Belisa	He means his son. He has the reputation 670
	Of a rake.
Batric.	I don't like the sound of that!
	A man who's rich and has that reputation
	Gives every cause for fear and suspicion.
	But how was it he got the information
	About our marriage?
Catal.	Just in passing, heading 675
	For Lebrija.
Batric.	I wouldn't put it past
	Him that the devil sent him straight to us.
	Still, what's the point of worrying about
	It? Let the whole world come! Let everyone
	Attend the celebration of our wedding! 680
	Though seeing this nobleman close to my dear
	Betrothed still gives me cause for utmost fear!

---

of divine perfection, was reflected imperfectly in the earthly world, and
the music of Nature was one example of it.

668   Don Juan Tenorio: Gaseno assumes that Catalinón is alluding to the
father, not the son. In the earlier version of *The Trickster* – see Act
II, 1, note – our Don Diego Tenorio was indeed called Don Juan
Tenorio, *viejo*.

Gaseno	Venga el Coloso de Rodas,	
	venga el Papa, el Preste Juan	
	y don Alfonso el Onceno	685
	con su corte, que en Gaseno	
	ánimo y valor verán.	
	Montes en casa hay de pan,	
	Guadalquivides de vino,	
	Babilonias de tocino,	690
	y entre ejércitos cobardes	
	de aves, para que las lardes,	
	el pollo y el palomino.	
	Venga tan gran caballero	
	a ser hoy en Dos Hermanas	695
	honra destas viejas canas.	
Belisa	El hijo del camarero	
	mayor. . .	
Batric.	[Ap.] Todo es mal agüero	
	para mí, pues le han de dar	
	junto a mi esposa lugar.	700
	Aun no gozo, y ya los cielos	
	me están condenando a celos.	
	Amor, sufrir y callar.	

Sale Don Juan Tenorio

D. Juan	Pasando acaso he sabido	
	que hay bodas en el lugar,	705
	y dellas quise gozar,	
	pues tan venturoso he sido.	
Gaseno	Vueseñoría ha venido	
	a honrallas y engrandecellas.	
Batric.	Yo, que soy el dueño dellas,	710
	digo entre mí que vengáis	
	en hora mala.	

---

683 We shall invite: given the initial idealization of country life, elements of doubt begin to intrude. Gaseno is seen to be foolishly over-proud and anxious that the nobility itself should be astonished by the feast that he has arranged. He lacks the dignity of a man like Pedro Crespo in Calderón's *El alcalde de Zalamea*. The implication is that in reality the peasants, though less deliberately malicious, are as flawed as the nobility.

689 Guadalquivirs: the Guadalquivir is one of Spain's longest rivers. It flows two hundred and twenty five miles in a south-westerly direction across the plains of Andalusia, through Seville, and enters the sea some fifty miles south of the city.

690 Babylons of ham: amongst other things the city of Babylon was famous in ancient times for its luxury. Subsequently any place distinguished by material wealth and comfort came to be referred to as Babylon.

Gaseno	We shall invite the Colossus of Rhodes	
	Itself. Why not the Pope? The Emperor	
	Of Ethiopia? Alfonso the Eleventh	685
	And all his courtiers? For in Gaseno	
	They shall discover spirit and true valour.	
	Mountains of bread we'll put upon their plates;	
	Guadalquivirs of wine shall pour into	
	Their mouths; Great Babylons of ham delight	690
	Their palates; and their stomachs shall be filled	
	With flocks of succulent and timid birds,	
	Chickens and tender doves fit for a King.	
	Go tell this honourable gentleman	
	He's welcome here, for here in Dos Hermanas	695
	His presence honours this grey head of mine.	
Belisa	He's son of the high chancellor!	
Batric.	[Aside] That means	
	They'll seat him at the table next to my	
	Sweetheart! And nothing could be worse than that!	
	I'm thinking everything is going badly.	700
	My happiness has turned to misery!	
	The heavens condemn me to this jealousy!	
	To love's to suffer in silent agony!	

Enter Don Juan Tenorio

D. Juan	A happy chance, my friends, to learn in passing	
	There's a wedding here! To be sure, a stroke	705
	Of luck, an opportunity for pleasure	
	And revelry that's quite unexpected.	
Gaseno	The arrival of your noble lordship serves	
	To add distinction to our humble feast.	
Batric.	[Aside] To think that all this here's supposed to be	710
	For me, designed to honour my good name!	
	I curse the day that this fine fellow came!	

---

695   **Dos Hermanas**: the town is to the south-east of Seville and is approximately half-way between the city and Lebrija, to which Don Juan has been banished by the King.

696   **His presence honours**: the peasant wedding is undoubtedly graced by the presence of a nobleman, especially by a nobleman who is the son of the High Chancellor. At the same time, however, Gaseno is shown to be a man who equates honour with nobility of birth and, as Don Juan's subsequent behaviour proves, is quite misguided in making that assumption.

711   **to honour my good name!**: like many peasants in Golden-Age drama, Batricio has a keen sense of his own good name and reputation. On the other hand, he does nothing to assert himself and to protect Aminta, and is therefore very different both from Lope's Peribáñez and Calderón's Pedro Crespo. He is presented by Tirso as a rather passive individual who is only too ready to think the worst of his bride.

Gaseno	¿No dais
	lugar a este caballero?
D. Juan	Con vuestra licencia quiero
	sentarme aquí.

Siéntase junto a la novia

Batric.	Si os sentáis	715
	delante de mí, señor,	
	seréis de aquesa manera	
	el novio.	
D. Juan	Cuando lo fuera,	
	no escogiera lo peor.	
Gaseno	¡Que es el novio!	
D. Juan	De mi error	720
	e ignorancia perdón pido.	
Catal.	[Ap.] ¡Desventurado marido!	
D. Juan	[Ap. a Catal.] Corrido está.	
Catal.	[Ap.] No lo ignoro;	
	mas si tiene de ser toro,	
	¿qué mucho que esté corrido?	725
	No daré por su mujer	
	ni por su honor un cornado.	
	¡Desdichado tú, que has dado	
	en manos de Lucifer!	
D. Juan	¿Posible es que vengo a ser,	730
	señora, tan venturoso?	
	Envidia tengo al esposo.	
Aminta	Parecéisme lisonjero.	
Batric.	Bien dije que es mal agüero	
	en bodas un poderoso.	735
Gaseno	Ea, vamos a almorzar,	
	por que pueda descansar	
	un rato su señoría.	

Tómale Don Juan la mano a la novia

D. Juan	¿Por qué la escondéis?	
Aminta	Es mía.	
Gaseno	Vamos.	
Belisa	Volved a cantar.	740
D. Juan	¿Qué dices tú?	

---

718   bridegroom: the situation of Aminta and Batricio is that they have taken their marriage vows before witnesses but the marriage has not yet been consummated. This is clearly what is meant by Catalinón's remark in 722.

724   playing the bull: once more, as in the earlier situation concerning Mota – see 505, note –, the allusions to the bull have to do with cuckoldry.

122

Gaseno	Make way there for our noble guest to sit.	
D. Juan	With your permission I should like to sit	
	Here.	

He takes his seat next to the bride

Batric.	If you sit there, sir, and take you place	715
	Before I do, it's just as if you've stepped	
	Into my shoes, taking my place as well	
	As bridegroom!	
D. Juan	My fine fellow, were I bridegroom	
	To this bride, who would dare condemn my choice?	
Gaseno	This is the bridegroom, sir!	
D. Juan	And for my error	720
	And sheer discourtesy, I beg forgiveness!	
Catal.	*[Aside]* A wretched fellow and before he's married!	
D. Juan	*[Aside]* The fellow's flummoxed and confused!	
Catal.	No wonder,	
	Master, playing the bull to your passes!	
	Are you surprised you've got him in a spin?	725
	[Aside] As for the girl, I wouldn't give a toss	
	For her virtue, nor for her suitor's honour!	
	Unfortunate the man whose fate it is	
	To fall into Lucifer's grasping hands!	
D. Juan	I can hardly believe that fortune smiles	730
	On me, oh lovely lady, with such favour!	
	Though envy of your husband moves me greatly.	
Aminta	I fancy, sir, you aim to flatter me.	
Batric.	And I was right to think a nobleman	
	Darkens a happy wedding with ill omen.	735
Gaseno	Come, then, let us begin the wedding-feast	
	And bid our gracious lord to take his ease	
	And join with us in our festivities.	

Don Juan takes Aminta's hand

D. Juan	But why remove your hand?	
Aminta	Because it's mine.	
Gaseno	Let's go!	
Belisa	And let the song begin again!	740
D. Juan	What's your impression?	

---

733   you aim to flatter me: although Aminta is dazzled by Don Juan's social position and the attention which he showers upon her, she distrusts him from the beginning and never leads him on. In the sense that she offers no encouragement, she is to be distinguished from the noblewomen who indulge in secret affairs. She is also totally unlike Tisbea. In general, it can be said of her that she is probably the least blameworthy character in the play of those who suffer at Don Juan's hands.

123

Catal.	¿Yo? que temo
	muerte vil destos villanos.
D. Juan	Buenos ojos, blancas manos,
	en ellos me abraso y quemo.
Catal.	¡Almagrar y echar a extremo! 745
	Con ésta cuatro serán.
D. Juan	Ven, que mirándome están.
Batric.	En mis bodas, caballero,
	¡mal agüero!
Gaseno	Cantad.
Batric.	Muero.
Catal.	Canten, que ellos llorarán. 750

*Vanse todos, con que da fin la segunda
jornada*

---

744   her beauty burns: although Aminta's hands are as white as snow, her
beauty burns Don Juan. See Act I, 632, note.

Catal.   Me? I'm scared to death
          These country fellows have our own deaths planned.
D. Juan   What lovely eyes she has! Her hands like snow!
          Already her beauty burns into my soul!
Catal.   You mark them out like sheep, master, before   745
          You turn them out. With her the total's four.
D. Juan   Come! They can't stop staring. I wonder why?
Batric.   This nobleman's presence at my wedding's
          A bad omen!
Gaseno   Begin the song!
Batric.   I die!
Catal.   All those who sing will soon be forced to cry.   750
     Exit all

---

746   the total's four: Catalinón's total consists of Isabela, Tisbea, Ana and
         Aminta. Clearly he is alluding only to those seductions or attempted
         seductions that take place during the action of the play, for the list of
         Don Juan's conquests is very much longer than that. His uncle, Don
         Pedro, refers in Act I, 80, to 'a Spanish lady of distinction' seduced
         by him, he himself alludes to his habit of seduction – Act I, 892 – and
         in Seville with his companion, Mota, he embarks on a new round of
         seductions.

JORNADA TERCERA

Sale Batricio, pensativo

Batric. Celos, reloj de cuidados,
    que a todas las horas dais
    tormentos con que matáis,
    aunque dais desconcertados;
    celos, del vivir desprecios,   5
    con que ignorancias hacéis,
    pues todo lo que tenéis
    de ricos, tenéis de necios;
    dejadme de atormentar,
    pues es cosa tan sabida   10
    que, cuando amor me da vida,
    la muerte me queréis dar.
    ¿Qué me queréis, caballero,
    que me atormentáis ansí?
    Bien dije cuando le vi   15
    en mis bodas, "¡mal agüero!"
    ¿No es bueno que se sentó
    a cenar con mi mujer,
    y a mí en el plato meter
    la mano no me dejó?   20
    Pues cada vez que quería
    metella la desviaba,
    diciendo a cuanto tomaba:
    "¡Grosería, grosería!"
    Pues llegándome a quejar   25
    a algunos, me respondían
    y con risa me decían:
    "No tenéis de qué os quejar;
    eso no es cosa que importe;
    no tenéis de qué temer;   30
    callad, que debe de ser
    uso de allá de la corte."
    ¡Buen uso, trato estremado!
    Más no se usara en Sodoma:
    que otro con la novia coma,   35
    y que ayune el desposado.
    Pues el otro bellacón

---

34 Sodom!: a city on the shore of the Dead Sea, destroyed by God on
  account of the excessive wickedness of its people. See *Genesis* xix.
37 this utter rogue: it is, of course, Don Juan's roguishness which carries
  the audience with him and ensures that it laughs at the deception of

Enter Batricio, pensive

Batric.   Jealousy, the timepiece of all our cares,
        You strike at every hour of the day,
        Not pleasing and harmonious sounds but discords
        That pierce and assault our very souls.
        Jealousy, you despise all happiness   5
        And life, and in your ignorance of it
        Make everything its opposite, transforming
        All our joy to pain, delight to anguish.
        I beg of you, spare me this awful torment!
        As everyone knows well, love gives new meaning   10
        To my existence, while you, despising
        Pleasure, conspire to bring about my death!
        As for you, nobleman, what do you want
        Of me that you should come and plague me so?
        The moment I set eyes on him arriving   15
        At my wedding, I thought it ominous!
        What else could it be when he sat himself
        Right next to my dear bride at our wedding
        Feast and, would you believe it, tried to stop
        Me eating from the plate in front of me!   20
        For every time I reached for food he knocked
        Away my hand, and every time I tried
        To grab the smallest morsel, he complained:
        'Who's ever seen gluttony as this?'
        I did protest, of course, to all the others,   25
        But, far from helping me, they only laughed
        At me, answering my grief with their mirth:
        'You have no cause for worry or complaint.
        You take the matter far too seriously.
        Why be afraid when there's no cause to fear?   30
        Just hold your tongue and be assured that this
        Is probably the custom of the Court'.
        Custom indeed! Oh, yes! You wouldn't find
        A custom more refined than that in Sodom!
        That he should sit down by the bride and eat,   35
        And I, the bridegroom, am denied my meat!
        Imagine! This fellow, this utter rogue,

---

men like Batricio. Almost every word uttered by Batricio here, though critical of Don Juan, backfires on Batricio himself. Needless to say, for a sophisticated city audience watching the play, the foolish country bumpkin was a ready source of humour.

a cuanto comer quería:
"¿Esto no come?", decía;
"No tenéis, señor, razón";   40
y de delante al momento
me lo quitaba. Corrido
estó; bien sé yo que ha sido
culebra y no casamiento.
Ya no se puede sufrir   45
ni entre cristianos pasar;
y acabando de cenar
con los dos, ¿mas que a dormir
se ha de ir también, si porfía,
con nosotros, y ha de ser,   50
el llegar yo a mi mujer,
"grosería, grosería?"
Ya viene, no me resisto.
Aquí me quiero esconder;
pero ya no puede ser,   55
que imagino que me ha visto.

   Sale Don Juan Tenorio
D. Juan   Batricio.
Batric.   Su señoría
          ¿qué manda?
D. Juan   Haceros saber. . .
Batric.   *[Ap.]* ¿Mas que ha de venir a ser
          alguna desdicha mía?   60
D. Juan   Que ha muchos días Batricio,
          que a Aminta el alma le di
          y he gozado. . .
Batric.   ¿Su honor?
D. Juan   Sí.
Batric.   *[Ap.]* Manifiesto y claro indicio
          de lo que he llegado a ver;   65
          que si bien no le quisiera
          nunca a su casa viniera.
          Al fin, al fin es mujer.
D. Juan   Al fin, Aminta celosa,
          o quizá desesperada   70
          de verse de mí olvidada
          y de ajeno dueño esposa,

---

63   Her honour?: highly conscious of his own good name, Batricio is quick
      to suspect the worst of Aminta. In this respect – as l. 68 confirms –
      he is remarkably like Duke Octavio, suspecting the worst of Isabela. In

128

No sooner do I try to grab some food,
Chastises me. 'You can't eat that', he says,
'You need to learn how to behave yourself!'   40
And there and then the food in front of me
Is gone, snatched right away, and there am I
Left open-mouthed, and made to look a fool!
Call this a wedding? It's a cruel joke,
An insult of the kind no man can bear   45
And still deserve respect from all his friends.
I'm sure when this nobleman has finished
Supper, and I and my fair bride are off
To bed, he's going to insist on coming
With us! And when I take her in my arms,   50
Drawing her close to me, he'll be there too,
Complaining that my love's indecency!
Talk of the devil, here the devil comes!
I'd better hide myself. I can't abide
Him! No, I can't do that! I've missed my chance.   55
Worse luck the fellow's caught a glimpse of me!

Enter Don Juan

D. Juan   Batricio!

Batric.   Oh, your lordship, there you are!
What would you have me do?

D. Juan   I'd have you know. . .

Batric.   *[Aside]* It's bound to be bad news! It can't be good,
He wouldn't want to see me otherwise!   60

D. Juan   For some days now, Batricio, Aminta has
Possessed my soul. I am her prisoner.
And as for her I have possessed. . .

Batric.   Her honour?

D. Juan   What else?

Batric.   *[Aside]* What more proof could I need of what
I have become, of everything I feared?   65
It's obvious too she loves him just as much.
Why else would she invite him to her house?
But then, what else could I expect of woman?

D. Juan   The truth of the matter is simply this.
Aminta, torn by jealousy and fear   70
Of seeing herself rejected and abandoned
By me, through marriage to another man,

---

short, the peasant's attempt to ape the nobleman in matters of honour
exposes him to precisely the same agonies and, given his
pretentiousness, renders those agonies comic.

129

```
                esta carta me escribió
                enviándome a llamar,
                y yo prometí gozar                        75
                lo que el alma prometió.
                Esto pasa de esta suerte.
                Dad a vuestra vida un medio;
                que le daré sin remedio
                a quien lo impida, la muerte.              80
Batric.         Si tú en mi eleción lo pones,
                tu gusto pretendo hacer,
                que el honor y la mujer
                son males en opiniones.
                La mujer en opinión                        85
                siempre más pierde que gana,
                que son como la campana,
                que se estima por el són.
                Y así es cosa averiguada
                que opinión viene a perder,                90
                cuando cualquiera mujer
                suena a campana quebrada.
                No quiero, pues me reduces
                el bien que mi amor ordena,
                mujer entra mala y buena,                  95
                que es moneda entre dos luces.
                Gózala, señor, mil años,
                que yo quiero resistir,
                desengañar y morir,
                y no vivir con engaños.                    100
        Vase Batricio
D. Juan    Con el honor le vencí,
           porque siempre los villanos
```

---

73   this letter: Batricio presumably cannot read. We may imagine Don Juan,
      sure in that knowledge, waving the letter in front of the bemused
      peasant's face. But if Batricio cannot read, it is even more probable
      that Aminta cannot write. His utter belief in Don Juan's assertion that
      she is the author of the letter is thus even more comic.

80   I shall kill him!: Don Juan's threat runs the risk of alienating an
      audience which throughout the scene delights in Batricio's confusion. It
      is important therefore that this phrase be delivered in a light-hearted
      and flippant manner, contrasting with the solemnity of Batricio's reply.

85   gossip: characters in the drama of the Golden Age are frequently
      concerned with the dangers of any gossip attaching to them, for to be
      talked about in a derogatory sense is tantamount to dishonour. Honour
      can thus be seen to have little to do with virtue and integrity and
      everything to do with the way the individual is perceived by others.
      Batricio, as we have seen, regards honour in this second sense, and is
      quick to abandon Aminta to Don Juan rather than have her, and thus
      himself, talked about. He is a complete contrast to Calderón's Pedro

	Wrote me this letter. It's an invitation,	
	A plea to call on her, and in reply	
	To it I merely promised that I would,	75
	In recognition of our heart's desires.	
	Such is the situation, my dear friend.	
	Accept it! Nothing else that you can do!	
	You see, if any man thinks that he can win	
	Her heart, he'd better know that I shall kill him!	80
Batric.	Since it's a choice I have to make, my lord,	
	I choose to do what you suggest I should.	
	Honour and woman have a lot in common:	
	They both go hand in hand on people's tongues,	
	Are bad companions when it comes to gossip,	85
	And any woman, given a bad name,	
	Is bound to lose much more than she can gain.	
	A woman's not much different from a bell:	
	Its quality is good if it rings well.	
	So it's a fact you have to take as proven	90
	That any woman's name, taken in vain	
	By others, is a bell that's cracked, no less!	
	As far as love's concerned, you've ruined it	
	For me, destroyed it's glitter, leaving me	
	A girl who, since her worth is now uncertain,	95
	Is like a coin in the dim light of evening.	
	You have her for eternity, my lord.	
	I'd rather give her up, accept the truth	
	For what it is and die resigned to it	
	Than be the butt of other people's jibes.	100

Exit Batricio

D. Juan	I've overcome this fellow through his honour!
	Easy enough, of course, for all these rustics

Crespo, the proud peasant of *El alcalde de Zalamea* for whom honour is
a spiritual thing, 'offspring of the soul', the province of God and not
of man. Yet even when a man like Crespo knows what true honour is,
he cannot isolate himself from other people's more worldly concept of
honour. The same is seen to be true of the peasant Peribáñez in the
play of the same name, for despite the fact that he knows his wife to
be innocent of any affair with the overlord of the village, he is
embarrassed by the fact that the latter's attentions to her should have
become public knowledge.

102   these rustics: an expression of scorn towards peasants who have regard
for their honour is often to be found in Golden-Age plays in the mouths
of those who consider themselves superior. In *El alcalde de Zalamea* the
Sergeant feels nothing but contempt for Pedro Crespo:

      I've heard it said this country fellow thinks
      Himself the finest fellow ever lived.
      He's so puffed up with pride and self-presumption,
      He has the manner of a nobleman. (Act I, 168–71)

tienen su honor en las manos,
y siempre miran por sí.
Que por tantas falsedades,   105
es bien que se entienda y crea,
que el honor se fué al aldea
huyendo de las ciudades.
Pero antes de hacer el daño
le pretendo reparar: 110
a su padre voy a hablar
para autorizar mi engaño.
Bien lo supe negociar:
gozarla esta noche espero.
La noche camina, y quiero   115
su viejo padre llamar.
Estrellas que me alumbráis,
dadme en este engaño suerte,
si el galardón en la muerte
tan largo me lo guardáis.   120

Vase. Salen Aminta y Belisa

Belisa   Mira que vendrá tu esposo:
entra a desnudarte, Aminta.

Aminta   De estas infelices bodas
no sé que siento, Belisa.
Todo hoy mi Batricio ha estado   125
bañado en melancolía,
todo es confusión y celos;
¡mirad qué grande desdicha!
Di, ¿qué caballero es éste
que de mi esposo me priva?   130
La desvergüenza en España
se ha hecho caballería.
Déjame, que estoy sin seso,
déjame, que estoy corrida.
¡Mal hubiese el caballero   135
que mis contentos me priva!

Belisa   Calla, que pienso que viene,
que nadie en la casa pisa
de un desposado, tan recio.

---

107   <u>night approaches</u>: see Act I, 10, note, for a comment on the way in
which the dialogue locates time and place. A brief consideration of the
play is sufficient to reveal that there is considerable movement in space
and time, but the observer is always kept informed through the
dialogue of any change of scene.

132   <u>no different from nobility</u>: Aminta's observation is a pointer to her own
perceptiveness and to one of the key issues of the play. On the

Hold their honour near to their hearts,
As though they hold it dear as life itself.
The truth is that the prevalence of cunning   105
And deceit has obliged honour to seek
A safer refuge in the countryside,
Forsaking all the ills of city-life.
But coming to this piece of trickery,
I'll cloak it in respectability.   110
I'll seek the father of the girl and let
Him give permission for her own deception.
What better way than that to set it up
And guarantee my pleasure for tonight?
The night approaches quickly now, it's time   115
I went to find the old man's whereabouts,
Oh, stars, you who illuminate my path,
Assist me carry out this cunning trick.
Though death may be my ultimate reward,
I'm sure there's time enough to pay that debt!   120

Exit Don Juan. Enter Aminta and Belisa

Belisa   Your husband will be here quite soon, Aminta.
You'd better go inside and get undressed.

Aminta   The wedding's turned out badly. I don't know
Belisa, whether I feel sad or happy.
The whole day long Batricio had a face   125
As long as this: a proper misery!
Confusion in his heart, and jealousy!
Oh, what a fine mess it's turned out to be!
Tell me, who is this nobleman who's turned
Up here and turned my man away from me?   130
As far as I can see, plain roguery
In Spain's no different from nobility.
You'd better leave me for a while, Belisa.
I'm all confused, and thoroughly ashamed.
That nobleman! A curse upon his head!   135
He's driven my Batricio from our bed!

Belisa   Listen! It sounds as if Batricio's coming.
Who else would dare to make his presence known
By boldly entering the bridegroom's home?

---

question of the morality of the Spanish nobility as it is presented to us
in the play, see Act II, 258, note.

136   from our bed!: the marriage is still to be consummated, see Act II, 718,
note. Don Juan's comment, Act III, 61, indicates that a few days have
passed since he first set eyes on Aminta. The action of Act III is not
therefore an unbroken continuation of the ending of Act II, for several
days have elapsed.

133

Aminta	Queda adiós, Belisa mía.	140
Belisa	Desenójale en los brazos.	
Aminta	¡Plega a los cielos que sirvan	
	mis suspiros de requiebros,	
	mis lágrimas de caricias!	

Salen Don Juan, Catalinón y Gaseno

D. Juan	Gaseno, quedad con Dios.	145
Gaseno	Acompañaros querría,	
	por dalle desta ventura	
	el parabién a mi hija.	
D. Juan	Tiempo mañana nos queda.	
Gaseno	Bien decís: el alma mía	150
	en la muchacha os ofrezco	

Vase

D. Juan	Mi esposa decid.	
	[A Catal.] Ensilla,	
	Catalinón.	
Catal.	¿Para cuándo?	
D. Juan	Para el alba, que de risa	
	muerta, ha de salir mañana,	155
	de este engaño.	
Catal.	Allá, en Lebrija,	
	señor, nos está aguardando	
	otra boda. Por tu vida,	
	que despaches presto en ésta.	
D. Juan	La burla más escogida	160
	de todas ha de ser ésta.	
Catal.	Que saliésemos querría	
	de todas bien.	
D. Juan	Si es mi padre	
	el dueño de la justicia,	
	y es la privanza del rey,	165
	¿qué temes?	
Catal.	De los que privan	
	suele Dios tomar venganza,	
	si delitos no castigan;	
	y se suelen en el juego	
	perder también los que miran.	170

---

150   I offer you: although, in reaching an agreement with Don Juan, Gaseno
shows himself to be unduly ambitious, he has no real reason to believe
that Don Juan will seduce and abandon his daughter.

157   another wedding in Lebrija: which wedding is this? In Act II, 14, the
King of Castile informs Don Juan's father that the young man is to
marry Isabela and immediately banishes him to Lebrija. When Isabela
arrives at Tarragona in Act III, she is on her way to Seville where her
marriage to Don Juan is presumably to take place. The latter is not

| Aminta | Oh, Belisa! Quickly! You'd better go! | 140 |

Aminta   Oh, Belisa! Quickly! You'd better go!   140
Belisa   Embrace him! Let your kisses soothe his sadness!
Aminta   I pray to Heaven above, please grant me this:
            That all my sighs be pure flattery,
            And every tear of mine a sweet carress!
     Enter Don Juan, Catalinón and Gaseno
D. Juan   Gaseno, God be with you! I'll take my leave.   145
Gaseno   My greatest wish, my lord, is to present
            My daughter with the news of her good fortune.
            I beg you grant a father this small favour.
D. Juan   Oh, time enough to tell her that tomorrow!
Gaseno   Well, I suppose you're right. I offer you   150
            My soul itself in the gift of my daughter.
     Exit Gaseno
D. Juan   You mean, of course, in the gift of my bride!
            [To Catalinón] Catalinón, the horses! Get them ready!
Catal.   When for, master?
D. Juan   The crack of dawn, for when
            The sun peeps out and sees what I have done,   155
            It's sure to split its sides with laughter.
Catal.   Then,
            My lord, another wedding in Lebrija
            Waiting for you. Take my advice, you'd better
            See to it this one is consummated quick!
D. Juan   Not only consummated, but a trick   160
            That in its artistry is consumate.
Catal.   Let's hope we get away with it! That's all
            I want to do!
D. Juan   Catalinón, my father,
            As you know, is chief justice in the land
            And very influential with the king.   165
            Why be afraid?
Catal.   Because, master, there's God
            To think about, and his vengeance always
            Gets those who think they've got away with it.
            And don't forget that when it comes to gambling,
            It's often those who watch who end up losing.   170

---

actually informed in the lines of the play of the proposed marriage to Isabela. Presumably lines have been lost in which he is told both of the marriage and of its celebration at Lebrija.

164   chief justice: what we know of Don Diego Tenorio is that he is High Chamberlain to the King – see Act I, 571, note. In Act II, after the murder of Don Gonzalo, it is Don Diego who commands the guards to arrest the Marquis of Mota in the name of the King and who throughout Act III is concerned that justice shall be done. See Act III, 240.

	Yo he sido mirón del tuyo,	
	y por mirón no querría	
	que me cogiese algún rayo	
	y me trocase en ceniza.	
D. Juan	Vete, ensilla, que mañana	175
	he de dormir en Sevilla.	
Catal.	¿En Sevilla?	
D. Juan	Sí.	
Catal.	¿Qué dices?	
	Mira lo que has hecho, y mira	
	que hasta la muerte, señor,	
	es corta la mayor vida,	180
	y que hay tras la muerte infierno.	
D. Juan	Si tan largo me lo fías,	
	vengan engaños.	
Catal.	Señor. . .	
D. Juan	Vete, que ya me amohinas	
	con tus temores estraños.	185
Catal.	Fuerza al turco, fuerza al scita,	
	al persa y al garamante,	
	al gallego, al troglodita,	
	al alemán y al japón,	
	al sastre con la agujita	190
	de oro en la mano, imitando	
	contino a la Blanca niña.	

Vase Catalinón

D. Juan	La noche en negro silencio	
	se estiende, y ya las cabrillas	
	entre racimos de estrellas	195
	el polo más alto pisan.	
	Yo quiero poner mi engaño	
	por obra. El amor me guía	

---

177   <u>You must be mad!</u>: the rashness of Don Juan's action has to be measured against the fact that any flouting of a royal edict of banishment constituted a capital offence. In addition, he is prepared to ignore the marriage which the King has arranged for him. It is little wonder that Catalinón reacts as he does, for his master's actions increasingly defy both earthly and heavenly authority.

186   <u>Admire the Turk</u>: in Act II, 332-37, Catalinón promises Don Juan that he will perform heroic and extraordinary deeds. He vows now that he intends to leave such reckless endeavours to Don Juan, listing in the process nations and people renowned for their ferocity. The Turks, for example, were a constant menace in the Mediterranean in the sixteenth century and were renowned for their cruelty and savagery before that. Similarly, the Scythians, an ancient and nomadic people dwelling on the

	Now, as for me, I've been a regular watcher	
	Of your game, and I don't aim on that	
	Account to be the target for any bolt,	
	Heaven-sent or not, that turns my bones to dust.	
D. Juan	Just get a move on! Saddle up! My plan's	175
	To spend tomorrow night back in Seville.	
Catal.	Seville?	
D. Juan	Of course!	
Catal.	You can't! You must be mad!	
	Remember what you've done there, and remember	
	Too that, though we think our life may last	
	Forever, it's over, gone, you're up the spout,	180
	And then the fires of hell to think about!	
D. Juan	All in good time, my friend, I'll meet that debt.	
	Plenty of fun in store as yet. . .	
Catal.	But master. . .	
D. Juan	Get moving! You've become a tedious fellow,	
	Extremely boring, and irrationally	185
	Fearful.	
Catal.	Admire the Turk, sir, and the Scythian!	
	Admire the Lybian, Persian and Galician!	
	The fierce caveman, the courageous German.	
	The Japanese with their reputation;	
	Admire, if you want, sir, the old tailor,	190
	His needle fashioning the well-known story.	
	Such bravery, master, but not for me!	

Exit Catalinón

D. Juan	The night, enveloped in darkest shadow, spreads	
	Its silence. The bright Pleiades, adorned	
	With starry clusters, treads the highest point	195
	Of heaven. Now comes the hour when I must seize	
	The opportunity to exercise	
	My cunning; when I, guided by the power	

---

north shore of the Black Sea about 100 B.C., were wildly feared. The
reference to the old tailor 'fashioning the well-known story' is
presumably to the well-known ballad which begins 'How white and
beautiful you are, my love' which recounts the story of a young
woman's adultery while her husband is away and his subsequent
vengeance. Clearly, the situation of the ballad has a relevance to Don
Juan, for his seduction of various women will, in Catalinón's view, lead
to trouble. In short, Catalinón is not anxious to face avenging
husbands or lovers.

194   The bright Pleiades: in Greek mythology the seven daughters of Atlas
and Pleïone. They killed themselves through grief over the death of
their sisters, the Hyades, and were set by Jupiter as a group of stars
in the heavens.

137

	a mi inclinación, de quien	
	no hay hombre que se resista.	200
	Quiero llegar a la cama.	
	¡Aminta!	

Sale Aminta como que está acostada

Aminta	¿Quién llama a Aminta?	
	¿Es mi Batricio?	
D. Juan	No soy	
	tu Batricio.	
Aminta	Pues ¿quién?	
D. Juan	Mira	
	de espacio, Aminta, quién soy.	205
Aminta	¡Ay de mí! ¡yo soy perdida!	
	¿En mi aposento a estas horas?	
D. Juan	Estas son las horas mías.	
Aminta	Volveos, que daré voces.	
	No excedáis la cortesía	210
	que a mi Batricio se debe.	
	Ved que hay romanas Emilias	
	en Dos-Hermanas también,	
	y hay Lucrecias vengativas.	
D. Juan	Escúchame dos palabras,	215
	y esconde de las mejillas	
	en el corazón la grana,	
	por ti más preciosa y rica.	
Aminta	Vete, que vendrá mi esposo.	
D. Juan	Yo lo soy; ¿de qué te admiras?	220
Aminta	¿Desde cuándo?	
D. Juan	Desde agora.	
Aminta	¿Quién lo ha tratado?	
D. Juan	Mi dicha.	
Aminta	¿Y quién nos casó?	

202+   Aminta appears . . . .: it seems very likely that Aminta emerges here
       from an area at the back of the stage which in the Golden-Age theatre
       was known as the 'discovery space' or inner stage. This was situated
       below the gallery which ran across the back of the stage, and between
       the two doors through which entrances and exits were made. The
       'discovery space', curtained off, was ideally suited to suggesting an
       inner room, such as a bedroom, or even a prison cell, as is the case in
       the opening scenes of Calderón's *La vida es sueño* where the
       man-beast, Segismundo, chained and attired in animal skins, is revealed
       to us in his dark prison-tower.

208   my special hours: another reference which has the effect of investing
       Don Juan with daemonic significance. See Act I, 15, note.

209   call for help: the point here is that if Aminta calls out, the presence of

```
              Of love, pursue its irresistible
              Attraction, faithful to my inclination.                 200
              I approach Aminta's bed. I'll call her name.
              Aminta!
        Aminta appears, as though she has been sleeping
Aminta          Who calls Aminta? Is that you,
              Batricio? Is it you?
D. Juan                            I assure you,
              Aminta, I'm not your sweet Batricio.
Aminta        Who are you?
D. Juan                     Look, observe, Aminta! Don't         205
              You recognize me?
Aminta                          You! And in my bedroom
              At this late hour! My reputation's ruined!
D. Juan       These late hours are my special hours.
Aminta        Leave me alone! Don't make me call for help!
              You dare to throw aside your obligation,           210
              Your debt and loyalty to my Batricio!
              Remember that in Dos Hermanas too,
              No less than in the world of ancient Rome,
              Lucretias and Emilias may be found
              Who will extract their vengeance!
D. Juan                                    Let me speak!         215
              No need to be afraid! The blush of your
              Cheeks, made lovlier still through being yours,
              Is better buried deep within your heart.
Aminta        Go quickly! My husband will soon be here!
D. Juan       I am your husband. Why this strange surprise?     220
Aminta        Since when are you my husband?
D. Juan                                    From today!
Aminta        And who's arranged the marriage?
D. Juan                                    My good fortune.
Aminta        Who's wedded you to me?
```

---

a stranger in her bedroom will become public knowledge and will lead to
her dishonour. A similar situation occurs in Act II of Lope de Vega's
Peribáñez when Casilda, startled by the appearance of the
Comendador in her bedroom, refrains from calling for assistance. See
Act III, 85, note, of *The Trickster*.

212   Dos Hermanas: see Act II, 695, note.

214   Lucretias and Emilias: Lucretia, wife of Collatinus, was violated by the
Roman Emperor, Sextus Tarquinius, and committed suicide. In literature
she is often mentioned as the epitome of wifely fidelity. The reference
to Emilia is less clear since there were several Roman Emilias. The wife
of Scipio Africanus was especially renowned for her fortitude in
adversity.

220   your husband: see Act II, 718, note.

D. Juan	Tus ojos.
Aminta	¿Con qué poder?
D. Juan	Con la vista.
Aminta	¿Sábelo Batricio?
D. Juan	Sí, 225
	que te olvida.
Aminta	¿Que me olvida?
D. Juan	Sí, que yo te adoro.
Aminta	¿Cómo?
D. Juan	Con mis dos brazos.
Aminta	Desvía.
D. Juan	¿Cómo puedo, si es verdad
	que muero?
Aminta	¡Qué gran mentira! 230
D. Juan	Aminta, escucha y sabrás,
	si quieres que te lo diga,
	la verdad, que las mujeres
	sois de verdades amigas.
	Yo soy noble caballero, 235
	cabeza de la familia
	de los Tenorios, antiguos
	ganadores de Sevilla.
	Mi padre, después del rey,
	se reverencia y estima, 240
	y en la corte, de sus labios
	pende la muerte o la vida.
	Corriendo el camino acaso,
	llegué a verte, que amor guía
	tal vez las cosas de suerte, 245
	que él mismo dellas se olvida.
	Vite, adoréte, abraséme
	tanto, que tu amor me anima
	a que contigo me case;
	mira qué acción tan precisa. 250

---

224 Why, sight: in Act I Don Juan observes that Tisbea's eyes destroy him with their gaze. See 941, note, on the way in which love and the power of love are communicated through the eyes. In Aminta's case, as in Tisbea's, Don Juan is, of course, putting on his stock performance.

229 away from you: on absence from the loved one, see Act I, 205, note.

231 A lie: as indicated previously, Aminta is probably the most moral character in the play, and certainly the one who least deserves to be

D. Juan	Your eyes, so bright!
Aminta	Who's given you authority?
D. Juan	Why, sight,
	Of course!
Aminta	Batricio hasn't!
D. Juan	But he knows. 225
	And wishes to forget you!
Aminta	Forget me?
D. Juan	Since I adore and worship you!
Aminta	But how?
D. Juan	With these two arms of mine!
Aminta	You stay away
	From me!
D. Juan	How can I when, away from you,
	I die?
Aminta	Because I know your every word's 230
	A lie.
D. Juan	Aminta, listen and you'll know
	I speak the truth, for women are the friends
	Of truth and thus are able to distinguish
	Clearly between the man whose only wish
	Is to deceive, and he who tells the truth. 235
	I am a nobleman, heir to the great
	Tenorio family, the ancient founders
	Of Seville. My father, second in fame
	And reputation only to the King,
	Is in the Court Chief Justice, on whose word 240
	There hangs the life or death of every man.
	And so it happened, as I was passing by,
	My eyes beheld you, guided by the hand
	Of love, whose influence so rules our lives
	By chance, that love itself, more often than not, 245
	Forgets the lovers conquered by its glance.
	I saw you, I adored you, you inflamed
	My passions so, that love for you ordained
	That I should seek your hand in marriage,
	Transforming adoration into action. 250

---

disgraced. On the other hand, while mistrusting Don Juan, she is also flattered by his intentions, naturally enough in the light of her inexperience and social position.

237　the ancient founders: various historical sources suggest that the Tenorio family, some of whom were stewards of the dukes of Osuna, had been involved in the conquest of Seville if not in its founding.

240　Chief Justice: see Act III, 164, note.

	Y aunque lo mormure el reino,	
	y aunque el rey lo contradiga,	
	y aunque mi padre enojado	
	con amenazas lo impida,	
	tu esposo tengo de ser.	255
	¿Qué dices?	
Aminta	No sé qué diga,	
	que se encubren tus verdades	
	con retóricas mentiras.	
	Porque si estoy desposada,	
	como es cosa conocida,	260
	con Batricio, el matrimonio	
	no se absuelve aunque él desista.	
D. Juan	En no siendo consumado,	
	por engaño o por malicia	
	puede anularse.	
Aminta	En Batricio	265
	puede anularse.	
D. Juan	Ahora bien: dame esa mano,	
	y esta voluntad confirma	
	con ella.	
Aminta	¿Que no me engañas?	
D. Juan	Mío el engaño sería.	270
Aminta	Pues jura que cumplirás	
	la palabra prometida.	
D. Juan	Juro a esta mano, señora,	
	infierno de nieve fría,	
	de cumplirte la palabra.	275
Aminta	Jura a Dios que te maldiga	
	si no la cumples.	
D. Juan	Si acaso	
	la palabra y la fe mía	
	te faltaré, ruego a Dios	
	que a traición y alevosía	280
	me dé muerte un hombre. . .	
	([Ap.] muerto: que, vivo, ¡Dios no	
	permita!)	

---

251   the kingdom disapprove: Don Juan's suggestion here is that opposition to the marriage would be on grounds of social inequality. He conveniently omits to mention his flouting of the arranged marriage to Isabela as another reason for the King's disapproval, were he to be aware of it.

255   I give my word: yet another example of a promise made.

263   unconsummated: how does Don Juan know this? Batricio does not speak about this aspect of his marriage to Aminta in the earlier conversation with Don Juan. Either Don Juan is guessing, and hoping for the

142

	And even though the kingdom disapprove	
	It and the King express his opposition	
	To our union, or my father's anger	
	Threaten to bring about our separation,	
	I give my word that I shall be your husband.	255
	Give me your answer!	
Aminta	How shall I answer?	
	I suspect that words which all seem truthful	
	Are just a pretty covering for lies.	
	In any case, if, as the whole world knows,	
	My marriage vows now tie me to Batricio,	260
	He's still my husband, that's a sure fact,	
	And nothing you can do destroys that pact.	
D. Juan	A marriage which remains unconsummated	
	Whether the cause be malice or deceit,	
	Is clearly a marriage null and void.	265
Aminta	Batricio's without malice or deceit.	
D. Juan	Come now. Enough of that. Give me your hand	
	And with it confirmation of your oath	
	And promise.	
Aminta	You promise you won't deceive	
	Me!	
D. Juan	Deceive you is to deceive myself!	270
Aminta	Then swear to me you'll never break your word,	
	And promise that our marriage is assured.	
D. Juan	I swear, my dearest, by this lovely hand,	
	White as the whitest snow yet full of fire,	
	That I, as you command, will keep my word.	275
Aminta	Then swear to God, for if you break that vow,	
	Your punishment is His to take.	
D. Juan	I swear	
	That if somehow I fail to keep my word	
	To you, all given in good faith, then God	
	Repay my treachery and bring about	280
	My death at someone else's hands. . . *[Aside]* Provided	
	That someone is already dead himself!	

---

confirmation which Aminta gives in 266, or the matter is common
knowledge.

270   Deceive you is to deceive myself!: Don Juan's words, taken at face
value by Aminta, are not as straightforward in meaning as they seem.
Put in a different way, the meaning could well be 'To seduce you is to
be the seducer myself', and in that sense Don Juan really does keep
his word. Clearly, the whole of his oath is ironic, the promise which he
vows to keep being the promise which he has made to himself that the
deception of Aminta will be his finest trick.

Aminta	Pues con ese juramento	
	soy tu esposa.	
D. Juan	El alma mía	
	entre los brazos te ofrezco.	285
Aminta	Tuya es el alma y la vida.	
D. Juan	¡Ay, Aminta de mis ojos!	
	Mañana sobre virillas	
	de tersa plata estrellada	
	con clavos de oro de Tíbar,	290
	pondrás los hermosos pies,	
	y en prisión de gargantillas	
	la alabastrina garganta,	
	y los dedos en sortijas,	
	en cuyo engaste parezcan	295
	trasparentes perlas finas.	
Aminta	A tu voluntad, esposo,	
	la mía desde hoy se inclina:	
	tuya soy.	
D. Juan	[Ap.] ¡Qué mal conoces	
	al Burlador de Sevilla!	300

Vanse. Salen Isabela y Fabio, de camino

Isabela	¡Que me robase el dueño,	
	la prenda que estimaba y más quería!	
	¡Oh, riguroso empeño.	
	de la verdad! ¡Oh, máscara del día!	
	¡Noche al fin, tenebrosa	305
	antípoda del sol, del sueño esposa!	
Fabio	¿De qué sirve, Isabela,	
	la tristeza en el alma y en los ojos,	
	si amor todo es cautela,	
	y en campos de desdenes causa enojos,	310

---

295   the whiteness of your skin: Don Juan addresses the peasant girl in
       language with which she is totally unfamiliar and offers her presents
       beyond her wildest dreams. It is little wonder that she should be
       overwhelmed by such an experience. In relation to language, the
       difference between Aminta and Don Juan in this respect is a pointer to
       the social gulf that separates them. Golden-Age dramatists frequently
       used the language of a play in order to make this point. Lope de
       Vega's *Peribáñez* is a particularly good example, for in the encounters
       of noblemen and peasants the different way in which they speak
       constantly underlines the theme of the unnaturalness of the overlapping
       of two very different social layers.
305   your darkness: several kinds of darkness are suggested here. First,
       the sea and the land are enveloped in darkness, for the weather is
       rough and the sun is hidden by dark clouds. Secondly, Isabela's life in

Aminta	Then I accept your vow and give my word
	I'll be your wife.
D. Juan	Within these arms of mine
	I offer you as well my very soul. 285
Aminta	And I to you my soul and life itself.
D. Juan	Aminta! As dear to me as life, as breath!
	Tomorrow you shall walk in shoes of pure
	And polished silver, whose beauty is enhanced
	By clasps and buttons of the finest gold 290
	From Africa. Your throat, whiter than
	The purest alabaster, shall be encased
	In necklaces, imprisoning its flesh,
	And on your fingers dazzling rings whose beauty
	Is eclipsed by the whiteness of your skin. 295
Aminta	From this day forth my will, oh dearest husband,
	Inclines to yours. Your wish is my command!
	Do with me as you will!
D. Juan	[Aside] Of that she can
	Be absolutely sure! I'll keep that promise
	And prove I am the trickster of Seville! 300

Exit both. Enter Isabela and Fabio dressed as travellers

Isabela	That he should rob me of the only master
	Of my soul; of the man I dearly love!
	That lies should cruelly masquerade as truth,
	And night assume the appearance of day!
	Oh, night, your darkness banishes the light, 305
	Obliterates the sun and allies you
	With sleep!
Fabio	But what's the point of all this weeping,
	Isabela? Of all these sighs and tears?
	I tell you, love's a maze, a cunning game
	That's full of tricks, disdain and cruel lies, 310

---

general has been darkened by the events that have overtaken her, and
the loss of her name and reputation is equivalent to the obliteration of
the sun. The correlation of man and the natural world, microcosm and
macrocosm, is, of course, highly characteristic of seventeenth-century
literature. Again the reader is referred to E.M.W. Tillyard. See Act I,
348, note.

307   With sleep!: if night is associated with sleep, sleep is also associated
with death. Isabela's dishonour is for her a kind of death, and she will
not truly live again until her honour is restored by marriage to the man
who has seduced her and deprived her of her good name.
    all this weeping: this passage is similar in its ironic tone and its
deflation of Isabela's weighty sentiments to Ripio's response to Octavio's
complaints in Act I, 191-242. It is another good example of the
juxtaposition of serious and comic elements in the drama of the Golden
Age.

	si el que se ríe agora	
	en breve espacio desventuras llora?	
	El mar está alterado	
	y en grave temporal, riesgo se corre.	
	El abrigo han tomado	315
	las galeras, duquesa, de la torre	
	que esta playa corona.	
Isabela	¿Dónde estamos ahora?	
Fabio	En Tarragona.	
	De aquí a poco espacio	
	daremos en Valencia, ciudad bella,	320
	del mismo sol palacio.	
	Divertiráste algunos días en ella,	
	y después a Sevilla,	
	irás a ver la octava maravilla.	
	Que si a Octavio perdiste,	
	más galán es don Juan, y de Tenorio	
	solar. ¿De qué estás triste?	
	Conde dicen que es ya don Juan Tenorio;	
	el rey con él te casa,	
	y el padre es la privanza de su casa.	330
Isabela	No nace mi tristeza	
	de ser esposa de don Juan, que el mundo	
	conoce su nobleza;	
	en la esparcida voz mi agravio fundo,	
	que esta opinión perdida	335
	es de llorar mientras tuviere vida.	
Fabio	Allí una pescadora	
	tiernamente suspira y se lamenta,	
	y dulcemente llora.	
	Acá viene, sin duda, y verte intenta.	340
	Mientras llamo tu gente,	
	lamentaréis las dos más dulcemente.	

Vase Fabio y sale Tisbea

---

317 towers: these would have been watchtowers, erected to warn of invasion by sea, especially by Turks and Moors. See Act I, 429, note.

324 Eighth wonder of the world: while Fabio applies the description to Seville, Don Gonzalo de Ulloa has previously spoken of Lisbon in exactly the same way. See Act I, 722. This suggests quite clearly that there is a deliberate intention in the play to compare and contrast the two cities.

335 blackening my reputation: that is to say, Isabela is still the subject of common gossip. Even though her marriage to Don Juan will provide her

	And in the end gets on your wick! Show me	
	The lover whose happy sighs won't soon become	
	His anguished cries! Look at the sea, how rough	
	It is! The waves whipped up! A real tempest!	
	The ships are making for the greater safety	315
	Of the harbour, lowering their anchor	
	Where those great towers overlook the shore.	
Isabela	What is this place?	
Fabio	This place is Tarragona,	
	Duchess. A few days' travelling, we'll reach	
	Valencia, the most beautiful of cities,	320
	Aboae and palace of the sun itself.	
	Spend a few days there, take in all the sights,	
	And then our journey's onward to Seville,	
	Eighth wonder of the world in all its glory.	
	As for Octavio, you may well have lost	325
	Him, but Don Juan's an even better catch,	
	So snatch him while you can! Don't be so sad!	
	That's madness when Don Juan's to be a count!	
	The King himself has called the marriage banns,	
	And Don Juan's father is his right-hand man!	330
Isabela	It's not the marriage to Don Juan that makes	
	Me sad. The whole world knows of his most noble	
	Birth and origins. I would gladly be	
	His wife on that account, but sadly they	
	Pursue me, blackening my reputation,	335
	And in lost honour there is no salvation.	
Fabio	My lady, look! A fishergirl approaches.	
	Like you she fills the air with anguished sighs.	
	Like you her tears fill her lovely eyes.	
	No doubt she wants to have a word with you.	340
	I'll disappear, fetch the others. Better	
	For you two if you bare your souls together!	

Exit Fabio. Enter Tisbea

---

with status, it will not prevent people from continuing to talk about her earlier disgrace.

343   I curse you: see Catalinon's similar attack on the sea and the invention of ships in Act I, 541. Tisbea's language here is as full of elaborate conceits as when we first saw her in Act I. Thus, the ocean contains not only water but fire – in the sense that it deposited the passionate Don Juan literally on her doorstep. His subsequent behaviour brought her grief, expressed in tears which not merely wet her cheeks but burn them, such is her shame. Once more the character of Tisbea's language can be described as Gongoresque. See Act I, 376, note.

Tisbea	Robusto mar de España,
	ondas de fuego, fugitivas ondas,
	Troya de mi cabaña, 345
	que ya el fuego, por mares y por ondas,
	en sus abismos fragua,
	y el mar forma, por las llamas, agua.
	¡Maldito el leño sea
	que a tu amargo cristal halló carrera, 350
	antojo de Medea,
	tu cáñamo primero o primer lino,
	aspado de los vientos
	para telas de engaños e instrumentos!
Isabela	¿Por qué del mar te quejas 355
	tan tiernamente, hermosa pescadora?
Tisbea	Al mar formo mil quejas.
	¡Dichosa vos, que en su tormento, agora
	dél os estáis riendo!
Isabela	También quejas del mar estoy haciendo. 360
	¿De dónde sois?
Tisbea	De aquellas
	cabañas que miráis del viento heridas
	tan vitorioso entre ellas,
	cuyas pobre paredes desparcidas
	van en pedazos graves, 365
	dando en mil grietas nidos a las aves.
	En sus pajas me dieron
	corazón de fortísimo diamante;
	mas las obras me hicieron,
	deste monstruo que ves tan arrogante, 370
	ablandarme de suerte,
	que al sol la cera es más robusta y fuerte.
	¿Sois vos la Europa hermosa?
	¿Que esos toros os llevan?
Isabela	A Sevilla
	llévanme a ser esposa 375
	contra mi voluntad.

---

351   <u>Medea's grief</u>: in Greek legend Medea helped Jason obtain the Golden Fleece and fled with him to Thessaly. He subsequently abandoned her for Creusa, the daughter of the King of Corinth, and Medea, overwhelmed by grief and hatred, took vengeance by murdering her children.

372   <u>melts hardest wax</u>: a contemporary audience, well-versed in classical legend, would have thought immediately of Icarus, whose father Daedalus constructed wings held together by wax in order to escape from Crete. In the course of the flight Icarus ventured too near the

Tisbea	I curse you, cruel sea, for your waves,	
	As full of blazing fire as of foam,	
	Destroyed my little cottage, burnt my home	345
	As if it were as great as ancient Troy!	
	Who would have thought that from your salty deep	
	Flames would emerge and tears scald my cheeks?	
	I curse the wood that, made into a boat,	
	Made your bitter surface its abode,	350
	In imitation of Medea's grief.	
	That canvas, that great sweep of sail and cloth	
	Nailed to a wooden cross, is but a spider's	
	Web in which all our dearest hopes are lost!	
Isabela	Sweet fishergirl, tell me why you complain	355
	So bitterly, and of the sea's treachery!	
Tisbea	Of the sea I complain a thousand fold,	
	While you, though buffeted by its assaults,	
	Can happily afford to laugh at it.	
Isabela	But I, like you, have good cause for complaint.	360
	Where are you from?	
Tisbea	You see that cottage there?	
	That tiny cabin was my home where now	
	The wind alone proclaims its victory.	
	Its poor walls reduced to dust or full	
	Of holes, where once I took my happy rest,	365
	Are now a ruin where only birds can nest.	
	There in its straw I lived a happy life,	
	My heart as hard as diamond to all	
	Men's sighs, until the sea in all its fury,	
	This fierce monster, conspired to bring	370
	About my ruin, softening my heart	
	As quickly as the sun melts hardest wax.	
	My friend, are you the beautiful Europa,	
	Borne by bulls to your cruel destiny?	
Isabela	Seville's my destination. My destiny	375
	A marriage now imposed on me against	
	My will.	

---

sun, the wax melted, and the boy plunged to his death in the sea. In Renaissance and post-Renaissance literature the fate of Icarus became a metaphor for excessive pride and confidence and in this context Tisbea's allusion is appropriately ironic.

373   the beautiful Europa: according to legend, Europa, virgin of Tyre, was abducted by Jupiter in the form of a bull. A version of the legend has it that Jupiter abandoned Europa on the coast of Tarragona. Tisbea's allusion to bulls may also have something to do with the fact that large boats arriving at Spanish destinations were pulled into the shore by oxen. Isabela has, of course, arrived by boat from Italy.

Tisbea	Si mi mancilla

Tisbea   Si mi mancilla
a lástima os provoca,
y si injurias del mar os tienen loca,
en vuestra compañía,
para serviros como humilde esclava   380
me llevad; que querría,
si el dolor o la afrenta no me acaba,
pedir al rey justicia
de un engaño cruel, de una malicia.
Del agua derrotado,   385
a esta tierra llegó don Juan Tenorio,
difunto y anegado:
amparéle, hospedéle en tan notorio
peligro, y el vil güésped
víbora fué a mi planta en tierno césped.   390
Con palabra de esposo,
la que de esta costa burla hacía,
se rindió al engañoso:
¡Mal haya la mujer que en hombres fía!
Fuese al fin y dejóme: 395
mira si es justo que venganza tome.

Isabela   ¡Calla, mujer maldita!
Vete de mi presencia, que me has muerto.
Mas si el dolor te incita,
no tienes culpa tú, prosigue el cuento.   400

Tisbea   La dicha fuera mía.

Isabela   ¡Mal haya la mujer que en hombres fía!
¿Quién tiene de ir contigo?

Tisbea   Un pescador, Anfriso; un pobre padre
de mis males testigo.   405

Isabela   [Ap.] No hay venganza que a mi mal tanto
Ven en mi compañía.   [le cuadre.

Tisbea   ¡Mal haya la mujer que en hombres fía!

*Vanse Tisbea y Isabela. Salen Don Juan
y Catalinón*

Catal.   Todo en mal estado está.

D. Juan   ¿Cómo?

Catal.   Que Octavio ha sabido   410
la traición de Italia ya,

---

390   a viper: there are many legends concerning the viper. The female was
said, for example, to conceive through its mouth, and in the very act
of conception to bite off the male's head. On giving birth, the female
herself suffered an equally horrible fate, for her offspring simply tore
their way through her breast. Acts of such ingratitude clearly led to
the association of the viper with any ungrateful or treacherous person.

Tisbea	Then if my plight moves you to feel
	Some pity for me, and the sea's injustice
	Is the source of your anguish, I beg you
	Take me with you. I'll be your loyal servant.	380
	My greatest wish, if only my anguish
	And dishonour allow me to survive,
	Is to obtain the justice of the King
	As punishment for such a vile deception.
	Don Juan Tenorio, spewed up by the waves,	385
	Set foot upon this shore, a man more dead
	Than living from the water still inside him.
	I cared for him, provided him with shelter
	Until he was much better, when he showed
	His gratitude, a viper at my feet!	390
	Believing his promise he'd be my husband,
	I, the girl whose pleasure was deceiving
	Others, was cruelly deceived by him!
	More fool the woman who puts her faith and trust
	In men! Finally he abandoned me.	395
	Surely there's justice in my claim for vengeance!
Isabela	I want to hear no more! A curse on you!
	Leave me alone! Your every word destroys
	Me! But no! No! For grief incites your anguish.
	The fault's not yours! Continue your story!	400
Tisbea	If only the story ended happily!
Isabela	More fool the woman who puts her faith and trust
	In men! And who are your two companions?
Tisbea	A fisherman, Anfriso, and a poor
	Father, both witnesses to my offence.	405
Isabela	*[Aside]* No vengeance is too great as punishment
	For this man's crimes! *[Aloud]* Let's go together then!
Tisbea	More fool the woman who puts her faith in men!

Exit Tisbea and Isabela. Enter Don Juan and Catalinón

Catal.	I fancy things are going from bad to worse!
D. Juan	Explain yourself!
Catal.	Well, first of all, Octavio	410
	Knows what really happened in Italy.

---

394   faith and trust: Tisbea's pronouncement about men can be compared
with the observations in the play made by men about women – by the
King of Naples, for example, Act I, 153-56, and by Octavio, Act I,
357-59.
398-9   destroys/Me!: Isabela's marriage to Don Juan will not, as she has
observed, prevent people from talking about her seduction. How much
more her peace of mind is endangered should Tisbea's fate also become
known!

	y el de la Mota ofendido	
	de ti justas quejas da,	
	y dice, que fué el recaudo,	
	que de su prima le diste	415
	fingido y disimulado,	
	y con su capa emprendiste	
	la traición que le ha infamado.	
	Dice que viene Isabela	
	a que seas su marido,	420
	y dicen. . .	

D. Juan   ¡Calla!
Catal.   Una muela
        en la boca me has rompido.
D. Juan   Hablador, ¿quién te revela
        tantos disparates juntos?
Catal.   ¡Disparate, disparate!   425
        Verdades son.
D. Juan   No pregunto
        si lo son. Cuando me mate
        Otavio: ¿estoy yo difunto?
        ¿No tengo manos también?
        ¿Dónde me tienes posada?   430
Catal.   En la calle, oculta.
D. Juan   Bien
Catal.   La iglesia es tierra sagrada.
D. Juan   Di que de día me den
        en ella la muerte. ¿Viste
        al novio de Dos-Hermanas?   435
Catal.   También le vi ansiado y triste.
D. Juan   Aminta, estas dos semanas,
        no ha de caer en el chiste.
Catal.   Tan bien engañada está,
        que se llama doña Aminta.   440
D. Juan   ¡Graciosa burla será!
Catal.   Graciosa burla y sucinta,
        mas siempre la llorará.

   Descúbrese un sepulcro de Don Gonzalo
   de Ulloa

D. Juan   ¿Qué sepulcro es éste?

---

422   <u>broken a precious tooth:</u> Don Juan, driven to distraction by Catalinón's
       prattling, suddenly loses control, hits him across the face and breaks
       one of his teeth. This is a finely observed moment on Tirso's part, for
       Don Juan's bravado is suddenly seen to be pierced by real doubt and
       uncertainty. He recovers quickly his former coolness, but the loss of

	Then Mota, your friend so grievously	
	Offended by you, bitterly complains	
	Of treachery. His claim is that the message	
	Which his cousin gave you, you passed to him	415
	In quite a different form, its meaning changed.	
	On top of that you took his cloak and tricked	
	His girl-friend, on account of which he stands	
	Accused himself. And then there's Isabela.	
	I've heard it said you'll have to marry her!	420
	The story has it too. . .	
D. Juan	Shut up!	
Catal.	You've gone	
	And broken a precious tooth! You have a look!	
D. Juan	You idle chatterbox! Who filled your head	
	With all that silly nonsense? Talk some sense!	
Catal.	But master, how can it be nonsense when	425
	It's common-sense and every word's the truth?	
D. Juan	Why should I care? If Octavio ever dares	
	To raise his hands against me, do I not	
	Have these hands for my defence? Stop your chatter	
	And show me where you've found us board and lodge.	
Catal.	It's down this street, a dark and quiet place.	
D. Juan	It suits me well.	
Catal.	This church is hallowed ground.	
D. Juan	Which means, my friend, that if I'm ever found	
	In it, I'm safe and sound! No need to worry!	
	Have you seen the bridegroom from Dos Hermanas?	435
Catal.	I saw him too. A sad and sorry sight!	
D. Juan	Aminta's not exactly bright! It's two	
	Weeks on. She doesn't believe she's been deceived.	
Catal.	You've tricked her good and proper, ain't yer?	
	She even calls herself Lady Aminta!	440
D. Juan	A real good laugh! Brings tears to my eyes!	
Catal.	No doubt, master! A sharp and cunning trick!	
	When she finds out, she'll laugh herself quite sick!	

They come across the tomb of Don Gonzalo de Ulloa

| D. Juan | Whose tomb is this? |

153

Catal.	Aquí	
	don Gonzalo está enterrado.	445
D. Juan	Este es al que muerte di.	
	¡Gran sepulcro le han labrado!	
Catal.	Ordenólo el rey ansí.	
	¿Cómo dice este letrero?	
D. Juan	"Aquí aguarda del Señor,	450
	el más leal caballero,	
	la venganza de un traidor."	
	Del mote reírme quiero.	
	¿Y habéisos vos de vengar,	
	buen viejo, barbas de piedra?	455
Catal.	No se las podrás pelar,	
	que en barbas muy fuertes medra.	
D. Juan	Aquesta noche a cenar	
	os aguardo en mi posada.	
	Allí el desafío haremos,	460
	si la venganza os agrada;	
	aunque mal reñir podremos,	
	si es de piedra vuestra espada.	
Catal.	Ya, señor, ha anochecido;	
	vámonos a recoger.	465
D. Juan	Larga esta venganza ha sido.	
	Si es que vos la habéis de hacer,	
	importa no estar dormido,	
	que si a la muerte aguardáis	
	la venganza, la esperanza	470
	agora es bien que perdáis,	
	pues vuestros enojo y venganza	
	tan largo me lo fiáis.	

Vanse y ponen la mesa dos Criados *

C. 1.*	Quiero apercebir la cena,	
	que vendrá a cenar don Juan.	475
C. 2.*	Puestas las mesas están.	
	¡Qué flema tiene si empieza!	
	Ya tarda como solía,	
	mi señor; no me contenta;	
	la bebida se calienta	480
	y la comida se enfría.	

---

455   your beard's hard and stony: Don Juan's pulling of the statue's beard
       suggests that the figure of Don Gonzalo de Ulloa is not standing but
       prone, as is often the case in Spanish churches. Given that the tomb
       is, in Don Juan's words, a 'splendid monument', it would probably be
       quite high, the stone figure placed on a large block of marble. In order
       to pull the beard Don Juan might well have to climb onto the block

Catal.	Whose tomb? I though you'd know.	
	This tomb belongs to your old friend, Gonzalo!	445
D. Juan	What? The very same Gonzalo I sent	
	Packing! For him this splendid monument?	
Catal.	They say they built it at the King's command.	
	They've put some lettering here. See what it says!	
D. Juan	'Here lies buried a noble gentleman,	450
	A loyal subject of the realm, whom God	
	Has promised vengeance on an evil traitor'.	
	Well isn't that a laugh? Foolish old man!	
	You really intend to avenge yourself on me?	
	You can't move! Even your beard's hard and stony!	455
Catal.	No point in pulling it! He only stares!	
	It's not the sort of beard that needs much care!	
D. Juan	[To the statue] Tonight, my friend, a special invitation.	
	Have dinner with me! A special celebration	
	Where I'm staying! There you can challenge me	460
	If you want, see if you can take your vengeance.	
	Though I can't see you making me atone,	
	Not when that sword of yours is made of stone.	
Catal.	Look, master, it's as black as night in here.	
	We ought to get back to our place I'm sure.	465
D. Juan	[To the statue] Your vengeance is a long time coming, sir!	
	If you intend to take it, best be sure	
	You aren't as still and sleepy as you seem.	
	A man in your state can only dream	
	Of vengeance and wait in hope till doomsday.	470
	A forlorn hope you'd just as well forget!	
	Plenty of time for me to pay that debt!	
	They leave. Two servants lay the table	
First	I'd better get a move on, warm his supper.	
Servant	If it's not done, I'm sure to come a cropper.	
Second	The table's laid. There's nothing else to do.	475
Servant	Don Juan's a cool one. You can be quite sure	
	He'll take his time, as usual, even though	
	The wine, instead of being cool, is hot,	
	And what was quite a supper's gone to pot!	

---

itself. The pulling of a man's beard was, of course, an insult, and had been from ancient times. There are frequent references to it in the medieval Spanish epic, the *Poema de Mío Cid*. As far as staging is concerned, a Golden-Age production in a public theatre would probably have the statue located in the 'discovery space'.

472+   lay the table: the scene changes here to the inn in which Catalinón has found a room.

```
                Mas, ¿quién a don Juan ordena
                esta desorden?
         Entran Don Juan y Catalinón
D. Juan                   ¿Cerraste?
Catal.     Ya cerré como mandaste.
D. Juan    ¡Hola! Tráigenme la cena.                    485
C. 2.°     Ya está aquí.
D. Juan                   Catalinón,
           siéntate.
Catal.              Yo soy amigo
           de cenar de espacio.
D. Juan                        Digo
           que te sientes.
Catal.                    La razón
           haré.
C. 1.°         También es camino                        490
           éste, si come con él.
D. Juan    Siéntate.
         Un golpe dentro
Catal.                  Golpe es aquél.
D. Juan    Que llamaron imagino;
           mira quién es.
C. 1.°                    Voy volando.
Catal.     ¿Si es la justicia, señor?                   495
D. Juan    Sea, no tengas temor.
         Vuelve el Criado, huyendo
           ¿Quién es? ¿De qué estás temblando?
Catal.     De algún mal da testimonio.
D. Juan    Mal mi cólera resisto.
           Habla, responde, ¿qué has visto?            500
           ¿Asombróte algún demonio?
           Ve tú, y mira aquella puerta:
           ¡presto, acaba!
Catal.                    ¿Yo?
D. Juan                       Tú, pues.
           Acaba, menea los pies.
Catal.     A mi agüela hallaron muerta                  505
           como racimo colgada,
           y desde entonces se suena
```

---

492   to share his food and drink: clearly, the servants are surprised by the
        fact that Catalinón should be ordered to share his master's table.
493+   *A mighty knock is heard:* the door which figures so prominently in this
        episode would have been, in a seventeenth-century production, one of

                    Anyway, who can order our Don Juan,   480
                    The very architect of all disorder?
          Enter Don Juan and Catalinón
D. Juan   Make sure you've shut the door!
Catal.   It's shut, master,
                    And bolted! Exactly as you ordered.
D. Juan   Hey, you two! Have you got my dinner ready?
Second Servant   Of course, sir! Here it is!
D. Juan   Catalinón!   485
                    Sit down! Pacing around! What is the matter?
Catal.   Truth is, master, I don't want to get fatter!
                    Besides, I like to take my time if you
                    Don't mind.
D. Juan   Sit down I said! Do what you're told!
Catal.   Alright! If you say so! I'm not so bold   490
                    As to disobey an order!
First Servant   This one
                    Travels with him to share his food and drink!
D. Juan   Sit!
          A mighty knock is heard
Catal.   Shit! What's that?
D. Juan   I fancy someone's knock.
                    See who it is!
First Servant   At once.
Catal.   Bit of a shock
                    If it's the law. . . you know. . . a raid!   495
D. Juan   What if it is? No need to be afraid!
          The servant returns running
                    Who's there? You look as if you've seen a ghost!
Catal.   Perhaps it is, my lord! A sign we'll roast
                    In Hell!
D. Juan   Come on, man! Tell us what you saw!
                    I'm losing patience! Out with it, before   500
                    I force it out of you! An evil spirit
                    Was it? Here, you! You go and open it!
                    And get a move on!
Catal.   Me?
D. Juan   Of course! Who else?
                    Your mouth is quick enough! Why not your feet?
Catal.   I had a grandmother. They found her dead,   505
                    Just hanging like a bunch of grapes they said
                    She was, and ever since, the story goes,

---

the two doors at the back of the stage. These were sometimes actual
doors, sometimes just a curtain. In the latter case the loud knock would
have to be made off-stage.

D. Juan	que anda siempre su alma en pena.	
	Tanto golpe no me agrada.	
D. Juan	Acaba.	
Catal.	Señor, si sabes	510
	que soy un Catalinón. . .	
D. Juan	Acaba.	
Catal.	¡Fuerte ocasión!	
D. Juan	¿No vas?	
Catal.	¿Quién tiene las llaves	
	de la puerta?	
C. 2.°	Con la aldaba	
	está cerrada no más.	515
D. Juan	¿Qué tienes? ¿Por qué no vas?	
Catal.	Hoy Catalinón acaba.	
	¿Mas si las forzadas vienen	
	a vengarse de los dos?	

*Llega Catalinón a la puerta, y viene
corriendo; cae y levantase*

D. Juan	¿Qué es eso?	
Catal.	¡Válgame Dios!	
	¡Que me matan, que me tienen!	
D. Juan	¿Quién te tiene, quién te mata?	
	¿Qué has visto?	
Catal.	Señor, yo allí	
	vide cuando. . . luego fuí. . .	
	¿Quién me ase, quién me arrebata?	525
	Llegué, cuando después ciego. . .	
	cuando vile, ¡juro a Dios!. . .	
	Habló y dijo, ¿quién sois vos?. . .	
	respondió, y respondí luego. . .	
	topé y vide. . .	
D. Juan	¿A quién?	
Catal.	No sé.	530
D. Juan	¡Cómo el vino desatina!	
	Dame la vela, gallina,	
	y yo a quien llama veré.	

---

508   full of pain and woe: if Catalinón's grandmother had indeed committed suicide, a mortal sin in the eyes of the Church, her soul would, of course, be damned. In typical *gracioso* fashion, Catalinón invents an absurd story in order to delay having to answer the door. He is less

	Her spirit wanders, full of pain and woe.	
	That knock! I'm scared it might be granny's soul!	

D. Juan   Stop prattling on!
Catal.   But master! If you know   510
          That I'm the greatest coward ever lived. . .
D. Juan   I said shut up!
Catal.   Oh, what a mess this is!
D. Juan   Are you defying me?
Catal.   Who's got the key?
          The bloody door's locked!
Second Servant   Only with the bolt,
          My friend! You are a dolt if you can't open   515
          It!
D. Juan   So get a move on! You can't sit there
          All night!
Catal.   Oh, poor Catalinón's all finished!
          What if the visitors are women you
          Raped, come to take their vengeance on us two?
          Catalinón goes to the door, comes running back, falls
          down, gets up again
D. Juan   So what's the verdict?
Catal.   God help me! I thought   520
          I was going to die! I thought they'd got
          Me!
D. Juan   Who got you? Why were you going to die?
          What did you see?
Catal.   Oh, master! There was I. . .
          My goodness!. . . Oh, my word!. . . What did I see?
          Who's trying to grab me, get hold of me?   525
          I got there, had a look. . . I must be blind!
          There, I see. . . suddenly. . . Oh, God be kind
          To me. . . It spoke and 'Who are you?' it said.
          I answered, God knows what, and bumped into. . .
D. Juan   Who?
Catal.   I don't know! I haven't got a clue!   530
D. Juan   Good God! The wine has driven him insane!
          Give me the candle! A coward through and through!
          I'll go myself and see who's at the door.

---

          concerned with his own dignity than with saving his skin in the event
          of the visitor's being the stone guest.
514   locked: we can well imagine Catalinón's fumbling with the door.
          Throughout the scene his physical actions combine with his absurd
          babbling to suggest very vividly a fearful state of mind.

Toma Don Juan la vela y llega a la puerta.
Sale al encuentro Don Gonzalo, en la forma que
estaba en el sepulcro, y Don Juan se retira atrás
turbado, empuñando la espada, y en la otra la
vela, y Don Gonzalo hacia el, con pasos menudos,
y al compas Don Juan, retirandose hasta
estar en medio del teatro

D. Juan	¿Quién va?	
D. Gon.	Yo soy.	
D. Juan	¿Quién sois vos?	
D. Gon.	Soy el caballero honrado	535
	que a cenar has convidado.	
D. Juan	Cena habrá para los dos,	
	y si vienen más contigo,	
	para todos cena habrá.	
	Ya puesta la mesa está.	540
	Siéntate.	
Catal.	¡Dios sea conmigo!	
	¡San Panuncio, San Antón!	
	Pues ¿los muertos comen, di?	
	Por señas dice que sí.	
D. Juan	Siéntate, Catalinón.	545
Catal.	No, señor, yo lo recibo	
	por cenado.	
D. Juan	Es desconcierto:	
	¡qué temor tienes a un muerto!	
	¿Qué hicieras estando vivo?	
	Necio y villano temor.	550
Catal.	Cena con tu convidado,	
	que yo, señor, ya he cenado.	
D. Juan	¿He de enojarme?	

---

532   the candle: again it is worth reminding ourselves that in the seventeenth-century public theatres the play would be performed in broad daylight. As we have seen previously, nocturnal episodes are suggested very often by the dialogue, which is usually the immediate spur to the audience's imagination. The suspension of disbelief was achieved as well, however, by the fact that the actors acted in these scenes as though it were in fact night – groping and stumbling, feeling their way around, as at the very beginning of Act I, or, as here, making use of appropriate props.

533+   a slow, measured step: the literal translation of the Spanish here is 'with small steps'. Whether 'small' or 'measured', the movement of the statue suggests the stiff, automaton-like advance of a non-human figure. How, in fact, would this have been done in a seventeenth-century production? On the one hand an actor could have played the part of the statue, perhaps wearing a mask or having had his face painted, and dressed in the same clothes as the recumbent

160

Don Juan takes the candle and goes to the door. Don
Gonzalo enters in the form of the stone statue above
the tomb. Don Juan steps back, disturbed, his sword
in one hand, the candle in the other. Don Gonzalo
advances towards him with a slow, measured step.
Don Juan retreats to centre stage

D. Juan   Who are you?

D. Gon.   Who am I? The honourable
Gentleman who's come to dine with you!   535
You haven't forgotten the invitation!

D. Juan   Of course not! For this occasion there's food
Enough for both of us, and more should any
Of your friends express the wish to join us.
As you can see, the table's set and ready.   540
So take a seat!

Catal.   Oh God above protect
Me! And Saint Panuncio! And Saint Anthony!
I'll ask him a question. Do dead men eat?
Good lord! He nods his head and says they do!

D. Juan   Catalinón! You'll join us. Take a seat!   545

Catal.   Oh, thank you, master! I'd rather not! I'm full
Already!

D. Juan   Full of what? Plain foolishness?
Scared as a rabbit of a man who's dead?
I wonder what you'd do were he alive!
Still, such a fear befits a common fool!   550

Catal.   You eat, sir, with your guest! I've got a rule
That having eaten once, I ought to rest.

D. Juan   You're asking me to lose my temper!

---

figure in the church. On the other hand, the actor might have worn a
suit of armour, and it is interesting to note in this respect that
stage-directions in the earlier version of the play, *Tan largo me lo
fiáis*, suggest this. Another possibility is that an actual automaton was
used. Golden-Age stage-designers and technicians often showed
themselves to be capable of quite ingenious effects, and it is certainly a
fact that the better-off acting companies could have afforded an
automatom. For interesting observations on the subject, see J.E. Varey,
*Historia de los títeres en España (desde sus orígenes hasta mediados del
siglo XVIII)* (Madrid, 1957), in particular pp. 24–90.

542   Panuncio: Catalinón's comic corruption of Pafnucio. The corruption or
mispronunciation of names by comic characters is a common feature of
Golden-Age drama. *Panuncio* presumably suggests both *pan*, 'bread',
and *anuncio* 'I proclaim' or 'I announce'.

544   He nods his head: again the indication that the actor should adopt the
movements and gestures of a non-human is quite clear.

Catal.	Señor,
	¡vive Dios que güelo mal!
D. Juan	Llega, que aguardando estoy.	555
Catal.	Yo pienso que muerto soy,
	y está muerto mi arrabal.

Tiemblan los Criados

D. Juan	Y vosotros, ¿qué decís?
	¿Qué hacéis? ¡Necio temblar!
Catal.	Nunca quisiera cenar	560
	con gente de otro país.
	¿Yo, señor, con convidado
	de piedra?
D. Juan	¡Necio temer!
	Si es piedra, ¿qué te ha de hacer?
Catal.	Dejarme descalabrado.	565
D. Juan	Háblale con cortesía.
Catal.	¿Está bueno? ¿Es buena tierra
	la otra vida? ¿Es llano o sierra?
	¿Prémiase allá la poesía?
C. 1.°	A todo dice que sí,	570
	con la cabeza.
Catal.	¿Hay allá
	muchas tabernas? Sí habrá,
	si Noé reside allí.
D. Juan	¡Hola! dadnos de beber.
Catal.	Señor muerto, ¿allá se bebe	575
	con nieve?

Baja la cabeza

	Así, que hay nieve:
	buen país.
D. Juan	Si oír cantar
	queréis, cantarán.

Baja la cabeza

C. 2.°	Sí, dijo.
D. Juan	Cantad.
Catal.	Tiene el seor muerto
	buen gusto.
C. 1.°	Es noble, por cierto,	580
	y amigo de regocijo.

---

554   the awful smell: a moment to delight the servants and soldiers, the equivalent of the 'groundlings' in the Elizabethan theatre, who would have been standing close to the stage. At the same time, the physical manifestation of fear in Catalinón is well observed on the part of the dramatist. We can compare the incident with another in *Don Quijote*,

Catal.	Well,
	Sir, you'll have to excuse the awful smell.
D. Juan	Stop dithering! Come over here and sit! 555
Catal.	The way I'm smelling sir, I must be dead.
	Or otherwise I've accidentally shit
	Myself!

The two servants are shaking with fear

D. Juan	What's wrong with you? Come. Answer me!
	Don't tell me you both suffer from weak knees!
Catal.	I can't say, master, I'm exactly pleased 560
	To dine with anyone from overseas.
	It's even worse to eat with this one here!
	A guest who's turned to stone!
D. Juan	A foolish fear!
	A man of stone, what can he do to you?
Catal.	Oh, only split my poor head wide open. 565
D. Juan	So when you speak to him, just be polite.
Catal.	Yes, well, let's see then. . . Oh, feeling alright
	Are you, mate? Often wondered what it's like
	Down there. . . you know. . . whether its flat or hilly. . .
	And whether or not they've got any poetry. . . 570
	Know what I mean. . .?
First Servant	Looks like he's keen to agree
	With everything, the way he nods his head.
Catal.	Got many taverns, have you? Course you have,
	Seeing old Noah lives there.
D. Juan	Bring some wine
	At once!
Catal.	Pretty refined as well, I expect, 575
	Mr Dead Man. . . you know. . . ice in your drinks
	Down there!

The statue nods its head

	Hell of a fancy place, I'd think!
D. Juan	You give the word, my friend, we'll have a song.

The statue nods its head

Second Servant	He fancies hearing one.
D. Juan	All of you sing
	To him!
Catal.	You can't go wrong with him! Such taste! 580
First Servant	All noblemen enjoy a bit of fun.

Part I, ch. 20, when Sancho Panza, terrified by hammering sounds during the night, reacts in identical fashion.

574   old Noah: according to Genesis, ix, 20-21, Noah was the first man to discover wine.

	Cantan dentro	
	Si de mi amor aguardáis,	
	señora, de aquesta suerte	
	el galardón en la muerte,	
	¡qué largo me lo fiáis!	585
Catal.	O es sin duda veraniego	
	el seor muerto, o debe ser	
	hombre de poco comer.	
	Temblando al plato me llego.	
	Poco beben por allá;	590

Bebe

yo beberé por los dos.
Brindis de piedra ¡por Dios!
menos temor tengo ya.
Cantan
Si ese plazo me convida
para que gozaros pueda,
pues larga vida me queda,
dejad que pase la vida.
Si de mi amor aguardáis,
señora, de aquesta suerte
el galardón en la muerte,   600
¡qué largo me lo fiáis!

Catal.   ¿Con cuál de tantas mujeres
          como has burlado, señor,
          hablan?
D. Juan   De todas me río,
          amigo, en esta ocasión.   605
          En Nápoles a Isabela. . .
Catal.   Esa, señor, ya no es hoy
          burlada, porque se casa
          contigo, como es razón.
          Burlaste a la pescadora   610
          que del mar te redimió,
          pagándole el hospedaje
          en moneda de rigor.
          Burlaste a doña Ana. . .
D. Juan   Calla,

581+   Singing: on songs in Golden-Age plays, see Act II, 633, note. It is
        also worth making the point that songs were used very dramatically in
        the religious plays, the *autos sacramentales*, of the Golden Age. A
        chorus sung off-stage often acted, for example, as a further stimulus
        to the character who is about to transgress, while another chorus
        sought to deter him from his course of action. Although Tirso's *El*

'The lady's foolishly deceived in love,
She waits for vengeance sent down from above.
Death to the faithless lover is her prayer,
But he enjoys himself without a care.'   585

Catal.   I wonder if this fellow's on a diet.
Perhaps he isn't eating 'cos it's hot,
Or maybe he's the sort don't eat a lot.
I'll have a go at eating, though my hand's
Still shaking. Seems he doesn't fancy drinking   590
Either. Perhaps I'd better sink the lot!

Catalinón drinks
Ah, well, me old stone feller, here's to you!
I'm feeling better now, give you your due!
[Singing off-stage]
'The time you've got on earth's a tidy span.
Enjoy as many women as you can.   595
And since most of your life's in front of you,
Eat, drink, make merry as you're passing through.
The lady's foolishly deceived in love,
She waits for vengeance sent down from above.
Death to the faithless lover is her prayer,   600
But he enjoys himself without a care.'

Catal.   Hey, master, of all those women you've gone through,
Which one d'you think the song's referring to?

D. Juan   How do I know? They're all the same to me,
My friend. A good laugh, even though I fancy   605
Them! Remember Naples and Isabela?

Catal.   Of course I do! But. . . you didn't fool her,
Did you? Not now she's fixed it that you marry
Her! She'll get her own back, make you feel sorry.
The fishergirl. . . oh, yes, you took her in,   610
After she'd helped you out and saved your skin.
Offered you lodging too. A sorry sight
She was! Oh, yes, you paid her back alright!
And then there was Dona Ana. . .

D. Juan   Don't speak

---

condenado por desconfiado is not a genuine *auto sacramental*, a similar
if not identical use of song may be noted in it, a very good example
occuring in Act III where the devil's exhortation to the criminal Enrico
to escape from the prison is answered by a chorus which advises him
not to yield to temptation. In this example in *The Trickster* the two
opposing strands – the exhortation to pleasure, the warning of
retribution – are neatly combined.

	que hay parte aquí que lastó	615
	por ella, y vengarse aguarda.	
Catal.	Hombre es de mucho valor,	
	que él es piedra, tú eres carne:	
	no es buena resolución.	

Hace señas que se quite la mesa y queden
solos

D. Juan	¡Hola! quitad esa mesa,	620
	que hace señas que los dos	
	nos quedemos, y se vayan	
	los demás.	
Catal.	¡Malo, por Dios!	
	No te quedes, porque hay muerto	
	que mata de un mojicón	625
	a un gigante.	
D. Juan	Salíos todos.	
	¡A ser yo Catalinón. . .!	
	Vete, que viene.	

Vanse, y quedan los dos solos, y hace señas
que cierre la puerta

D. Juan	La puerta	
	ya está cerrada. Ya estoy	
	aguardando. Di, ¿qué quieres,	630
	sombra o fantasma o visión?	
	Si andas en pena o si aguardas	
	alguna satisfación	
	para tu remedio, dilo,	
	que mi palabra te doy	635
	de hacer lo que me ordenares.	
	¿Estás gozando de Dios?	
	¿Dite la muerte en pecado?	
	Habla, que suspenso estoy.	

Habla paso, como cosa del otro mundo

| D. Gon. | ¿Cumplirásme una palabra | 640 |
| | como caballero? | |

---

621 all his gestures: see Act III, 533 and 544, notes.
633 your soul's in torment: it has to be borne in mind that Don Gonzalo died suddenly, without confession, and was not therefore absolved of his sins. For that reason his soul is still in purgatory. A comparison may be made with Hamlet's father, poisoned in his sleep, whose ghost haunts the castle battlements at night. When Hamlet has the opportunity to avenge his father's death, he draws back from killing the murderer, Claudius, precisely because Claudius is at that moment praying, and to kill him in a state of grace would merely be to guarantee his soul a place in heaven.

615

So loudly! This fellow's resolved to keep
His word and take his vengeance if he can.

Catal.   I'm not surprised. Just look at him! A man
Of stone, and you of ordinary flesh.
I tell you straight, you're in a proper mess!

*The statue indicates that the table should be cleared
and that he and Don Juan should be left alone*

D. Juan   You there! Make sure the table's cleared quickly!   620
If I interpret all his gestures rightly,
He wants to be alone with me. You'd better
Leave us.

Catal.   Oh, master! I'm scared stiff for you!
Don't stay with him all on your own! One blow
From a man of stone's enough to finish   625
Off a giant!

D. Juan   Come on! All of you out!
I'm no Catalinón! No cause to doubt
My nerve! Away now! Our guest approaches.

*The others leave. The two men are alone. The statue
indicates that the door be closed*

D. Juan   Well now, sir. The door's firmly shut behind
You and here you have me at your disposal,   630
Eager and willing to please. What would you
Ask of me? Ghost, phantom, fantastic vision,
Can it be your soul's in torment or do
You seek from me some kind of satisfaction
To ease your suffering? I beg you say   635
What's on your mind. You have my word and promise
I shall obey whatever you command.
Do you enjoy the grace of God, my friend,
Or could it be you died in mortal sin?
I'm eager to know, sir. Give me your answer.   640

*The statue speaks slowly, like something from another
world*

D. Gon.   One thing I ask of you. Give me your word
As a gentleman.

640+   <u>The statue speaks slowly</u>: the first occasion on which the statue
speaks. Clearly, the stage-direction calls for a voice that will
distinguish the stone-guest from the human characters of the play and
at the same time evoke the horrors of the other world. Dan Rogers,
Tirso de Molina, El burlador de Sevilla. . . p.23, notes that the
stage-direction 'seems to call for some kind of hollow whisper. If so, it
would have had to be a good "stage whisper": his words are so
important that they must be heard all over the house'. Indeed they
must. Moreover, a hollow whisper would need to be done in a way
which did not merely provoke laughter.

D. Juan	Honor
	tengo, y las palabras cumplo,
	porque caballero soy.
D. Gon.	Dame esa mano, no temas.
D. Juan	¿Eso dices? ¿Yo temor?	545
	Si fueras el mismo infierno
	la mano te diera yo.

Dale la mano

D. Gon.	Bajo esta palabra y mano,
	mañana a las diez estoy
	para cenar aguardando.	650
	¿Irás?
D. Juan	Empresa mayor
	entendí que me pedías.
	Mañana tu güésped soy.
	¿Dónde he de ir?
D. Gon.	A mi capilla.
D. Juan	¿Iré solo?	655
D. Gon.	No, los dos;
	y cúmpleme la palabra
	como la he cumplído yo.
D. Juan	Digo que la cumpliré;
	que soy Tenorio.
D. Gon.	Yo soy
	Ulloa.
D. Juan	Yo iré sin falta.	660
D. Gon.	Yo lo creo. Adiós.

Va a la puerta

D. Juan	Adiós.
	Aguarda, iréte alumbrando.
D. Gon.	No alumbres, que en gracia estoy.

Vase muy poco, mirando a Don Juan,
y Don Juan a él, hasta que desaparece, y
queda Don Juan con pavor

D. Juan	¡Válgame Dios! todo el cuerpo
	se ha bañado de un sudor,	665
	y dentro de las entrañas
	se me hiela el corazón.
	Cuando me tomó la mano,
	de suerte me la apretó,
	que un infierno parecía:	670
	jamás vide tal calor.

---

644   your hand: this is the first occasion in the play on which Don Juan offers his hand as a token of keeping his promise, and actually keeps it.

D. Juan	I, sir, am a man
	Of honour who always keeps his word faithfully.
D. Gon.	Then give me your hand! Don't be afraid!
D. Juan	Afraid of you? I'm not some silly maid.

645

My friend, I tell you I'd give you my hand
Were you the burning fires of Hell itself.

Don Juan holds out his hand

D. Gon.   I accept it as I accept your word.
Promise me this. Tomorrow night at ten
You'll dine with me. Now can you guarantee   650
You'll come and join me?

D. Juan   Of course! I guarantee
It! I must admit I thought your plans
For me were somewhat more ambitious. Where
Shall I find you?

D. Gon.   Come straight to the chapel.

D. Juan   Should I come alone?

D. Gon.   No. The two of you.   655
And don't forget! Be sure you keep your word
To me, my friend, as I kept mine to you.

D. Juan   My word's my bond, sir! Do you think I make
A promise – I a Tenorio – I'll not keep?

D. Gon.   And I, sir, an Ulloa!

D. Juan   I shall be there,   660
Without fail!

D. Gon.   I believe you. Fare you well!

He goes to the door

D. Juan   Wait a moment! I'll light the way in case
You fall.

D. Gon.   My way is lit, sir, by God's grace.

*The statue withdraws very slowly, observing Don Juan,
as he observed it. It disappears, leaving Don Juan in
a state of fear*

D. Juan   Oh, God assist me! The whole of my body's
Suddenly bathed in sweat. And deep inside   665
Here, it's as if my heart's been stilled and frozen
Into a solid block of ice. The moment
He took my hand and held it in his grip,
So hard, so like a vice, I had a vision,
A sudden premonition of the agony   670
Of Hell, as though the hand itself burned me.

---

650   You'll dine with me: on the motif of the double-invitation, see the
Introduction.

Un aliento respiraba,
organizando la voz,
tan frío, que parecía
infernal respiración.   675
Pero todas son ideas
que da la imaginación:
el temor y temer muertos
es más villano temor;
que si un cuerpo noble, vivo,   680
con potencias y razón
y con alma, no se teme,
¿quién cuerpos muertos temió?
Mañana iré a la capilla
donde convidado soy,   685
por que se admire y espante
Sevilla de mi valor.

Vase
Salen el Rey y Don Diego Tenorio y
acompañamiento

Rey	¿Llegó al fin Isabela?
D.Diego	Y disgustada.
Rey	Pues ¿no ha tomado bien el casamiento?
D.Diego	Siente, señor, el nombre de infamada. 690
Rey	De otra causa procede su tormento. ¿Dónde está?
D.Diego	En el convento está alojada de las Descalzas.
Rey	Salga del convento luego al punto, que quiero que en palacio asista con la reina más de espacio.
D.Diego	Si ha de ser con don Juan el desposorio, manda, señor, que tu presencia vea.
Rey	Véame, y galán salga, que notorio quiero que este placer al mundo sea.

---

674   And deathly sound: see 640+ above, note. This line gives a much
clearer indication of the way in which the actor playing the stone-guest
is required to speak. Evidently the voice must have a hoarse quality,
lacking the resonance and intonation of the voice of a living person.

679   the mark of pure cowardice!: to act in a cowardly manner was, of
course, to act dishonourably, and Don Juan is never willing to let
himself down in the eyes of the world or, in the last resort, the other
world. A somewhat similar situation occurs in the final Act of Lope de
Vega's *El caballero de Olmedo* when the protagonist, Alonso, warned by
a ghostly figure of impending doom, refuses to heed the warning on the
basis that to do so would be to compromise his name and reputation.

And yet his breath and voice contained the coldness
Of some frozen wasteland, the icy blast
And deathly sound of some forbidden place,
As if, a mortal man, I gazed upon   675
The face of Hell!. . . But this is pure fancy,
Imagination's silly trickery!
To be afraid is bad enough. To fear
Dead men's worse: the mark of pure cowardice!
Have I been known to fear any man,   680
Though he be noble, strong, endowed with reason,
In full possession of his faculties?
Then why this fear of a man who's dead?
Tomorrow I shall appear in the chapel
And fulfil my obligation to my host.   685
The city of Seville shall be amazed
By Don Juan's confrontation with this ghost.

*Exit Don Juan. Enter the King, Don Diego Tenorio and
their retinue*

King   So Isabela's here at last?   '
D. Diego   Against
            Her will, I fear.
King   Not displeased with the marriage?
D. Diego   The loss of her good name distresses her.   690
King   Perhaps her anguish has another cause.
            Where is she now?
D. Diego   Lodged, I think, in the convent
            Of the Descalzas.
King   Have the lady brought
            To the palace as quickly as you can.
            Here she can be of service to the Queen.   695
D. Diego   My lord, if her marriage is to Don Juan,
            Command him to present himself before
            You.
King   Indeed I shall. We'll have this nobleman
            Appear here at Court, and as a measure

---

690   The loss of her good name: see Act III, 335, note.
693   the Descalzas: there seem to have been twenty-one or so convents in
       Seville at or around the time of the play's composition but none of them
       was known by this name. It is possible that the allusion is to the
       Convento de las Descalzas Franciscas in Madrid, whose founder was
       Princess Juana, the daughter of Charles V, and which was opened in
       1559. This convent may have been chosen by Tirso simply because it
       would be well known to a Madrid audience watching the play who, like
       the dramatists of the Golden Age, would have been indifferent to
       geographical and historical accuracy. The convent in question was one
       where distinguished people ofteń stayed and it was frequently visited
       by both Philip III and Philip IV.

	Conde será desde hoy don Juan Tenorio	700
	de Lebrija; él la mande y la posea,	
	que si Isabela a un duque corresponde,	
	ya que ha perdido un duque, gane un conde.	
D.Diego	Todos por la merced tus pies besamos.	
Rey	Merecéis mi favor tan dignamente,	705
	que si aquí los servicios ponderamos,	
	me quedo atrás con el favor presente.	
	Paréceme, don Diego, que hoy hagamos	
	las bodas de doña Ana juntamente.	
D.Diego	¿Con Octavio?	
Rey	No es bien que el duque Octavio	710
	sea el restaurador de aqueste agravio.	
	Doña Ana con la reina me ha pedido	
	que perdone al marqués, porque doña Ana,	
	ya que el padre murió, quiere marido;	
	porque si le perdió, con él le gana.	715
	Iréis con poca gente y sin ruido	
	luego a hablalle a la fuerza de Triana;	
	por su satisfacción y por su abono	
	de su agraviada prima, le perdono.	
D.Diego	Ya he visto lo que tanto deseaba.	720
Rey	Que esta noche han de ser, podéis decille,	
	los desposorios.	
D.Diego	Todo en bien se acaba.	
	Fácil será al marqués el persuadille,	
	que de su prima amartelado estaba.	
Rey	También podéis a Octavio prevenille.	725
	Desdichado es el duque con mujeres;	
	son todas opinión y pareceres.	
	Hanme dicho que está muy enojado	
	con don Juan.	
D.Diego	No me espanto si ha sabido	
	de don Juan el delito averiguado,	730
	que la causa de tanto daño ha sido.	
	El duque viene.	

---

717   the castle of Triana: a Moorish castle situated across the river from Seville. It served as a prison but was also used by the dreaded Inquisition. The building is no longer in existence.

723   Be put right: the various marriages, arranged or otherwise, signify the restitution of harmony and order. Throughout the play Don Juan constantly denies the importance of marriage as a social institution, for in following his impulses and desires he represents the anarchic force

	Of my good faith, the world shall know my pleasure's	
	This: that Don Juan now become Count of Lebrija.	
	If Isabela's worthy of a duke	
	And he is lost to her, a count should be	
	Sufficient compensation.	
D. Diego	Your majesty	
	Honours me greatly.	
King	Your loyal service	705
	Deserves such favour, Don Diego. I hardly	
	Think this recompense or adequate reward	
	For your life-long sacrifice towards	
	Your king. I fancy too that Doña Ana	
	Should be married.	
D. Diego	To Octavio?	
King	I think not.	710
	It's not appropriate that he should be	
	The saviour of her good name when she herself,	
	Assisted by the queen, has intervened	
	With me and sought forgiveness for the Marquis.	
	Her father's death requires that she be married.	715
	His loss to her shall now become her gain.	
	Proceed at once to the castle of Triana;	
	Inform the Marquis that the restoration	
	Of Ana's name's the source of his salvation.	
D. Diego	And as for me, your majesty, the true	720
	Fulfilment of my hopes.	
King	The marriages	
	Will be performed tonight.	
D. Dieg.	And all injustice	
	Be put right. The Marquis is sure to agree	
	To that. He loves his cousin dearly.	
King	Inform Octavio too of our intention.	725
	As far as women are concerned, the duke's	
	Been out of luck. And so he thinks all women	
	Superficial and fit for common gossip.	
	They tell me he's quite furious with Don Juan.	
D. Dieg.	He'll know about the trick my son has played	730
	On him, the source of all his great misfortune.	
	Why, here he comes!	

---

of sexuality outside marriage. The King, the representative of God on earth and the source of society's well-being, attempts to restore order where Don Juan disrupts it. Even so, as has been pointed out, King Alfonso is always a step behind events as they occur, is ever trying to patch things up, and is certainly not the idealized monarch that is to be found in many Golden-Age plays.

| Rey | No dejéis mi lado. |
| | que en el delito sois comprehendido. |

Sale el Duque Octavio

Octav.	Los pies, invicto rey, me dé tu alteza.
Rey	Alzad, duque, y cubrid vuestra cabeza. 735
	¿Qué pedís?
Octav.	Vengo a pediros,
	postrado ante vuestras plantas,
	una merced, cosa justa,
	digna de serme otorgada.
Rey	Duque, como justa sea, 740
	digo que os doy mi palabra
	de otorgárosla. Pedid.
Octav.	Ya sabes, señor, por cartas
	de tu embajador, y el mundo
	por la lengua de la fama 745
	sabe, que don Juan Tenorio,
	con española arrogancia,
	en Nápoles una noche,
	para mí noche tan mala,
	con mi nombre profanó 750
	el sagrado de una dama.
Rey	No pases más adelante.
	Ya supe vuestra desgracia.
	En efeto: ¿qué pedís?
Octav.	Licencia que en la campaña 755
	defienda como es traidor.
D.Diego	Eso no. Su sangre clara
	es tan honrada. . .
Rey	¡Don Diego!
D.Diego	Señor.
Octav.	¿Quién eres que hablas
	en la presencia del rey 760
	de esa suerte?
D.Diego	Soy quien calla
	porque me lo manda el rey;
	que si no, con esta espada
	te respondiera.
Octav.	Eres viejo.
D.Diego	Ya he sido mozo en Italia, 765
	a vuestro pesar, un tiempo;

---

751 Go no further: Octavio does not realize that Don Diego is Don Juan's father. Presumably, the King wishes to spare the old man further pain and for that reason cuts Octavio short.

King	Then you shall stay with me,

For you too share responsibility.

Enter Duke Octavio

Octav.   Great majesty, I humbly kneel before
You.

King   Arise, Octavio, and replace your hat.   735
What would you ask of me?

Octav.   Your majesty,
I ask one favour only that you, in your
Great mercy and in answer to the justice
Of my petition, must consider worthy
Of your approval.

King   Should your case prove just   740
Octavio, you have my word that I as king
Must give you satisfaction. State your case.

Octav.   My lord, you'll know from your ambassador
In Italy, as surely as the whole
World knows through common gossip and malicious   745
Tongues, that Don Juan Tenorio has recently,
And with true Spanish arrogance, betrayed
A certain lady. In Naples one dark night
The fellow took advantage of my name
To take advantage of this same lady,   750
Depriving her of honour.

King   Go no further,
Octavio. The details of your great misfortune
Are known to me already, so it's best
You simply state the nature of your request.

Octav.   Permission of your majesty to challenge   755
Him! Confront him with his treachery
And make him pay for it!

D. Diego   My lord, his blood
Is noble! I beg of you!

King   Don Diego!

D. Diego   Your majesty!

Octav.   Who is this person dares
To speak like this, and in the royal presence?   760

D. Diego   A man, sir, loyal to the king who therefore
Holds his tongue. Were it not so, this sword of mine
Would answer for me.

Octav.   Come now! Fury ill
Becomes old age!

D. Diego   I'll have you know, my youth
Was spent in Italy, and there the man   765

	ya conocieron mi espada	
	en Nápoles y Milán.	
Octav.	Tienes ya la sangre helada.	
	No vale fuí, sino soy.	770
D.Diego	Pues fuí y soy.	

Empuña

Rey	Tened; basta;	
	bueno está. Callad, don Diego,	
	que a mi persona se guarda	
	poco respeto. Y vos, duque,	
	después que las bodas se hagan,	775
	más de espacio hablaréis.	
	Gentilhombre de mi cámara	
	es don Juan, y hechura mía;	
	y de aqueste tronco rama:	
	mirad por él.	
Octav.	Yo lo haré,	780
	gran señor, como lo mandas.	
Rey	Venid conmigo, don Diego.	
D.Diego	*[Ap.]* ¡Ay, hijo! ¡qué mal me pagas	
	el amor que te he tenido!	
Rey	Duque.	
Octav.	Gran señor.	
Rey	Mañana	785
	vuestras bodas se han de hacer.	
Octav.	Háganse, pues tú lo mandas.	

Vanse el Rey y Don Diego, y salen Gaseno y Aminta

Gaseno	Este señor nos dirá	
	dónde está don Juan Tenorio.	
	Señor, ¿si está por acá	790
	un don Juan a quien notorio	
	ya su apellido será?	
Octav.	Don Juan Tenorio diréis.	

---

767   <u>Naples and Milan:</u> as has been indicated previously, only Sicily belonged to Spain at the time of the play's action. See Act I, 20+, note. During the Golden Age, of course, Spain had much greater influence in Italy, and many Spanish writers spent part of their youth or early manhood there. The most notable example is, perhaps, Cervantes whose short-story, *El licenciado vidriera*, clearly recalls his own experience of various Italian cities which he visited when serving in the Spanish army.

176

	Who dared to cross me had good cause to regret	
	His folly. In Naples and Milan, sir,	
	This sword became a by-word for my bravery.	
Octav.	But now you're old, sir, and your blood runs cold.	
	You have to say 'I am', sir, not 'I was'.	770
D. Diego	I am, sir, what I was!	

He seeks to draw his sword

King	Enough! No cause
	For all this squabbling! You, Don Diego,
	Show scant respect for me, and in my presence!
	And as for you, Octavio, once your marriage
	Has been arranged, you'll need to speak	775
	With me of this at greater length. For now,
	I'll have you know Don Juan's a nobleman,
	An honoured member of my Court and under
	My protection: a branch of this great tree.
	You shall not harm him.
Octav.	Your majesty,	780
	I promise to obey your every word.
King	Don Diego, come with me!
D. Diego	[Aside] This boy of mine!
	A fine way to repay a father's love
	When he has put concern for him above
	All else!
King	Octavio!
Octav.	Yes, my lord?
King	Tomorrow	785
	Your marriage to the lady shall take place.
Octav.	Obedience is, sire, my greatest solace.

Exit the King and Don Diego. Enter Gaseno and Aminta

Gaseno	Ah, this kind gentleman will likely know
	The whereabouts of Don Juan Tenorio.
	Excuse me, sir! I'm looking for a certain	790
	Fellow, his name's Don Juan. You ought to know
	Him, seeing he's well known around these parts.
Octav.	You'll be referring to Don Juan Tenorio.

---

779   a branch of this great tree: the reference is not to the King himself
but to Don Diego.

786   Your marriage: there is some confusion here. The King, having
promised Octavio that he will marry Doña Ana, has subsequently stated
that she, at her own request, is to marry Mota, while Isabela is, as we
have seen, on her way to her marriage to Don Juan. To whom,
therefore, is Octavio to be married? The confusion is clearly not the
King's but the dramatist's. He is already looking forward to the series
of marriages with which the play ends.

Aminta	Sí, señor; ese don Juan.	
Octav.	Aquí está: ¿qué le queréis?	795
Aminta	Es mi esposo ese galán.	
Octav.	¿Cómo?	
Aminta	Pues, ¿no lo sabéis	
	siendo del alcázar vos?	
Octav.	No me ha dicho don Juan nada.	
Gaseno	¿Es posible?	
Octav.	Sí, por Dios.	800
Gaseno	Doña Aminta es muy honrada.	
	Cuando se casen los dos,	
	que cristiana vieja es	
	hasta los güesos, y tiene	
	de la hacienda el interés,	805

. . . .

	más bien que un conde, un marqués.	
	Casóse don Juan con ella,	
	y quitósela a Batricio.	
Aminta	Decid cómo fué doncella	
	a su poder.	
Gaseno	No es juicio	810
	esto, ni aquesta querella.	
Octav.	[Ap.] Esta es burla de don Juan,	
	y para venganza mía	
	éstos diciéndola están.	
	¿Qué pedís, al fin?	
Gaseno	Querría,	815
	porque los días se van,	
	que se hiciese el casamiento,	
	o querellarme ante el rey.	
Octav.	Digo que es justo ese intento.	
Gaseno	Y razón y justa ley.	820
Octav.	[Ap.] Medida a mi pensamiento	
	ha venido la ocasión.	
	En el alcázar tenéis	
	bodas.	
Aminta	¿Si las mías son?	
Octav.	[Ap.] Quiero, para que acertemos,	825
	valerme de una invención.	

---

801   Doña Aminta's: we can well imagine how a Madrid audience of the seventeenth century would roar with laughter at Gaseno's claim, moreso if he were to make it in a broad rural accent.

801   ancient Christian stock: that is to say, without any Moorish or Jewish blood, a matter of concern in the Spain of the Golden Age when,

Aminta	Yes, that's the one! The very Don Juan we're looking
	For.
Octav.	Look no further! What do you want of him? 795
Aminta	I need to find him, sir, seeing he's my husband.
Octav.	He's what?
Aminta	Oh, yes, sir! Nothing could be truer!
	And you a courtier should know that for sure.
Octav.	Don Juan has told me nothing! Not a word!
Gaseno	I can't believe that!
Octav.	Heavens above, it's easy 800
	To believe;
Gaseno	The fact is Doña Aminta's
	Honourable. And when she marries him
	She honours him, being herself of pure
	And ancient Christian stock. He can be sure
	Too her fortune's quite considerable. 805
	My land, you see! I'm like a count or marquis
	On his estates! That's why Don Juan Tenorio
	Pinched my daughter from her betrothed Batricio.
Aminta	You tell him she was a virgin before
	He took her from him!
Gaseno	That's no argument 810
	On which to base the righting of this wrong.
Octav.	[Aside] Another of his tricks! This fellow's song
	And dance gives me the chance to get Don Juan
	Hoist well and truly on his own petard!
	Then tell me, sir, what you intend to do. 815
Gaseno	Time's marching on, sir, I want him to keep
	His promise to my daughter and marry her.
	If not, the King shall hear about the traitor.
Octav.	Your case, my friend's entirely reasonable.
Gaseno	For reason's on my side and justice too. 820
Octav.	[Aside] Who would have dreamt that mere destiny
	Could offer me this opportunity?
	Today, of course, the palace celebrates
	A wedding.
Aminta	Looks as if he's fixed the date
	Then, don't it?
Octav.	[Aside] Now, I think, we'll nail our man. 825
	He shan't escape the cunning of this plan!

---

especially during the reign of Philip II and a feared Inquisition, religious orthodoxy became an obsession.

807   On his estates!: peasant pride in property and status is also a marked feature of Calderón's *El alcalde de Zalamea* and its protagonst, Pedro Crespo. See Act III, 102, note.

	Venid donde os vestiréis,	
	señora, a lo cortesano,	
	y a un cuarto del rey saldréis	
	conmigo.	
Aminta	Vos de la mano	830
	a don Juan me llevaréis.	
Octav.	Que de esta suerte es cautela.	
Gaseno	El arbitrio me consuela.	
Octav.	[Ap.] Estos venganza me dan	
	de aqueste traidor don Juan	835
	y el agravio de Isabela.	

Vanse
Salen Don Juan y Catalinón

Catal.	¿Cómo el rey te recibió?	
D. Juan	Con más amor que mi padre.	
Catal.	¿Viste a Isabela?	
D. Juan	También.	
Catal.	¿Cómo viene?	
D. Juan	Como un ángel.	840
Catal.	¿Recibióte bien?	
D. Juan	El rostro	
	bañado de leche y sangre,	
	como la rosa que al alba	
	revienta la verde cárcel.	
Catal.	Al fin, ¿esta noche son	845
	las bodas?	
D. Juan	Sin falta.	
Catal.	Si antes	
	hubieran sido, no hubieras,	
	señor, engañado a tantas;	
	pero tú tomas esposa,	
	señor, con cargas muy grandes.	850
D. Juan	Di: ¿comienzas a ser necio?	
Catal.	Y podrás muy bien casarte	
	mañana, que hoy es mal día.	
D. Juan	Pues ¿qué día es hoy?	
Catal.	Es martes.	
D. Juan	Mil embusteros y locos	855
	dan en esos disparates.	
	Sólo aquel llamo mal día,	
	aciago y detestable,	
	en que no tengo dineros;	
	que lo demás es donaire.	860

836+   *Enter Don Juan*: as the two men enter, they are, to judge from 861, in
the process of getting ready to leave the inn, yet by 873 they are

	You shall in that case now accompany me	
	From here, assume the garments of a courtly	
	Lady, and at the court appear with me	
	As my companion.	
Aminta	You mean you'll take me	830
	With you and present me to my Don Juan?	
Octav.	The best plan I can think of, don't you see?	
Gaseno	I do agree, sir! You make an old man happy!	
Octav.	[Aside] These two offer me the opportunity	
	For vengeance on Don Juan. He'll pay as well	835
	For his offence against my Isabel.	

They leave. Enter Don Juan and Catalinón

Catal.	How did his majesty take to you, master?	
D. Juan	Oh, much more lovingly than my own father!	
Catal.	What about Isabela? See her, did you?	
D. Juan	Of course!	
Catal.	How is she then?	
D. Juan	She's like an angel.	840
Catal.	I bet she gave you hell!	
D. Juan	A face like heaven	
	Itself, my friend. The white of milk tinged pink,	
	As when at dawn the lovely rose emerges	
	From the leafy prison of its green cell.	
Catal.	Ah, well! The wedding's fixed for tonight then,	845
	Master?	
D. Juan	Without fail.	
Catal.	It's quite clear to me,	
	If you'd got hitched before, you'd not be lumbered	
	With all those women you deceived. But now,	
	Taking a wife's a very different matter,	
	And you with those responsibilities!	850
D. Juan	Don't start to play the fool again with me!	
Catal.	Marry tomorrow's my advice to you!	
	Marry today you're sure to be sorry!	
D. Juan	What day is it today?	
Catal.	You know it's Tuesday!	
D. Juan	Don't be a fool! A silly superstition,	855
	A piece of nonsense fit for fools and madmen!	
	As far as I'm concerned, the only day	
	I'd call unfortunate's the day I'm short	
	Of ready money. As for all the rest,	
	A sheer waste of time and best forgotten.	860

---

outside the church – a fine example of the fluidity of movement in the drama of the Golden Age.

854   You know it's Tuesday!: in Spain Tuesday is associated with bad luck.

Catal.	Vamos, si te has de vestir,
	que te aguardan, y ya es tarde.
D. Juan	Otro negocio tenemos
	que hacer, aunque nos aguarden.
Catal.	¿Cuál es?
D. Juan	Cenar con el muerto. 865
Catal.	Necedad de necedades.
D. Juan	¿No ves que di mi palabra?
Catal.	Y cuando se la quebrantes,
	¿qué importa? ¿Has de pedirte
	una figura de jaspe 870
	la palabra?
D. Juan	Podrá el muerto
	llamarme a voces infame.
Catal.	Ya está cerrada la iglesia.
D. Juan	Llama.
Catal.	¿Qué importa que llame?
	¿quién tiene de abrir, que están 875
	durmiendo los sacristanes?
D. Juan	Llama a este postigo.
Catal.	Abierto
	está.
D. Juan	Pues entra.
Catal.	Entre un fraile
	con su hisopo y estola.
D. Juan	Sígueme y calla.
Catal.	¿Que calle? 880
D. Juan	Sí.
Catal.	Dios en paz
	destos convites me saque.

Entran por una puerta y salen por otra

      ¡Qué escura que está la iglesia,
      señor para ser tan grande!
      ¡Ay de mí! ¡Tenme, señor,   885
      porque de la capa me asen!

Sale Don Gonzalo como de antes, y
encuéntrase con ellos

D. Juan	¿Quién va?
D. Gon.	Yo soy.

---

882   *from the opposite side of the stage*:   a fine example of the use of the two back-stage doors in a Golden-Age theatre. *They exit* in this stage-direction means, of course, that Don Juan and his servant leave the stage by one of the doors which represents the postern. In other words they enter the church whose interior at this moment is behind the back-stage area. When the two men reappear through the door at the opposite side of the stage, they are in fact inside the church,

Catal.	Alright then, master. Time for getting dressed.
	They're waiting for you and you're late already.
D. Juan	We've other business to attend to first,
	My friend. They'll have to wait until we're ready.
Catal.	What other business?
D. Juan	Dinner with the dead, 865
	Of course!
Catal.	You must be off your bloody head!
D. Juan	You know I gave the man my solemn word!
Catal.	You better break it while you can then, master!
	I'm sure he won't mind! In any case,
	How can a man of stone start arguing 870
	With you if you don't keep his silly bargain?
D. Juan	No dead man shall call me, Don Juan, a coward.
Catal.	Anyway, looks as if the church is locked.
D. Juan	Then knock them up!
Catal.	But what's the point in knocking,
	Master? Who's going to open up? Flat out 875
	They'll be, those sacristans, tucked up in bed.
D. Juan	Try the postern!
Catal.	Oh, Lord above! It's open.
D. Juan	In you go then!
Catal.	What? Me in there? A priest's
	What you need, sprinkling his holy water!
D. Juan	Out of my way! And stop your silly chatter! 880
Catal.	I will, I will! I pray God save this sinner!
	Deliver him safely from this dinner!

They exit and enter from the opposite side of the stage

	Oh, master! Have you ever seen a church
	As big as this and yet as black as pitch?
	Oh, God! Where are you? Answer! It's no joke 885
	In here! I swear that someone grabbed my cloak!

Enter Don Gonzalo as before. He stands before them

D. Juan	Who's there?
D. Gon.	Your host.

---

which is now represented by the stage itself. We have here a very good example indeed of the freedom of movement and changes of location that are characteristic of Golden-Age drama.

884   as black as pitch?: once more the reader should recall that in the seventeenth-century public theatres the action on the stage took place in the afternoon and that most theatres, including those in Madrid, were not covered.

Catal.		¡Muerto estoy!	

Catal.   ¡Muerto estoy!

D. Gon. El muerto soy, no te espantes.

No entendí que me cumplieras

la palabra, según haces   890

de todos burla,

D. Juan   ¿Me tienes

en opinión de cobarde?

D. Gon. Sí, que aquella noche huíste

de mí cuando me mataste.

D. Juan Huí de ser conocido;   895

mas ya me tienes delante.

Di presto lo que me quieres.

D. Gon. Quiero a cenar convidarte.

Catal.   Aquí escusamos la cena,

que toda ha de ser fiambre,   900

pues no parece cocina.

D. Juan Cenemos.

D. Gon.   Para cenar

es menester que levantes

esa tumba.

D. Juan   Y si te importa,

levantaré esos pilares.   905

D. Gon. Valiente estás.

D. Juan   Tengo brío

y corazón en las carnes.

Catal.   Mesa de Guinea es ésta.

Pues ¿no hay por allá quien lave?

D. Gon. Siéntate.

D. Juan   ¿Adónde?

Catal.   Con sillas   910

vienen ya dos negros pajes.

Entran dos enlutados con dos sillas

¿También acá se usan lutos

y bayeticas de Flandes?

D. Gon. Siéntate tú.

Catal.   Yo, señor,

he merendado esta tarde.   915

D. Gon. No repliques.

---

904   <u>move the stone</u>: food for the dead was apparently kept beneath the stone placed over the tomb in the floor of the church.

Catal.	Oh, Christ! The bloody ghost!	
D. Gon.	The dead man! There's no need to be afraid	
	Of me. I am surprised, my friend, to see	
	You've kept your promise, seeing how remiss	890
	You've been, so often breaking it with others.	
D. Juan	You aren't accusing me of cowardice!	
D. Gon.	Was it not fear made you seek safety	
	In flight the night you chose to murder me?	
D. Juan	Not fear of you! Merely the fear of being	895
	Identified! But now I stand before	
	You! Call that a sign of fear, do you?	
	Just tell me quickly what you ask of me.	
D. Gon.	Merely that you agree to dine with me.	
Catal.	Master, you'd better think of some excuse.	900
	Tell him you like hot food. It's all cold here.	
	Ask him where he does his cooking, seeing	
	There's no sign of any bloody kitchen!	
D. Juan	We shall eat with you, sir.	
D. Gon.	Then move the stone	
	That covers the tomb.	
D. Juan	Just give the word, I'll move	905
	These pillars too.	
D. Gon.	How brave you are, my friend!	
D. Juan	To the very marrow, if you need proof.	
Catal.	The table looks as if it's from the coast	
	Of Guinea! Black as toast that's burnt! Maybe	
	He hasn't got a servant.	
D. Gon.	Take a seat.	910
D. Juan	Where?	
Catal.	There, master! Two servants black as pitch	
	And bringing chairs.	

Enter two figures in black with chairs

	Must be the case down there	
	They're all in mourning, draped in flanelling	
	From Flanders.	
D. Gon.	Take a seat!	
Catal.	Don't need to eat	
	Again, sir, if you don't mind. I've had my dinner.	915
	More than enough! I went and stuffed. . .	
D. Gon.	Will you	
	Shut up!	

---

909   Of Guinea!: black servants were transported to Spain from Guinea.
914   From Flanders: the kind of material described here was particularly associated with Flanders. It was used especially to cover coffins.

Catal.	No replico.
	Dios en paz de esto me saque.
	¿Qué plato es éste, señor?
D. Gon.	Este plato es de alacranes
	y víboras.
Catal.	¡Gentil plato!

920

D. Gon.	Estos son nuestros manjares.
	¿No comes tú?
D. Juan	Comeré,
	si me dieses áspid y áspides
	cuantos el infierno tiene.
D. Gon.	También quiero que te canten.

925

Catal.	¿Qué vino beben acá?
D. Gon.	Pruébalo.
Catal.	Hiel y vinagre
	es este vino.
D. Gon.	Este vino
	esprimen nuestros lagares.
	Cantan
	Adviertan los que de Dios
	juzgan los castigos grandes,
	que no hay plazo que no llegue
	ni deuda que no se pague.

930

Catal.	¡Malo es esto, vive Cristo!
	que he entendido este romance,
	y que con nosotros habla.

935

D. Juan	Un hielo el pecho me parte.
	Cantan
	Mientras en el mundo viva,
	no es justo que diga nadie:
	¡qué largo me lo fiáis!
	siendo tan breve el cobrarse.

940

Catal.	¿De qué es este guisadillo?
D. Gon.	De uñas.
Catal.	De uñas de sastre
	será, si es guisado de uñas.

---

928   Rioja: in the Spanish text Catalinon words are, literally: 'This wine is gall and vinegar.' I have taken the liberty of introducing the allusion to Rioja in order to up-date the lines and, indeed, to make them more comic.

930+ *[Singing off-stage]*:the song that follows is precisely in the tradition of the *auto sacramental* alluded to previously. See Act III, 581+ note.

945   tailor's . . .: clearly an allusion to the greed of tailors. In the literature of the Golden Age the professions provided a rich vein of

Catal.	I am shut up, sir. Well and truly. . .
	Oh, God! Please save me! What nice dish is this,
	Sir?
D. Gon.	A plain dish for you. It's only snake
	And roasted scorpion!
Catal.	Oh, a fine concoction! 920
D. Gon.	Typical of the food the dead must eat.
	Won't you try some?
D. Juan	Of course! I've said I will.
	Pile snakes and scorpions on my plate, I'd still
	Devour them, all the snakes that Hell contains.
D. Gon.	I'll have them sing a song to entertain 925
	You.
Catal.	Drink real vintage stuff down there, do you?
D. Gon.	Taste it and you shall see.
Catal.	Oh, yes. A fine
	Rioja, an exquisite blend of gall and vinegar.
	Bit on the sharp side really to caress
	The palate.
D. Gon.	Made by our finest presses. 930
	[Singing off-stage]
	'Let all men know God's punishment is great.
	Take note all men who live below and wait,
	For everyone the day of judgement's set,
	And no one can escape the final debt.'
Catal.	In God's name that's a song to make us fear. 935
	The meaning of its every word is clear
	Enough. Look how it speaks to both of us.
D. Juan	My blood freezes and feels as cold as ice.
	[Singing off-stage]
	'As long as man lives out his total span,
	Let him avoid this boast, as best he can: 940
	"Plenty of time to pay the final debt".
	No sooner said, the payment must be met.'
Catal.	This stew here. What ingredients does it have?
D. Gon.	Mainly fingernails.
Catal.	By the way they jab
	And grab at me, they're obviously some tailor's 945
	Nails.

---

satire. Thus, Francisco de Quevedo in his highly satirical work, *Los sueños*, portrays professional men condemned to Hell for their sins or called to account for them on the Day of Judgement. In the *Sueño de las calaveras* a tailor is shown attempting to justify himself: '"What could I steal if I was always dying of hunger myself?" And the others told him, seeing that he denied having been a thief, that it really was the limit to despise his own profession.'

187

D. Juan	Ya he cenado; haz que levanten	945
	la mesa.	
D. Gon.	Dame esa mano;	
	no temas, la mano dame.	
D. Juan	¿Eso dices? ¿Yo temor?	
	¡Que me abraso! ¡No me abrases	
	con tu fuego!	
D. Gon.	Este es poco	950
	para el fuego que buscaste.	
	Las maravillas de Dios	
	son, don Juan, investigables,	
	y así quiere que tus culpas	
	a manos de un muerto pagues,	955
	y si pagas desta suerte,	
	esta es justicia de Dios:	
	"quien tal hace, que tal pague".	
D. Juan	¡Que me abraso, no me aprietes!	
	Con la daga he de matarte.	960
	Mas ¡ay! que me canso en vano	
	de tirar golpes al aire.	
	A tu hija no ofendí,	
	que vió mis engaños antes.	
D. Gon.	No importa, que ya pusiste	965
	tu intento.	
D. Juan	Deja que llame	
	quien me confiese y absuelva.	
D. Gon.	No hay lugar; ya acuerdas tarde.	
D. Juan	¡Que me quemo! ¡Que me abraso!	
	¡Muerto soy!	970

Cae muerto

Catal.	No hay quien se escape,	
	que aquí tengo de morir	
	también por acompañarte.	
D. Gon.	Esta es justicia de Dios:	
	"quien tal hace que tal pague".	

Húndese el sepulcro con Don Juan y Don Gonzalo, con mucho ruido, y sale Catalinón arrastrando

---

964 **She has her honour**: see Act II, 513, note.
968 **No time, my friend!**: the point is made for the benefit of a contemporary audience that Don Juan has had time to change his ways and has been warned of the dangers of not doing so. He has assumed unwisely that he can confess his sins at the very last moment and is therefore guilty of presumption. A contrast can be made in that sense with Enrico, the sinner of *El condenado por desconfiado* who, though

D. Juan	All finished then. Shall we clear the table?
D. Gon.	Give me your hand! No need to be afraid.
	Don't be afraid, my friend. Give me your hand!
D. Juan	I fear nothing. Your hand's on fire,
	It's burning me. . .
D. Gon.	But nothing, my dear friend, 950

D. Gon.   But nothing, my dear friend,   950
Compared with all the agony that lies
Ahead of you. God's workings are, Don Juan,
Intelligible to each and everyone.
I am the man through whom you meet your doom,
Your life the sacrifice for all your sins.   955
God gives man life that he can call his own,
But he must reap the harvest he has sown.

D. Juan Your hand burns! Let me go! Before this knife
Of mine puts paid again to your life.
The blow strikes home. It hits its target square.   960
But nothing! Nothing! Where it falls, it falls
On empty air! Your daughter. . . I did not
Seduce her. . . There was no offence against
Her. . . She has her honour. . . She saw the trick
In time!

D. Gon.   Nothing excuses your intention.   965
Her seduction was firmly in your mind.

D. Juan Give me confession! Grant me absolution!

D. Gon. No time, my friend! No time! Your time runs out.

D. Juan My body is on fire! Your flames destroy
Me!

Don Juan falls dead

Catal.   There's no escape for me either. My fate's   970
Bound to be his, and death my ultimate
Reward for being the servant and companion
Of Don Juan.

D. Gon.   His fate provides the lesson
You should heed, for each man reaps the harvest
Of his deeds.

The tomb sinks with much noise. Don Juan and Don Gonzalo disappear with it. Catalinón drags himself to safety.

---

more evil than Don Juan, undergoes a conversion, confesses in time, and is saved.

974+   The tomb sinks: this is the only mechanical effect called for in the play. The trapdoor in the stage itself, a characteristic feature of the public theatre of the seventeenth-century, would have been used to allow the tomb to sink below stage-level. The noise alluded to in the stage-direction would probably have been produced by exploding thunderflashes.

Catal.	¡Válgame Dios! ¿Qué es aquesto?	975
	Toda la capilla se arde,	
	y con el muerto he quedado	
	para que le vele y guarde.	
	Arrastrando como pueda	
	iré a avisar a su padre.	980
	¡San Jorge, San Agnus Dei,	
	sacadme en paz a la calle!	

Vase
Salen el Rey, Don Diego y acompañamiento

D.Diego	Ya el marqués, señor, espera	
	besar vuestros pies reales.	
Rey	Entre luego y avisad	985
	al conde, porque no aguarde.	

Salen Batricio y Gaseno

Batric.	¿Dónde, señor, se permite	
	desenvolturas tan grandes,	
	que tus criados afrenten	
	a los hombres miserables?	990
Rey	¿Qué dices?	
Batric.	Don Juan Tenorio,	
	alevoso y detestable,	
	la noche del casamiento,	
	antes que le consumase,	
	a mi mujer me quitó;	995
	testigos tengo delante.	

Salen Tisbea y Isabela y acompañamiento

Tisbea	Si vuestra alteza, señor,	
	de don Juan Tenorio no hace	
	justicia, a Dios y a los hombres,	1000
	mientras viva, he de quejarme.	
	Derrotado le echó el mar;	
	dile vida y hospedaje,	
	y pagóme esta amistad	
	con mentirme y engañarme	
	con nombre de mi marido.	1005
Rey	¿Qué dices?	
Isabela	Dice verdades.	

Salen Aminta y el Duque Octavio

Aminta	¿Adónde mi esposo está?	
Rey	¿Quién es?	
Aminta	Pues ¿aun no lo sabe?	
	El señor don Juan Tenorio,	
	con quien vengo a desposarme,	1010

| Catal. | Heavens above! What's going on? | 975 |
| | The chapel's full of smoke and flames. Don Juan's | |

Catal.   Heavens above! What's going on?   975
              The chapel's full of smoke and flames. Don Juan's
              A gonner by the look of things, and here
              Am I, him dead, left to look after him.
              I'll creep away from here as best I can.
              I'll have to break the news to his old man.   980
              I pray to you Saint George, the Holy Lamb,
              Please get me out of such a bloody jam.
        Exit Catalinón. Enter the King, Don Diego, attendants
D.Diego   The Marquis is outside, your majesty.
              He seeks an audience with you urgently.
King   Then bid him enter. I'll see the Count Don Juan   985
              As well. No need for him to wait out there.
        Enter Batricio and Gaseno
Batric.   Oh where on earth, your majesty, are such
              Atrocities, such hideous deeds as these
              Permitted, when such men as you protect
              And favour take advantage of your loyal   990
              Subjects?
King   Which men? Explain.
Batric.   Don Juan Tenorio,
              Resorting to the vilest treachery,
              On the night of my wedding and before
              Its consummation, took my bride from me,
              Deprived her of her pure chastity.   995
              I have witnesses to prove it to you.
        Enter Tisbea, Isabela and companions
Tisbea   Oh, your majesty, I bring to you
              This earnest plea. Punish Don Juan Tenorio,
              For otherwise both God and all the world
              Shall know, as long as I have breath, of his   1000
              Offence. This traitor, washed up by the sea,
              I cared for, took into my house, restored
              To life again. The hospitality
              That I gave him he cruelly abused,
              And promsing to be my husband, tricked   1005
              Me.
King   Another complaint?
Isabela   She tells the truth.
        Enter Aminta and Duke Octavio
Aminta   Where is my husband?
King   And who would he be?
Aminta   Who would he be? I thought your majesty
              Would surely know that he's Don Juan Tenorio
              Who's promised faithfully to marry me.   1010

porque me debe el honor,
y es noble y no ha de negarme.
Manda que nos desposemos.

Sale el Marqués de la Mota

Mota   Pues es tiempo, gran señor,
que a luz verdades se saquen,   1015
sabrás que don Juan Tenorio
la culpa que me imputaste
tuvo él, pues como amigo,
pudo el crüel engañarme;
de que tengo dos testigos.   1020

Rey   ¿Hay desvergüenza tan grande?
Prendelde y matalde luego.

D.Diego   En premio de mis servicios
haz que le prendan y pague
sus culpas, porque del cielo   1025
rayos contra mí no bajen,
si es mi hijo tan malo.

Rey   ¡Esto mis privados hacen!

Sale Catalinón

Catal.   Señores, todos oíd
el suceso más notable   1030
que en el mundo ha sucedido,
y en oyéndome, matadme.
Don Juan, del Comendador
haciendo burla, una tarde,
después de haberle quitado   1035
las dos prendas que más valen,
tirando al bulto de piedra
la barba por ultrajarle,
a cenar le convidó:
¡nunca fuera a convidarle!   1040
Fué el bulto y convidóle;
y agora porque no os canse,
acabando de cenar,
entre mil presagios graves,

1029   <u>Advantage of the King</u>: the moral and political point is made very clearly for the benefit of a contemporary audience. Throughout the play criticism has been made of the irresponsible behaviour of noblemen –

I'm sure a man of such nobility
Is bound to act towards me honourably.
Will your majesty arrange the marriage?

Enter the Marquis of Mota

Mota   It's time, your majesty, that certain facts
Should see the light of day. On that account   1015
I'm forced to say the crime of which I stood
Accused was never mine. Don Juan Tenorio's
The man to blame for that, for he abused
My friendship and used for his advantage
My good name. These two witnesses will speak   1020
On my behalf.

King   Enough. Such shamelessness
Condemns itself. Arrest him. Have him put
To death.

D. Diego   I've served you long, your majesty.
You'll honour me by punishing this son
Of mine, for then perhaps the Heavens will spare   1025
A poor father, forgive him for the birth
Of such a worthless child.

King   It shall be done.
Let no one think that noblemen can take
Advantage of the King.

Enter Catalinón

Catal.   My lords, my lords,
I've come as quickly as I can to bring   1030
You news of the most strange and terrible thing
The world has ever witnessed. Believe me,
It's all true, cross my heart and hope to die
Right here, struck down by God upon this spot.
My news involves Don Juan who, having robbed   1035
The good Commander of precious life and honour,
Encountered his statue, upon which he
Pulled his beard, insulting him further,
And there and then invited him to dinner.
Oh what a stupid, idiotic thing   1040
To go and offer him that invitation!
Anyway, so as not to bore you more,
The man of stone turned up and asked if we
Would like to sup with him. To be polite

---

not only Don Juan, but Mota, Duke Octavio, and even Don Pedro
Tenorio. Ideally, of course, the nobility should be setting an example
for others to follow, but this was far from the case in Tirso's lifetime.
See Act I, 26+, note.

	de la mano le tomó,	1045
	y le aprieta hasta quitalle	
	la vida, diciendo: "Dios	
	me manda que así te mate,	
	castigando tus delitos.	
	Quien tal hace que tal pague."	1050
Rey	¿Qué dices?	
Catal.	Lo que es verdad,	
	diciendo antes que acabase,	
	que a doña Ana no debía	
	honor, que le oyeron antes	
	del engaño.	
Mota	Por las nuevas	1055
	mil albricias pienso darte.	
Rey	¡Justo castigo del cielo!	
	Y agora es bien que se casen	
	todos, pues la causa es muerta,	
	vida de tantos desastres.	1060
Octav.	Pues ha enviudado Isabela,	
	quiero con ella casarme.	
Mota	Yo con mi prima.	
Batric.	Y nosotros	
	con las nuestras, porque acabe	
	El Convidado de piedra.	1065
Rey	Y el sepulcro se traslade	
	en San Francisco en Madrid,	
	para memoria más grande.	

1060   Let order reign again: see Act III, 723, note.
1067   San Francisco's church: San Francisco in Madrid became a church in the fifteenth century, having been founded as a hermitage two centuries earlier. It was renovated in 1617 – around the time of the play's composition – and rebuilt in 1761.

	We went and, when we'd finished, he commands	1045
	Don Juan give him his hand, which he then grips
	And squeezes till my master has no breath
	At all left in him, and the stone man says:
	'Death is God's punishment. Let each man heed
	The sinner reaps the harvest of his deeds'	1050
King	What are you saying?
Catal.	Just the honest truth,
	Your majesty. Oh, and there's one thing more.
	I heard my master say that Doña Ana
	Didn't lose her honour. They spotted him
	Before he could seduce her.
Mota	Oh, thank you, sir,	1055
	For news like this I willingly embrace
	You.
King	How justly God punishes Don Juan!
	But now, my friends, let marriage make amends
	For all the wrongs inflicted by this man,
	Their cause is dead. Let order reign again.	1060
Octav.	Now Isabela has no husband, I,
	Your majesty, can hope to satisfy
	Her need.
Mota	And I, your majesty, shall marry
	Doña Ana.
Batric.	All of us, as this play ends,
	Shall marry our girl-friends.
King	My last command	1065
	Is this. The tomb of Don Gonzalo shall
	be moved, from here to San Francisco's church.
	Madrid shall be his final resting-place.